Peter Caton was born in 1960 and has always lived in Essex. He is married with two children. Trained as a polymer chemist, he ran a business manufacturing adhesives which he sold in 2018, allowing more time for his interests in walking, the countryside and conservation. Peter holds season tickets at both West Ham and Torquay United and is a member of Upminster Methodist Church. He has written books covering themes of walking, travel and railways.

Peter's previous books include:

Essex Coast Walk

Peter walks the whole length of the Essex coastline, the longest of any English county. He writes of the beauty, wildlife and history of this little known coast, and includes many amusing observations along the way. Many readers have contacted Peter to say how the book inspired them to follow his footsteps onto the Essex coast paths.

No Boat Required – Exploring Tidal Islands

Peter becomes the first person to visit the 43 tidal islands that can be walked to from the UK mainland. He writes of the challenges faced reaching remote islands, the beauty of the islands and unearths many little known facts and stories.

Remote Stations

Combining a love of remote places and of travelling on our more interesting trains, Peter visits forty of Britain's most lonely railway stations. Written not just for the railway enthusiast but also for anyone who enjoys travel books, it includes a chapter on the Southwold railway.

SUFFOLK
COAST WALK

Peter Caton

Copyright © 2015 Peter Caton
Reprinted 2018, 2021
Reprinted 2026 with updates

The moral right of the author has been asserted.

Apart from any fair dealing for the purposes of research or private study, or criticism or review, as permitted under the Copyright, Designs and Patents Act 1988, this publication may only be reproduced, stored or transmitted, in any form or by any means, with the prior permission in writing of the publishers, or in the case of reprographic reproduction in accordance with the terms of licences issued by the Copyright Licensing Agency. Enquiries concerning reproduction outside those terms should be sent to the publishers.

Matador
9 Priory Business Park
Kibworth Beauchamp
Leicestershire LE8 0RX, UK
Tel: (+44) 116 279 2299
Fax: (+44) 116 279 2277
Email: books@troubador.co.uk
Web: www.troubador.co.uk/matador

ISBN 978-1784620-967

British Library Cataloguing in Publication Data.
A catalogue record for this book is available from the British Library.

Printed and bound in the UK by TJ Books, Padstow, Cornwall
Typeset in 11pt Adobe Garamond Pro by Troubador Publishing Ltd, Leicester, UK

Matador is an imprint of Troubador Publishing Ltd

To all the friendly, interesting and knowledgeable people I met on the way.

Thanks to my wife Debbie and my parents for their help and support.

And thanks to Jeremy Scott of Swan Books, Upminster's excellent independent bookshop, for his invaluable advice. www.swanbooks.co.uk

And to Naomi Green of Matador for her help in producing this book.

The author is always pleased to hear from readers through his website:

www.petercatonbooks.co.uk

Facebook – Peter Caton Books

Contents

Chapter One	Corton to Kessingland	1
Chapter Two	Kessingland to Southwold	17
Chapter Three	Blythburgh to Southwold	27
Chapter Four	Southwold to Dunwich	39
Chapter Five	Dunwich to Aldeburgh	51
Chapter Six	Aldeburgh to Snape	71
Chapter Seven	Snape to Iken to Orford	81
Chapter Eight	Orford to Butley	97
Chapter Nine	Orford Ness	105
Chapter Ten	Havergate Island	117
Chapter Eleven	Butley to Hollesley	125
Chapter Twelve	Hollesley to Bawdsey Ferry	133
Chapter Thirteen	Bawdsey to Woodbridge	145
Chapter Fourteen	Woodbridge to Waldringfield	159
Chapter Fifteen	Waldringfield to Felixstowe	169
Chapter Sixteen	Felixstowe to Trimley	181
Chapter Seventeen	Trimley to Ipswich	189
Chapter Eighteen	Ipswich to Chelmondiston	203
Chapter Nineteen	A Walk Around Ipswich	211
Chapter Twenty	Chelmondiston to Shotley Gate	219
Chapter Twenty One	Shotley Gate to Lower Holbrook	229
Chapter Twenty Two	Lower Holbrook to Cattawade	235
Updates 2026		245

INTRODUCTION

'You'll like Suffolk'; 'Southwold's lovely'; 'good fish and chips at Aldeburgh'; 'Dunwich is interesting'. That's what everyone said when I told them I was walking the Suffolk coast. No one mentioned the winding river estuaries, haunting shingle, remote creeks, enigmatic marshes, remarkable wildlife, history and mysteries that I would find on my way.

I'd walked the coast of Essex, my home county, been to forty three tidal islands and travelled ten thousand miles around Britain by train, but had rarely visited our neighbour across the Stour. I'd been intrigued by Orford Ness on the map, seen photos of the heather-covered Dunwich Heath and read tales of eroding coastline. Now it was time to explore this coast that everyone had spoken so highly of.

I would walk from north to south, a day or two at a time, staying over to get a flavour of its towns and villages, and taking a year to see Suffolk in all seasons. For environmental reasons and to prove that it is possible, I would travel to and from each walk by public transport. The excellent website *www.traveline.info* provided timetables for the county's rural buses.

Where practical I would take the closest path to the coast, but wouldn't always follow dead ends or beach walking. Rather than taking ferries across the rivers, I would walk to the first fixed crossing point, which was generally around the tidal limit, so covering all 162 miles of what I was to find is a surprisingly varied and wonderful coastline.

Much of the walk would be through The Suffolk Coast and Heaths Area of Outstanding Natural Beauty, which includes three National Natures Reserves and is one of the UK's most important areas for wildlife. Whilst most famous for its birds, I was to find that the coast supports vital populations of all kinds of lesser known creatures and to learn something of the management required to maintain biodiversity across a range of habitats. I would visit Suffolk's only island, taking a rare opportunity to meet some of its remarkable wildlife.

The Suffolk coastline has a number of waymarked paths, which I was to find were well signposted and generally made for easy walking. The Suffolk Coast Path runs for about sixty miles from Lowestoft to Felixstowe, from where The Stour and Orwell Walk took me another forty three miles mostly along river walls. Sometimes these bypassed interesting places and frequently I found my own routes, most notably along the River Deben. Often the paths would wander inland, but these diversions through woods, marshes, heaths and fields added to the variety and enjoyment of the whole walk.

The book tells the story of my walk, the people I met, the places I saw, the history, wildlife and many mysteries of Suffolk's coast. It is intended as an easy read rather than specifically a guidebook but I've aimed to include enough details on the route that others may follow it. The approximate mileage for each section is shown at the start of chapters.

Maps at the start of each chapter show the route I took, sometimes suggesting alternatives that others may prefer to follow. Note that the scales of the maps vary and as you will read, although they show the route I took, this is not always to be recommended. I must add the caveat that the author and publisher make no warranties as to the existence of rights of way and will not accept liability for any errors found. It is recommended that the maps are used in conjunction with the relevant ordnance survey (OS) map, although as I was to find, not all the paths shown on the OS actually exist.

I've researched information as much as reasonably possible and made every effort to ensure that all facts are accurate, but will be happy to be corrected. Where sources gave conflicting information, unless one is overwhelmingly in a minority, I've either stated this or been less than definite in my wording.

Information was obtained from numerous sources, too many to mention, although I've put the occasional acknowledgement in the text and included a bibliography at the end. This isn't the sort of book to include lots of references, but I would like to note particular acknowledgment to Simon Knott whose excellent website *www.suffolkchurches.co.uk* provided information on churches and villages.

My observations are recorded as they happened. Many travel writers make up or exaggerate incidents to add interest or humour, but with a scientific rather than journalistic training, I have kept to the truth, resisting the temptation to embellish.

Each chapter describes a day's walk, with lengths depending on public transport access points and suitable overnight stops. I have included black and white photos in the text illustrating the story of the walk, with a central colour section that helps portray the beauty of Suffolk's coast. Other than cropping, none of the photos have been digitally altered – that's cheating!

I make no apologies for using mixed imperial and metric units, as this is one of the idiosyncrasies of the current English language. Like most people I say miles, so that's what I've written. Being of the generation who were bought up on yards, it feels right to use these rather than metres, but in most contexts 'a few yards' or 'a few metres' is pretty much the same. Being yet to meet anyone who has any idea how big a hectare is, for area I've stuck to square miles or acres.

Like much of our east coast, Suffolk's is a changing coast, both in human activity and geography. I was to walk through many tiny settlements where once busy commercial wharves lie derelict or taken over by leisure craft, and through towns and villages whose economy is now largely based on tourism rather than fishing, but I was also to find a few places where industry still thrives.

Suffolk's coastal erosion is well known, the retreating shore having claimed whole towns and villages, but I was to find that this is very much an ongoing process, with winter storms and the highest tidal surge for sixty years closing some of the paths that I walked a few months earlier. I knew that it was a changing coast, but I didn't think it would change so much in just one year. Hence, to keep the book as up to date as possible I went back to several areas, repeating walks and adding post scripts to chapters, so that anyone walking the section will have the most recent information on the paths.

You will read how sometimes I deliberated and chose to ignore signs saying that paths were closed. Obviously I can't advise others to do likewise, but it should be noted that some of these signs were years out of date. Where paths were 'closed' or 'private' I've suggested alternative routes.

As well as a coast of beauty, of wildlife, of history and of people, I was to find that Suffolk's is a coast of mystery, the highlight perhaps a truly unforgettable walk around Orford Ness. Legends of invading Germans, Crazy Mary, UFOs, Anne Boleyn, church bells ringing under the sea, elephants on a ferry and a half man half fish creature, all provided intrigue, and I've tried to give a little insight into whether or not they may be true.

Nice as they are, I was to find that there's much more to the Suffolk coast than Southwold, Dunwich and Aldeburgh. It was perhaps the enigmatic marshes, the desolate yet haunting shingle, the winding rivers, unique heathland and crumbling cliffs that I shall remember most. I hope that I have been able to portray the beauty, charm and history of this wonderful coast, and perhaps inspire others to walk its paths.

Reprints

This book has been reprinted several times, with updates made in 2018, 2021 and 2026. For this latest reprint I went back to Suffolk once more, re-walking at least part of most of the walks. Brief notes on changes noted for each chapter are included at the end of the book.

Please note however, that as I didn't repeat the whole walk, it is possible that there have been some changes to footpaths on this dynamic coastline since the book was originally published, which I have not mentioned in the updates.

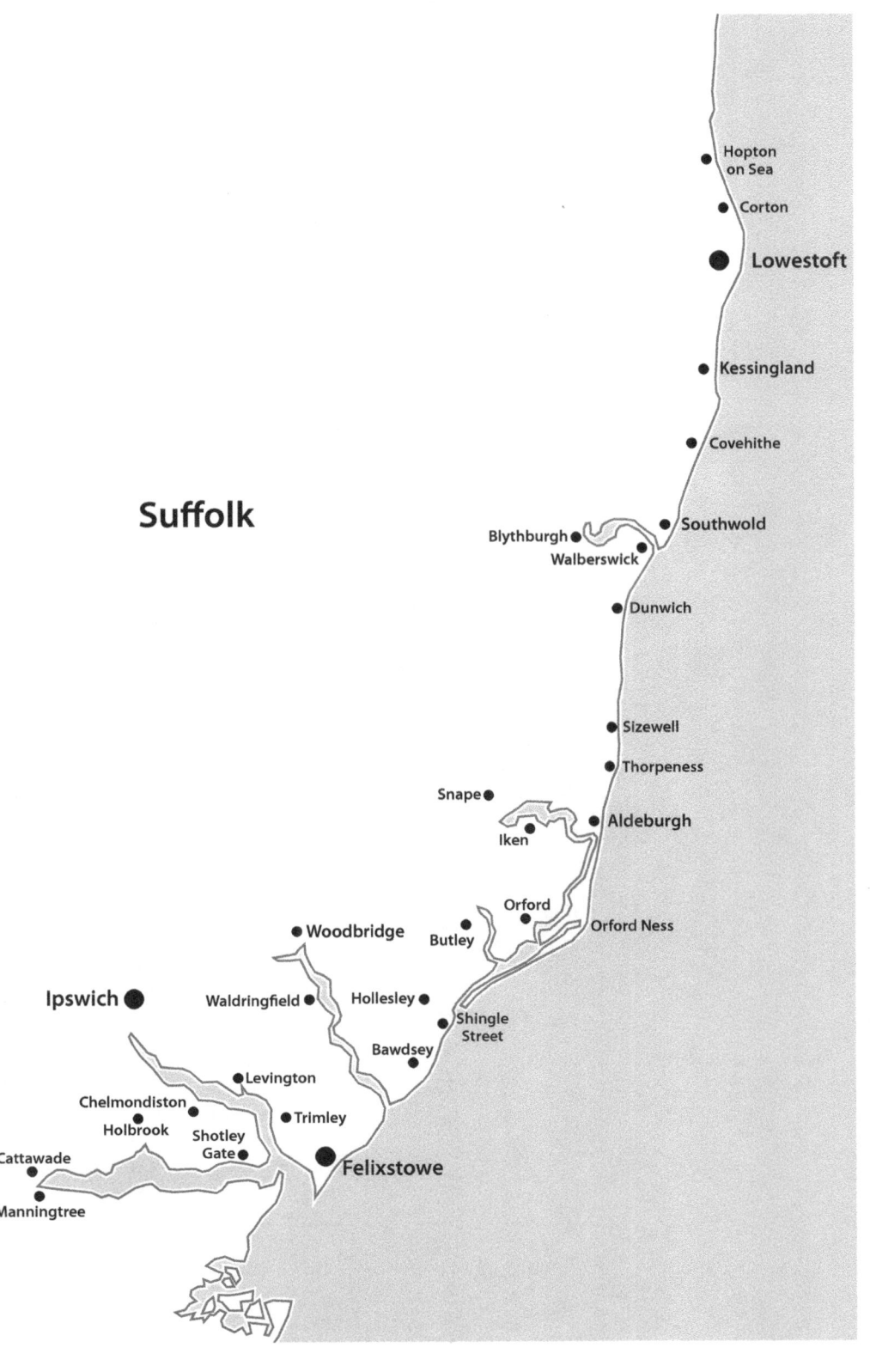

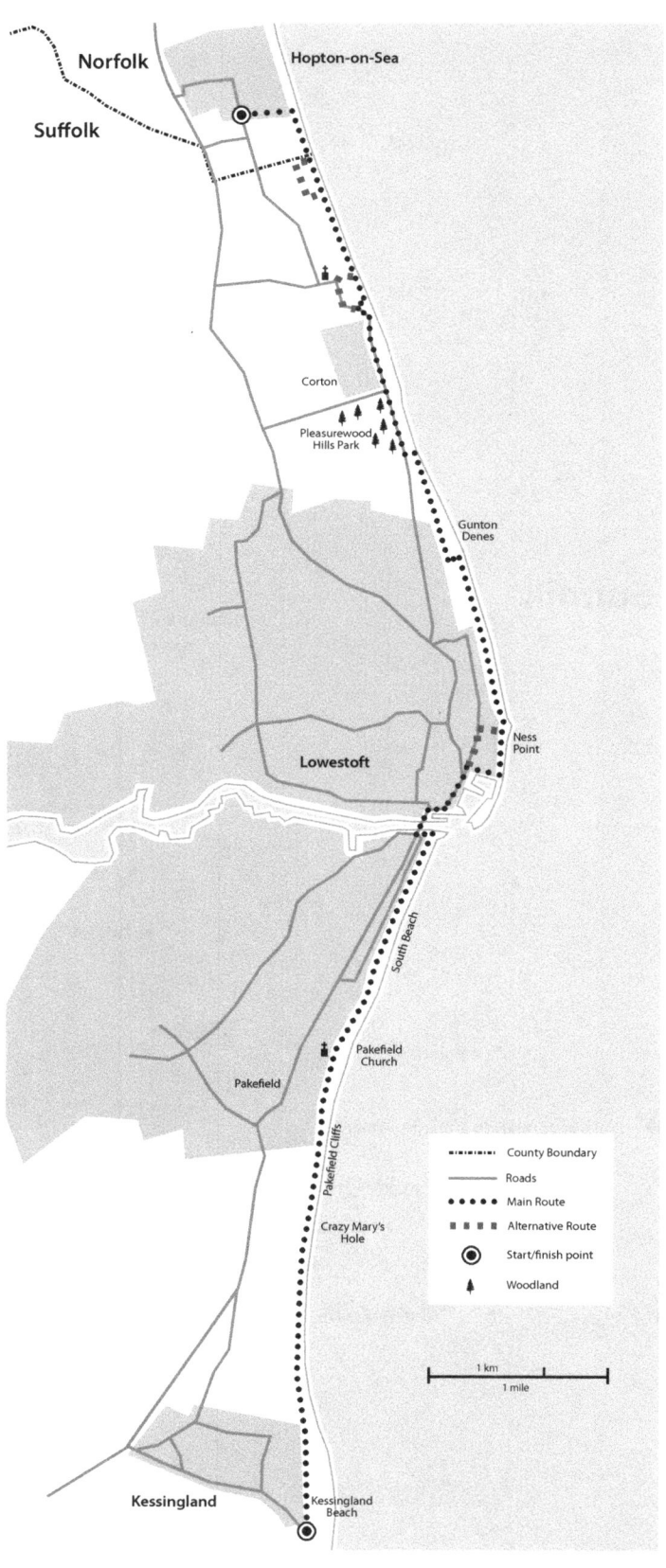

CHAPTER ONE
CORTON – KESSINGLAND

(10 Miles) 4th March

DANGER EXTREMELY DANGEROUS CLIFF FALL

DO NOT GO PAST THIS NOTICE

EXTREME DANGER CLIFF EROSION KEEP OUT

These weren't the signs I wanted to see as I tried to enter Suffolk. WELCOME TO SUFFOLK would have been nice, but I'd have been quite happy to have walked into the county with no signs at all. Five notices telling me I couldn't go past wasn't quite the greeting I had in mind.

I'd started in Norfolk. It seemed right to commence the walk by crossing Suffolk's border, so I caught a Number One bus the six miles from Lowestoft to the seaside village of Hopton-on-Sea. On the train to Norwich I'd passed the county's southern border, the White Bridge over the Stour, from where I'd started my Essex Coast Walk and was to end the Suffolk walk 162 miles later. The northern boundary is however less defined. Until 1974 Hopton-on-Sea had been in Suffolk, but now the border runs along the River Waveney, through Fritton Decoy, then in the absence of any natural barriers, takes a straight line from the A12 to the coast.

A short walk from the bus stop took me to the cliff top and past Potters Leisure Resort, now a luxury holiday village, but originally a holiday camp set up in army Nissan huts by Herbert Potter in 1919 with £500 he won in a newspaper competition.

A tall barbed wire topped fence marks the boundary between Norfolk and Suffolk. More rolls of barbed wire lay inside the fence. I know there's rivalry, and football matches between Norwich and Ipswich can get a bit lively, but I didn't expect this! Looking more like the Korean border than the division between two rural East Anglian counties, the fence surrounds what was once RAF Hopton. Originally a Second World War radar station, the site was chosen as part of a network of improved radar sites which were hurriedly built in the Cold War to give early warning of approaching Russian bombers. Changes in technology and the advent of supersonic aircraft meant that the Hopton was redundant within a few years of opening, and it has lain derelict for many years.

To the left of the fence was a narrow strip of land running to the cliff edge. It was here that the path was closed. As I studied the map considering alternative routes, a man walking two dogs, one white one black, approached. He told me that the path had been closed since a landslip in January, but that the plastic fence around the fall had been taken down and I could get past it with care. With suitable caution I walked beyond the five forbidding signs to inspect the situation. There was still three or four feet of land, but some of this was overhang and it wasn't easy to tell how much. Footprints showed that others had walked across. Mangled steel and concrete at the base of the cliff

Welcome to Suffolk!

were the remains of Corton promenade, which was also closed with fears of further landslides. It was on this that I would land if the cliff gave way.

This is where I say – Don't try it at home. As I had when visiting some of the islands for *No Boat Required*, I carried out my own risk assessment, ignored all official advice, and pressing myself up to the fence, edged very carefully past the landslip. Was I a naughty boy? Yes. Was I reckless? No – I assessed the risk for myself and decided that with care it was safe. Should anyone else do the same? No – you should of course obey warning signs that are put up to ensure your safety.

The path continued on the cliff edge and at another landslip disappeared over it, as I passed the first of Suffolk's many caravan parks, then agricultural land with misty views to Corton's distinctive St Bartholomew's church. In 1986 the new vicar here complained that his first sermon was not well received, with parishioners trying to shout him down and asking him to leave. This was not as he thought because he was a socialist, but a local Corton tradition known as 'vicar bating'!

There's no cliff top path at Corton, so with the promenade closed I headed inland through the village. Away from the sea breeze it seemed that in an instant winter had turned to spring. Locals tended their allotments in the sunshine, and I swapped my woolly hat and scarf for a baseball cap – all in the claret and blue of West Ham of course.

Sea Defences & Erosion – Corton Cliffs

Many of Corton's houses show the initials JJC in brickwork, indicating that they were built for Jeremiah James Colman, founder of the Norwich based mustard company. His friend William Gladstone gave a clock to the village, which can still be seen inside the village hall. Colman financed the pretty flint and red-brick Methodist church, which stands in a tree-lined churchyard in the centre of the village. By the school is a memorial to Lieutenant Commander Roy Edwards and Ensign John Howard, who were killed in June 1942 defusing a magnetic mine on Corton Beach, plus the twenty one people from Corton who died in the two World Wars.

A sign 'To Beach' pointed me down a short path, but the gate at the end was locked, the beach closed by more landslides. Despite unsightly wooden defences running parallel to the shore, the beach is unsafe, its closure impacting on both tourism and locals. A cottage 75 yards from the cliff edge was aptly named 'Near Enough'. East Anglia has the fastest eroding coastline in Europe and a combination of the power of the North Sea and some of the youngest and softest rocks in the UK, means that 54% of Suffolk's coast is eroding – more than any other county.

One consequence of coastal erosion was the controversial closure of Corton Naturist Beach. The 200 yard stretch of beach became one of Britain's first official nudist beaches in 1979, but the designation was removed by Waveney District Council in 2009, on the basis that erosion over twenty years had reduced the size of Corton's beach by 80%. Anyone using the village's beach now had little option but to enter the designated area and some may have seen sights that they would rather not. A spokesman for British Naturism, whose 14,000 members represented an estimated 1.5 million nudists, claimed that the council's report was misleading and suggested a hidden agenda to get rid of the naturists.

The controversy continued the following year when British Naturism challenged the sign which advised that the beach was now not designated as 'naturist' or 'clothes optional'. Whilst correct that the beach was no longer designated as naturist, the byelaw requiring clothing to be worn on all beaches except Corton had been revoked, so one can now be *'unclothed'* on all beaches within the Waveney District. Locals complained of *'inappropriate behaviour'* by a *'fringe element'*, and Suffolk police published guidance which I shall repeat should any readers wish to bare all on the county's beaches:

'You can go on any beach and naturism is not illegal, however, any behaviour which is deemed to be exhibitionist or offensive would be dealt with. Any form of overt sexual behaviour is the easiest way of explaining it. A naturist walking down a beach to go for a swim is not in itself exhibitionism. On a vast, empty stretch of beach, if a naturist chooses to sit down in very close proximity to a non-naturist, that could be seen as exhibitionism. Some people may find naturism difficult to deal with, but we're asking all sides to respect each other.'

With the beach closed and no coastal path, I followed the road which runs through woodland. Behind the woods is Pleasurewood Hills, the largest theme park in East Anglia, where those who so desire can pay to be spun, twisted, dropped and accelerated around a selection of rides which apparently possess the power to turn your knuckles white.

A path at the end of the woods took me onto Gunton Cliffs and Warren – a lovely walk through gorse, heather and bracken covered cliffs, heath, scrub and sand dunes. This was just the sort of Suffolk coastal environment that I'd been looking forward to. It is a designated nature reserve with varied bird populations, including occasional rare migrants.

I chatted to a couple walking their dog, our conversation adhering to convention – the weather (good for walking) and the coast (very nice). They told me that I'd be able to walk by the sea all the way into Lowestoft, following the sea wall beyond the car park for Gunton Denes Beach. A sign indicated that this was part of the North Sea Cycle Route. No ordinary cycle path, at 6000km and passing through eight countries, this is the world's longest cycle route.

The cliff here is some way back from the shore and amongst trees on the cliffside stands Lowestoft High Lighthouse. This was originally erected in the 17th century, when it was linked with a Low Lighthouse on the foreshore, enabling vessels to line up the two lights and steer a path through Stamford Channel. When the channel disappeared the Low Light served no purpose, so was extinguished, but the High Light still operates, the beam from the tower that was rebuilt in 1874 visible 20 miles out to sea.

The walk along the sea wall was not exactly scenic. The beach was closed, because of '*concrete debris and sharp spikes*'. The old promenade and some small stone buildings had been claimed by the sea. Ahead was a huge Birds Eye factory. To my right was an area of wasteland, then a rather sad caravan park. I can think of better places to stay than by a closed beach next to a food processing factory.

Two men were fishing from the sea wall in front of the factory. They'd had no luck. I'm not surprised. If I were a fish the last place I'd want to be swimming is near a Birds Eye plant. Perhaps they'd have done better to have cast their lines the other way and hook a fish finger.

Lowestoft is the most easterly place in the UK. The area is marketed as the Sunrise Coast and the town as the first place to see the sun each morning (although in mid-summer it's actually the Shetland Isles and in mid-winter it's Dover), but no one seems to know what to do with Ness Point, our most easterly point. Rather than the dramatic cliffs or grassy headland one expects, it's simply a flat piece of concrete behind a sea wall and in front of a Birds Eye factory.

All that marks the point is the 'Euroscope', a large flat concrete wheel showing approximate bearings and distances to various places around Europe. It was reasonably interesting to learn that I was 472 miles from Dunnet Head, 352 miles from Lizard Point and 451 miles from Ardnamurchan Point, the most northerly, southerly and westerly points on the UK mainland, but all in all it seemed rather inadequate.

Euroscope

Gulliver

More spectacular is 'Gulliver', the largest onshore wind turbine in the UK. The 125 metre tall structure produces enough electricity to power 1,500 homes, saving over 6,000 tonnes of greenhouse emissions each year. The tips of the ten tonne blades cut through the air at around 150mph, with the turbulence generated accounting for the pulsating whooshing noise audible from underneath. Adjacent is OrbisEnergy, a centre of excellence for environmentally friendly technology, conference venue and home to businesses involved in offshore renewable energy.

At the North Pier I turned right along Hamilton Dock, then left into Lowestoft centre on the A12. This wasn't a place I particularly wished to dwell. Lowestoft is Suffolk's second largest town but it's far from the nicest.

I walked through the pedestrianised centre, which could have been any not very prosperous medium-sized town around the country (same shops – different order), then crossed the Bascule Bridge – the gateway to Lowestoft by both road and water. Built in 1974, the bridge lifts to allow boats to enter the North Docks and inner harbour, a stretch of water known as Lake Lothing. Although commercial shipping is discouraged from passing under the bridge in the rush hours, and smaller vessels using the marina may only pass if it's already opened for a commercial one, locals complain of the congestion it causes on the busy A12. The problem has become worse since Lowestoft became the main port servicing North Sea wind farms and Waveney District Council is considering various solutions. The most likely of these is a new four lane bridge across a broader part of the harbour.

The bridged stretch of water is man-made. It was cut through the shingle beach in 1831, the initiative coming from Norwich merchants, annoyed by the way they felt Yarmouth took advantage of its navigational stranglehold. A miscalculation meant that on the first high tide the wooden lock gate floated off its sockets and drifted out to sea. Whilst this link gave Lowestoft its harbour, it was the coming of the railway in the 1840s, brought here by the enterprise of the engineer Samuel Morton Peto (who built Nelson's Column), which turned Lowestoft into a busy fishing port and holiday resort.

At the southern end of the bridge is a statue of a lifeboatman looking out to sea, dedicated to '*All Lowestoft lifeboatmen, past, present and future, for their sterling duty to seafarers of the world*'. Lowestoft is one of the oldest lifeboat stations in

Britain, the first boat being placed here in 1801, twenty three years before the RNLI was founded. A fund was set up by Robert Sparrow of Worlingham Hall and Reverend Francis Bowness, Rector of Gunton, who were distressed at the loss of life in shipwrecks along the treacherous coast. A thirty foot boat was built by Greathead of South Shields at a cost of £160, but what most books omit to mention is that it was a complete failure. In two years it failed to carry out a single rescue, for the simple reason that Lowestoft men considered her unfit for the purpose. Her form they said, was totally unsuitable for the steep shingle shore, as it couldn't be launched without filling with water. Undeterred, Robert Sparrow offered the men more money; ten guineas for a mission and fifteen if lives were saved, but Lowestoft men knew an unseaworthy vessel. In six years it was recorded to have attended just one wreck and in 1807 the boat was sold to Harwich for a mere ten pounds.

The town's maritime history goes back to the Anglo-Saxons, who had a small fishing community here, and expanded in the 13th century when Kessingland's harbour began silting. By the 19th century it was the world's busiest herring port. Two numbers in the town's history that are hard to comprehend are the 90% of the population killed by bubonic plague in 1349, and the 1,044,001,200 herring landed at Lowestoft and Great Yarmouth in 1909. Most of the catch was sent by train to London, with thirty to forty wagons leaving Lowestoft every hour. Such fishing was not sustainable and by the Second World War North Sea stocks were becoming depleted. It remained Lowestoft's main industry until the 1960s, but now just a handful of small boats fish from the town. North Sea gas and more latterly offshore wind farms have however maintained some employment and its role as a working port.

Rivalry between the Lowestoft and Yarmouth has continued for hundreds of years, although no longer do residents of the Suffolk town call Yarmouthians 'Duff Chokers' and the Norfolk people refer to Lowestoft fishermen as 'Pea Bellies'. The derivation of the former is unknown, but the latter is believed to come from fishermen being so poor that they lived chiefly on pea soup.

The southern part of Lowestoft is more of a traditional holiday resort, with a wide promenade, sandy beaches and the usual entertainments. On Royal Plain, opposite the attractive Edwardian clubhouse of the Royal Suffolk and Norfolk

Yacht Club, are seventy four new fountains with interactive jets and variable lighting, providing a play area for children and an illuminated spectacle on summer evenings. Inside the East Point Pavilion a coach party of senior citizens sat drinking tea. This focal point of the seafront was built in traditional Edwardian glass winter gardens style and opened in 1997.

I enjoyed a chicken roll sitting on the promenade, watching the world pass by: a man from the council filling holes with tarmac, four young men with beer cans heading for a shelter, elderly people in buggies towing dogs, two gulls who stood watching my every bite but gave up just as I finished and a fat pigeon who was rewarded for staying by hoovering up a few crumbs under the seat.

Continuing along the esplanade I passed Claremont Pier, which dates from 1903, but like so many of our seaside piers, is now a shadow of its former self. The shore end boasts modern facilities – amusement arcade, restaurant, casino and roller skating rink, but the wooden head of the pier where steamers once brought day trippers, has been claimed by the sea. The remaining boards, where well dressed Edwardian holiday-makers promenaded above the waves, are now unsafe and closed to the public.

Leaving the town I followed a path along the top of the cliffs, until diverting a few yards inland to the thatched Pakefield church. It is actually two churches, with two altars, chancels and naves, although the dividing wall was taken down at least two centuries ago. Hence it is dedicated to both All Saints and St Margaret. Until the 18th century both churches had their own parish, but the

South Pier – Lowestoft

easterly one has now been entirely taken by the sea. Stocks and a whipping post at the gate remind of how local miscreants would have been dealt with years ago.

Pleased to find the door open, I wandered in to find that this mediaeval church still thrives and moves with the times. It was good to see modern instruments used in worship and a range of activities for all ages. A friendly parishioner told me that they get congregations of a hundred and that installing modern chairs in place of pews had not detracted from the history of the building, as the latter dated from only the 1950s. The originals were lost when the church was completely gutted by a bomb in 1941. I was glad to have stopped here for a while.

The path continued on the cliff top, until a large chalet park where the Suffolk Coast Path headed inland. Preferring to stay by the shore, I carried on amongst the chalets until a short road led to the cliff edge. Here a sign said there was no path – but there was! It was only narrow and right at the edge of the cliff, so with concerns for my safety and whether there'd be a way through at the end, after a couple of hundred yards I reluctantly turned back – see I'm not really reckless!

From here to Kessingland I walked on the beach, initially on a path under the cliff, then when this disappeared, on a strip of firm sand by the sea. Exposed at the base of the cliffs is part of the Cromer Forest Bed, a series of fossil-rich freshwater sediments which were formed between 450,000 and 780,000 years ago. Bones of mammoth, sabre tooth cat, hippopotamus and giant deer have been found here, and in 2005 Pakefield Cliffs became a sight of national importance with the discovery of flint tools dating from more than 700,000 years ago. Until older tools were found up the coast at Happisburgh in 2010, these were the earliest evidence of human occupation in the UK.

If you study any Ordnance Survey map it doesn't take long to find an intriguing place name, wonder how it came about and if there's a story behind it. Looking at the map before setting out I'd found *Crazy Mary's Hole*, a gully beneath the old Pakefield Lighthouse (now a Coastwatch Station). A little research told me the story, or as is often the case, two versions of a story.

Many years ago a woman named Mary had a husband who was a fisherman. One afternoon he went to sea but never returned. In her grief, every evening at about

9 o'clock Mary walked along the cliff top, hoping against hope that one day she would again see the sails of his boat on the horizon. Alas it was never to be and the poor woman finally went mad with grief and walked down the gully into the sea to join her husband. That's the first version. The second says that she waited for his return on the cliffs, where she eventually died of starvation, but her ghost still waits and was seen in 1981 by an employee of a local holiday camp.

There was no sign of Mary as I walked along the deserted beach, looking back occasionally to the now distant buildings of Lowestoft beneath the towering Gulliver. Approaching Kessingland the beach broadens and having stayed by the sea I found myself a long way from the cliffs. It was a strange walk back across a desert-like landscape of shingle, sand and occasional clumps of marram grass. This is one of the few beaches in East Anglia to be growing, reputedly thanks to the author Rider Haggard spotting the erosion problem and planting marram grass to protect the beach house where he used to write. I suspect though that it has more to do with the process of longshore drift, the transport of sediment along the coast. All these eroded cliffs have to go somewhere. If it continues to grow Kessingland Beach will eventually overtake Ness Point as our most easterly point.

Anglian Buses' cheerful blue and yellow Number 601A was waiting at the top of the beach. The driver told me he'd be leaving in ten minutes. A small picnic area by the bus stop is dedicated to Roynon Brown MBE, who served on Kessingland Parish Council for 45 years and sadly died a few weeks before he was to be presented with Freedom of the Village on his 96th birthday. Opposite is a pub, Sailors Home. I've thought about it for twelve months but can think of only one meaning for the two words that wouldn't need an apostrophe – the somewhat unlikely explanation that the second word is a verb and it's a statement referring to mariners possessing the instinct to return to their place of abode (as in pigeons home).

A rather uncomfortable and circuitous bus ride (it was one of those drivers who believe that their foot must always be hard down on either the accelerator or brake), passing *Africa Alive* (formerly *Suffolk Wildlife Park*) twice and diverting into Morrisons, took me back to Lowestoft. It stopped a few yards from Edingworth Guest House, my bed for the night.

Sailors Home – Kessingland

Owners Viv and Mike were interested in my books and I told them I'd be mentioning accommodation, but only by name if it was good. They'd have to wait for the book to see if they were named! My report is positive – a quiet and comfortable room, good breakfast and friendly proprietors. I nearly didn't stay there though – it seemed too cheap – about 25% less than many apparently similar establishments in the town. Initially attracted by the lower price, concern that you usually get what you pay for led me to reconsider. Excellent internet reviews swayed my choice. Viv said that the only bad one was a very large lady who complained that the towels were too small to fit round her. That she'd found the lady had posted a string of poor hotel reviews perhaps tells us more about this guest than any deficiency in the towels.

Dinner presented a similar dilemma. The carvery advertised by Hatfield Hotel at £3.79 seemed just too cheap and again I thought twice. The lady on reception said it was good, so in I went. Let's say £3.79 was a fair price.

Lowestoft isn't a rich town. Rates of unemployment and crime are above the national average and compare unfavourably to much of Suffolk. It seems to be a town that doesn't know quite what it wants to be. It's a holiday resort, but finds it hard to compete with the more genteel Suffolk towns to the south, or the brasher Great Yarmouth to the north. It would like to be a fishing port, but suffers from the short-sightedness of previous generations who decimated North Sea stocks. It has industry and commercial shipping, but neither enhance the town's tourist appeal. It has a unique geographical landmark, but pretty much ignores it. Its position means that few people pass through and most of those who do find little to entice them to stop for long. Lowestoft isn't a bad place, but pushed to say what's good about it all that comes to mind is – it's cheap!

Post Script

Repeating my walk from Hopton-on-Sea to Lowestoft a year later, I found both the lane to the shore and the beach to be closed. A digger working on the shingle suggested this was temporary. Keep Out signs still greeted walkers at Suffolk's boundary, but now a wooden fence blocked the cliff-top path. I walked around the old radar site, which a couple told me is now owned by Potters Leisure. There's no path or right of way, but it was easy walking, although two rather fierce guard dogs inside the wire fence made it clear they weren't happy to see me. Back at the cliff edge it was clear why the path was closed – it had gone. Last year I'd squeezed by along the fence. Now the path and fence were in the sea.

The cliff-top in front of the caravan park was fenced off but a strip of grass made for easy walking. How much longer will this and the caravans remain I wondered. More erosion had left the next section of path precariously close to the edge and the only safe walking was on a ploughed field. To avoid further tramping on the farmer's ploughed land, at the next field boundary I took a track that runs towards Corton church, meeting up with the road which took me into Corton. I had found a way through from Hopton, but anyone wishing to walk the Suffolk coast may find it easier to start from Corton.

At Lowestoft I turned right by Ness Point, following signs to the 'Historic High Street'. Somewhat rundown, although with a few interesting buildings, like the Euroscope, it delivered less than it promised. Lowestoft was still cheap. Hatfield Hotel had slightly raised their carvery price but also the quality, and the Edingworth provided another comfortable night at a bargain rate.

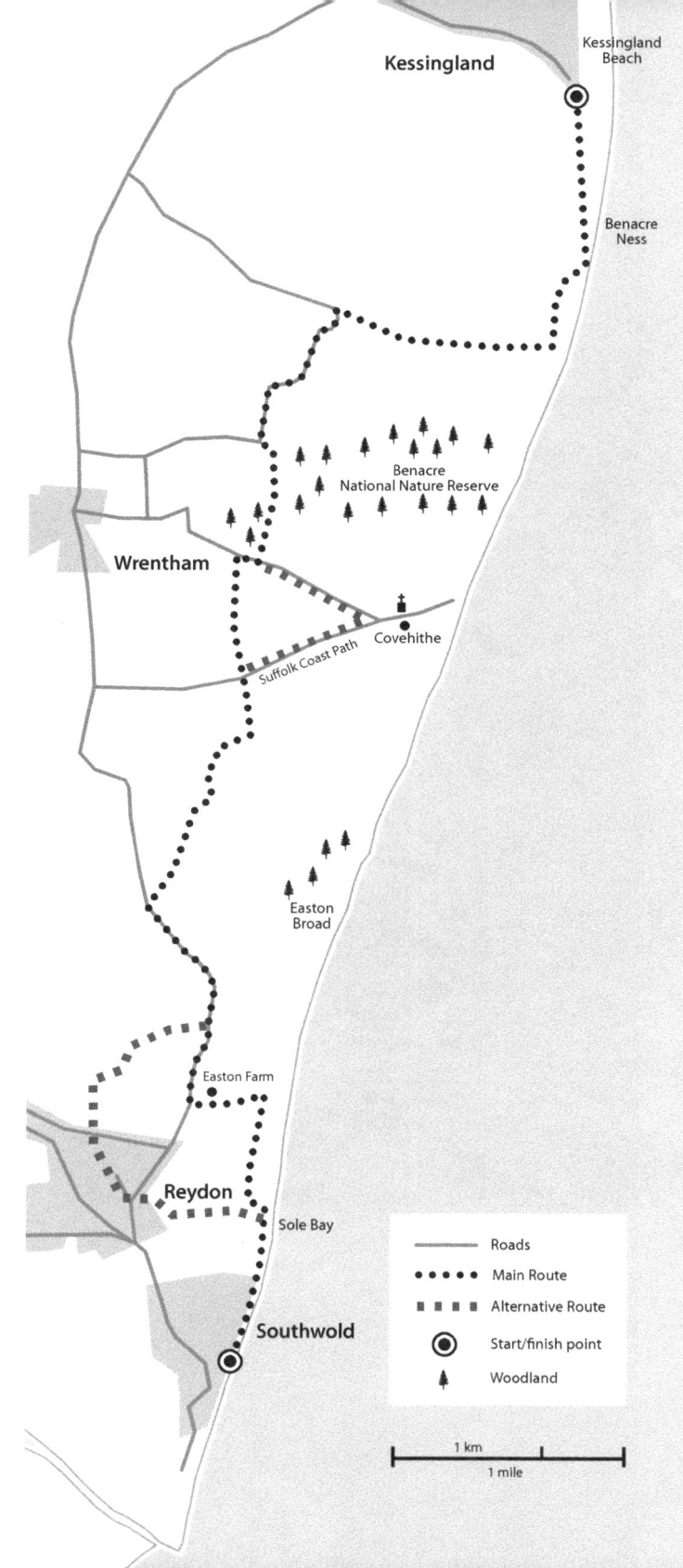

CHAPTER TWO
KESSINGLAND – SOUTHWOLD

(8 Miles) 5th March

At 10 o'clock the next morning I was back at Kessingland, pondering again the apostrophe status of the Sailors Return. I'd been the only person to leave Kessingland on the bus last night, and the only one to arrive this morning.

Today's walk started on the Suffolk Coast Path, which I was to follow on and off to Southwold. A concrete path at the top of the beach soon gave way to what I was already finding to be typical Suffolk walking – sand, shingle, grass and dunes. I caught up with a lady with her dog, and we walked together, chatting for a while. She told me that thirty years ago people used to swim from the top of the beach but now only occasional storms bring the sea up here. As I continued towards what the map marked as 'Ppg Sta', she headed off into the dunes where her dog liked to look for rabbits. It wasn't until examining the map on the train home that it dawned on me what the initials stood for – Pumping Station.

This is Benacre Sluice, where the Hundred River enters the North Sea. A sign directed walkers inland, warning of 'Deep Fast Flowing Water'. The stream was all of two inches deep and two feet wide. I should not have scoffed. Exactly a week after my visit Lowestoft Coastguard issued a warning to keep clear as gushing water had washed away a slice of the beach.

My plan anyway was to head inland, following an embankment around Benacre Pits, an attractive lake just behind the beach. With the appearance of a natural lagoon, this was actually man-made, formed by the extraction of gravel to construct nearby concrete runways and bunkers in World War Two. Two other pits have been consumed by the sea, which continues to erode the area, depositing sediment to the north on Kessingland's growing beach.

The path took me almost back to the shore, where I detoured onto the beach to investigate some strange brick-built constructions on the sand – a dome resembling a small kiln or large beehive, and several other mysterious remains. I had absolutely no idea what they were and initial research drew a blank. It was Stacie at Southwold Tourist Information Centre who found their origin. Someone had sent a photo to the *Lowestoft Journal* and two readers replied with the same rather unromantic answer. The remains were of a humble septic drainage system, with the domed construction a brick soak-away chamber, all exposed by erosion. Mr P.J. Harrold wrote, *'Beach walkers of a delicate disposition can be reassured that Mother Nature has long since removed any trace of anything which might have more obviously indicated its original purpose!'*

Looking south, the beach stretched away into the distance beneath low cliffs. At low water it's usually possible to walk all the way to Southwold, but this should never be attempted when the tide is rising. Even at low tide the Benacre, Covehithe and Easton Broads can all be impassable, especially in winter months. With a rising tide there was no way I would have attempted it (see that's twice I haven't been reckless!), but in any case I didn't fancy walking five miles on shingle and preferred a more varied inland route.

Brick Soak-away Chamber – Benacre Beach

A narrow path headed inland, becoming a paved track at Beach Farm and crossing huge ploughed fields towards Benacre church. After about a mile it reached The Street, a narrow country lane. To the left were woods which surround Benacre Broad. I'd considered cutting off a corner by following tracks through the trees but signs advised this was a conservation area with access barred. Whilst I might be prepared to ignore a private sign that I felt was unjustly limiting my freedom to roam, if wildlife needs to be left alone, so it should be.

It is part of Benacre National Nature Reserve, which is recognised as one of the finest wildlife sites in Britain. The three saline lagoons (the broads) were formed in shallow valleys when ice age glacial drift blocked the outflow to the sea. They are the reserve's main interest and support specialist species such as lagoon shrimp and starlet sea-anemone. Over a hundred bird species breed on the reserve, reedbeds supporting marsh harriers, water rail and bittern, heathlands providing home to woodlarks, and shingle beaches nesting sites for avocets and terns. In summer butterflies abound, including the recently discovered brown argus.

The reedbeds are home to the very rare white-mantled wainscot moth, which was considered extinct in Britain after habitat in Sussex, its only known site, was destroyed during World War Two. The moth was rediscovered at Benacre and other than a recent sighting in Norfolk, is only found on the Suffolk coastal marshes. Light brown in colour, after over-wintering as an egg it flies from July to early August, fluttering over the tops of reedbeds at dusk and amongst the reeds later in the night.

Turning left into a quiet lane (just one car passed me in fifteen minutes) I headed south once more. Perhaps in protest at having to walk on tarmac, my legs decided that they wanted to go slowly. They know what speed they are comfortable with and don't like being told to go faster or slower. Once I'd turned left onto a very pleasant track beside the woods they sped up, but by the corner of Holly Grove I stopped. A mysterious old shed required investigating. The door looked as if it hadn't been opened for years and inside was an array of pipes, valves and electrical boxes. I presumed it was once used in connection with draining the marshes.

Every few minutes the peace of the countryside was interrupted by gunfire. Several signs warned of shooting in progress, one rather incongruously on a gate saying 'Conservation Area'. Turning the corner, I met a pheasant on the path and had a quiet word suggesting he'd be best to lie low for a while. Heeding my advice he scuttled off into the undergrowth.

A tall fence had recently been erected around the ancient woodland of Holly Grove, enabling the hazel and sycamores to be coppiced, the traditional method by which such woods have been sustainably managed for centuries. Felling selected trees at the stump allows multiple new shoots to grow, which without the grazing from fallow and muntjac deer, brings a new layer of growth to the woodland and more nesting places for birds such as nightingales. It is hoped that this intervention will allow wildlife that has lived in the woods for thousands of years to recover from the effect of the grazing; an example of man's helping hand being needed to encourage biodiversity which he upset in the first place – neither muntjac or fallow deer are indigenous British species and of course we wiped out deer's natural predators.

At the end of the wood the Suffolk Coast Path turns left onto a lane into Covehithe, but preferring to avoid more road walking I went the other way for a couple of hundred yards, during which I nearly got run over. As I wandered down the middle of the lane an urgent whistle caused me to turn to see a yellow lycra clad cyclist rapidly approaching. With a cheery *'alright'* he whizzed by, but I was glad to leave the road, turning left down a wide track between trees. Marked on the OS map as 'Green Lane', it is shown on Hodskinson's 1783 Suffolk map as forming the boundary between enclosures to the west and what was then Covehithe Common to the east.

The track made ideal walking and near Field Farm I found a suitable spot for lunch. Sitting at the edge of a field as a tractor drove to and fro sowing seeds and with truly not a cloud in the sky, this was an almost idyllic English rural scene. It would have been perfect but for the rather disconcerting sound of sporadic gunshots that were a little too close for comfort.

At Crossways Cottages I met up with the Suffolk Coast Path which had followed lanes in and out of Covehithe, most of which has been lost to the sea. The coastline here has been calculated to have retreated 500 metres since the

1830s, and the road now simply falls away to the beach. It's likely that within another fifty years the whole village, including the magnificent ruin of St Andrew's Church, will have been claimed by the sea.

The Suffolk Coast Path continues along Air Station Road (there was a First World War airfield here which was used for anti Zeppelin patrols but later returned to agricultural land), then takes a route to Southwold that runs a couple of miles inland. I preferred the shorter route along a track opposite Green Lane, which became a lovely grassy path between fields. It was easy walking; a contrast to some of the inland paths I'd followed in Essex.

The track ended at the busy B1127, which I followed for a mile, the least enjoyable section of walking so far. At Potter's Bridge the road crosses the Easton channel, around which is the second largest area of reedbeds in England. Reeds up to eight foot high form a landscape that is as inaccessible to man as it is ideal for some of our rarest birds, including in some years, bittern. This thick-set heron relies on such reedbeds and with a breeding population of less than a hundred, is one of the UK's most endangered birds.

The area is threatened by coastal erosion, with Easton Broad protected from the sea by only the shingle beach, which is regularly breached during high tides and storms (hence the option of beach walking from Covehithe to Southwold is not always possible even at low tide).

To protect the upper part of the marsh and be sure of retaining some freshwater on which the bittern rely (they only eat freshwater fish which will die when the area inevitably becomes flooded with seawater), the Environment Agency has plans to build a 400 metre clay bank along the B1127. Inland of this the freshwater reedbeds will be protected, while the rest will eventually become salt marsh. Having drained so much natural habitat over many centuries, it is now necessary for man to intervene in order to ensure that some of our rarest wildlife can survive. Much care however is required to ensure that such intervention is to the benefit of overall biodiversity, and not just the more celebrated species such as bittern. Our humble friend the white-mantled wainscot moth requires drier reedy ditches for its larvae and these can be lost as part of conservation management for other species.

Just beyond the bridge two men were loading bundles of reeds onto a trailer. This commercial harvesting of the reeds for thatching has taken place for centuries – a sustainable way for man, wildlife and marsh to live in harmony.

As I rounded a bend the town of Southwold with its iconic white lighthouse, came into view. Rather than follow the road into Reydon where it meets the Suffolk Coast Path, I turned left down Easton Lane, an unadopted road passing farm buildings. Here I was almost back at the sea. The map showed a path running across a field on the cliff top. A sign said 'No Footpath' but it looked like one to me, so I carried on. It took me through Southend Warren, where rabbits scampered about on the short grass, happy in the knowledge that they were no longer here to be fattened for the pot. The path ended on the edge of the cliff where I passed two signs, and looked back to read, 'PRIVATE ACCESS ONLY' and 'NO PUBLIC RIGHT OF WAY'. Oh dear, I'd been naughty again.

This stretch of sea is known as Sole Bay, although the coastline is actually quite straight, with no sign of a bay. However, before the sea carved away Easton Ness to the north and Dunwich to the south, Southwold was in a bay. It was here on 28th May 1672, that England fought a major sea battle with the Dutch – the Battle of Sole Bay.

At 2.30 in the morning a French frigate reported that the Dutch fleet was two hours away. The English fleet had assembled at Southwold to refit and most of the crews were enjoying shore leave. With an immediate call to arms, 90 ships, carrying 24,000 men and over 5,500 guns, set sail at 5.30am, under the command of James, Duke of York (later to become James II) and Admiral Edward Montagu the First Earl of Sandwich. The French fleet, an ally of England in this third Anglo-Dutch War, managed by accident or design to sail off, leaving the English ships to do battle with a similar number of Dutch. The thunder of guns brought crowds onto the cliffs as the battle raged all day, with smoke billowing from fire ships deliberately set ablaze to destroy enemy vessels. When the battle appeared to be turning against the English an order was put out that no one may leave Southwold, in case they were needed to repel a Dutch invasion.

Both sides lost two ships and many men; 2,000 English and 1,800 Dutch, but as the Dutch withdrew both claimed victory. The people of Southwold tended 800 injured men and dealt with bodies which were washed up on the beaches for weeks after. These included the Earl of Sandwich, who had drowned when the sloop in which he was escaping from his burning flagship collapsed under the weight of panicked sailors. His body was only recognised by scorched clothing which still showed the Shield of the Garter.

After stopping to pass the time of day with a lady who was feeding cabbage to her sheep, I completed the final short stretch past Easton Marshes, meeting up with the Suffolk Coast Path which had completed its inland meanderings, much of which are on roads. I'd recommend my route to anyone walking this section, although maybe you should avoid the private path through Southend Warren, and take an alternative path on the right just after Potter's Bridge. This links with the official route at Reydon Smear, follows roads for half a mile, then runs alongside Easton Marshes, coming out just south of the warren.

On such a sunny day Southwold was busy, but my exploring had to wait for the next trip. There was just time for a toasted teacake before catching the Number 520 bus to Halesworth. Like most rural buses, this dived in and out of little villages with no one getting on or off, before dropping me at the station in time for the Ipswich train.

The East Suffolk Line from Ipswich to Lowestoft runs parallel to the coast and was to be my route to and from Suffolk for most of the walks. Had Beeching got his way the line would have closed in the 1960s, but the route survived, albeit with economies made. My father spoke at a meeting in Halesworth opposing its closure. Ironically Beeching hadn't proposed closing the Lowestoft to Great Yarmouth line, which served Hopton-on-Sea and Corton, but with through services withdrawn, the by then very rundown line was closed in 1970. Having recently lost its through trains to London, in 2012 the East Suffolk Line received a major boost with the construction of a passing loop at Beccles, allowing an hourly service to be run.

It was a surprisingly modern and comfortable train that took me on the

Southwold Lighthouse

pleasant ride through Suffolk countryside, with a glimpse of the sea at Woodbridge and the paths I'd be taking here in a few months time.

Post Script

As I progressed down the coast more and more people were asking me what I thought of Covehithe. When I had to confess that I'd missed it out, they told me how I should have seen the church and the lane that disappears over the cliff. So on a sunny October morning I came back to the northern end of Suffolk's coast.

The lane which drops off the edge of the cliff was a bit of a disappointment. Signed as private and with warnings of danger, cars have been barred for years and walkers positively discouraged. Nevertheless a well trodden path round the barrier suggested that many do walk the few hundred yards to the edge of the cliff. Although still marked as a lane on the map, bushes spreading from each side now accommodate only those on foot or cycle. It ends with a mass of bramble bushes, spreading ten yards or so back from the cliff edge. Photos showing the spectacular drop over the cliff must have been taken a good number of years ago.

The church is quite remarkable – a 17th century chapel inside the dramatic ruins of a huge 15th century church. Out of all proportion to Covehithe's population, which never exceeded three hundred souls, the original building was funded by the generosity of the very wealthy William Yarmouth. It was not as many suppose the action of Cromwell's puritans that reduced the magnificent building to ruin, but simply that it was too large for the parish to maintain. Permission was granted to use materials from the church to erect a much smaller chapel within the current shell. The original curtain wall remains, as does the fine tower, which for many years was maintained by Trinity House as a landmark for shipping. Weekly services are still held here, but with the dull, cold and damp interior, and green algae growing on the west wall, I hope the vicar keeps his sermons short.

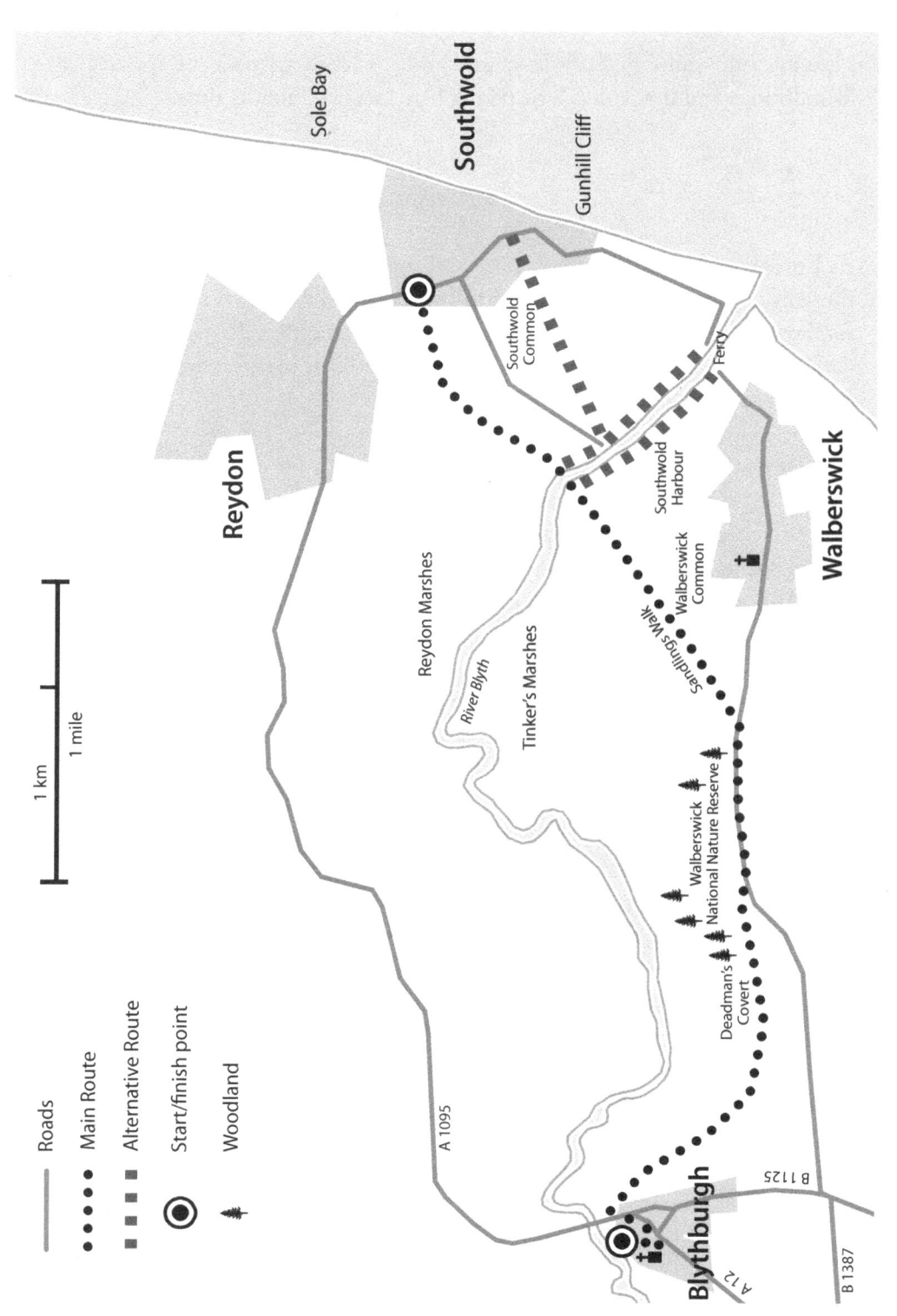

CHAPTER THREE
BLYTHBURGH – SOUTHWOLD

(6 Miles) 8th April

Having reached Southwold, I now had a dilemma. A footbridge over the River Blyth meant that to follow my rule of walking to the first fixed crossing point of rivers would entail leaving out the large tidal estuary west of Southwold. More importantly it would miss the village of Blythburgh, which is generally considered to be on Suffolk's coast. A compromise seemed to be in order, hence I alighted from the bus at Blythburgh, with the plan to walk south of the estuary to Southwold. There is no path to the north, and this way I could avoid lengthy road walking, following a combination of footpaths and an old railway line.

Although aware of the somewhat eccentric Southwold Railway, it was a visit to the Railway Shop whilst waiting for the bus back from my last walk that inspired me to find out more. The three foot gauge line from Halesworth ran for just fifty years. Whilst successful for most of its existence, carrying locals, holidaymakers, coal, fish, farm produce and ale, the branch struggled to compete with the rise of the motor vehicle. Not helped by trains being limited to sixteen miles per hour, so taking forty one minutes for the nine mile journey, it closed as long ago as 1929.

The Southwold Railway Trust (*www.southwoldrailway.co.uk*) aims to preserve the memory of this unique little railway and hopes to reopen part of the route. A replica of locomotive *No. 3 Blythe* is being built and at the time of my visit a planning application had just been submitted to rebuild a half mile section of track at Wenhaston, one of the three intermediate stations. The Trust is based at the shop in Southwold High Street, where I had purchased its guide to walking the route.

Of the four trains and a bus it took me to reach Blythburgh, only one was late – the Norwich express between Colchester and Ipswich. The guard apologised no less than six times for the five minute delay and the *'inconvenience it may cause.'*

Alighting in the village, I made my way straight to the magnificent Holy Trinity Church, 'The Cathedral of the Marshes', which dominates Blythburgh. Simon Knott, whose excellent website provides detailed descriptions of all Suffolk's churches, describes it as *'the most beautiful church in Suffolk – a wonderful art object'* and *'one of the most significant medieval buildings in England'*. With its clerestory windows, beautiful wooden roof, exquisite carvings, stone arches and an unusual sense of spaciousness and light, this is truly a special church.

But why should a Suffolk village with around three hundred inhabitants have such a large and splendid church? The answer is not as is commonly thought, that it's a 'wool church' or that Blythburgh was once far larger. It is more to do with 15th century local rivalry, with Blythburgh competing with the other coastal settlements of Southwold, Covehithe and Walberswick to build the largest and most beautiful church. Housing the congregation was in many ways a secondary aim; the buildings were raised to the glory of God, funded by generous local benefactors, in Blythburgh's case, Lord of the Manor, John Hopton. The churches' size reflected less the wealth of the community as a whole, than the deliberately

Holy Trinity Church – Blythburgh

conspicuous expenditure of wealthy individuals who wished to be remembered after their deaths. In a form of life insurance for the soul, their hope was that the prayers of the living would ensure their entry to heaven.

On a cold day I was almost tempted by The White Hart as I walked through the village. This large 16th century inn is witness to Blythburgh's importance as a thoroughfare on the A12, one of the most important roads in medieval England. It was however the bowls of chips on dining tables inside that interested me.

A short track took me to the old railway line along the shore. This narrow grassy embankment running along the estuary's bank seemed too small to have held a railway, but doubts as to whether I'd misread the map were dispelled when I found two pieces of old rail. Photographing these led to one of those, 'I'm glad no one was watching' moments. Crouching low to get the rail in the foreground, I overbalanced, rolling part way down the embankment into some bushes. Luckily birds were my only witnesses and I don't think they'll tell.

Southwold Railway Line

The Blyth Estuary is a haven for birds and I was walking through the Walberswick section of the Suffolk Coast National Nature Reserve, which is managed by English Nature in conjunction with the RSPB and Suffolk Wildlife Trust. The reserve's importance is illustrated by the numbers of species that can be found here, including 300 birds, 500 butterflies and moths and 100 crane flies.

A wooden walkway over the marshes leads to a hide, which made an ideal spot not only to view birds, but also shelter from the cold wind to eat my lunch. Initially just a pair of pheasants poking about in the reeds provided interest as I looked through the narrow slats across the water. With the tide high most of the wading birds would have been roosting, but soon a curlew appeared, seemingly oblivious to me a few yards away. As the tide fell exposing food-rich mud at the water's edge, birds started arriving in numbers. Without binoculars and with limited recognition skills, I managed to pick out shelduck, dunlin, lapwing and an egret, but wished I could have put names to more. Black and white birds in the distance may well have been avocet, who frequent the estuary, but I was too far away to be sure that I'd seen these iconic birds, which as the RSPB emblem symbolise the bird protection movement. Mind you, my bird knowledge is better than a man in Southwold who thought a juvenile herring gull was a hybrid of a seagull and duck!

After a mile or so the embankment moved away from the water's edge, running between an area of marsh and a small wood, and passing through another of those names on the map that suggest a story – *Deadman's Covert*. Possibly related to *Deadman's Cross*, a heap of stones marking a suicide's grave, or *Deadman's Corner*, where it's said a man was once burnt at the stake, the path here is claimed to be the haunt of an 'evil presence'. Local riders have apparently reported that their horses have shied at the spot and refused to proceed.

Now climbing away from the shoreline, the railway ran through List's Cutting, passing Keeper's Cottage, where estate head gamekeeper John List once lived. Although only a gentle rise for walkers, the 31 foot gain in height over half a mile of track represented a gradient of 1 in 88, which is quite steep for a railway. It must have been a sight to see the little steam engines puffing hard as they pulled their trains up through the woods.

Deciduous woods changed to coniferous, with the path strewn with pine cones. As on my last trip, the disconcerting sound of nearby gunfire was all that detracted from perfect walking. I simply fail to understand how anyone can gain pleasure from killing animals. I'd seen no one on the walk, but stuck in the fence as the path crossed an area of heath was litter of the worst sort – a plastic bag containing dog poo, left by someone who believes their civic duty extends to picking up the mess, but not taking it home. I'd gladly have taken it home for them --- and posted it through their letter box.

The next stretch of railway line isn't accessible and for half a mile walkers have to use the B1387 road, before turning left onto a path across Walberswick Common. This is the Sandlings Walk, a fifty five mile path through inland Suffolk heaths and forests. It was another lovely section of walk across the open common, running parallel to the railway embankment and heading towards Southwold's distinctive water tower.

Just beyond a cattle creep (a small gap in the embankment to allow animals to pass under the line) the path rejoined the old railway track. After passing through a gorse-lined cutting I reached the site of Walberswick station. More than a mile from the village and with no houses nearby, this must have been a lonely spot to leave the train on a dark evening. All that remains is a concrete base with a more recent seat looking out across the reed covered marshes.

From here the path was paved and suddenly there were people – enough that to say hello would have seemed as odd as it would have been not to have done so had I passed anyone earlier. Approaching Southwold a Bailey bridge crosses the River Blyth, where a swing bridge had once taken the railway over the water. With time to spare, I took a detour along the river, which becomes Southwold Harbour as it approaches the sea, returning on the other bank having crossed on the foot ferry.

Quite different from the traditional picture postcard harbour enclosed with stone jetties, Southwold's harbour is long, narrow and ramshackle. It is however a busy, interesting and picturesque harbour, and most significantly a working harbour, with a variety of workshops, sailing and commercial fishing activities. Freshly caught fish are sold from wooden shacks to take home for tea, or enjoyed in cafes fried in batter with chips. Southwold was mentioned in the Domesday Book as being a prosperous fishing port. It was good to see that despite the industry's decline some can still make a living from the sea, albeit far from the scale of the early 20th century, when large numbers of people could be seen gutting fish on the harbourside. A fisherman mending his nets by the water provided more evidence that this is a real working harbour where people earn their livelihoods and not just for leisure or tourists.

With no harbour wall, water frequently overtops the banks, putting the Harbour Inn, in, rather than alongside the River Blyth. Floods force it to close on a regular basis, however, it seems generally agreed that to build big concrete barriers would spoil the harbour. After nine closures in two months, pub landlord Nick Attfield told the BBC, *'I knew what I was taking on and it's part of the charm here'*. The pub has plug sockets near the ceiling, fridges with electrics at the top and kitchen equipment on wheels so it can easily be moved, but even this couldn't cope with a flood on the scale of 1953, when the river rose by ten feet. As seawater swept across the marshes, the landlord, five customers and six (unspecified) pets were marooned here for a day. A plaque on the wall, inches below the first floor windows, shows the level reached by these tragic floods which killed five people in Southwold and more than three hundred along the East Coast.

Back at the Bailey bridge I sat by the river for a while, watching a regular succession of walkers, cyclists and strolling families cross the narrow bridge. Just upstream on Reydon marshes is Blackshore Mill, a pump mill which was built by Beccles millwright Robert Martin in 1890. Unfortunately it only worked for four years until a gale blew off the sails and broke the windshaft. Repaired in 2002 to conserve the attractive brick-built structure, the mill is one of many historic buildings in and around Southwold.

I followed the railway track for its final mile into Southwold. As this passes the sewage works and ends as a dusty road to a recycling centre, it would have been a nicer walk on one of two paths which cross the common. Nothing remains of Southwold station, which was opposite the Blyth Hotel, on land now occupied by the police and fire stations. From here I turned right to explore the town.

The Harbour Inn – Southwold

With its sandy beach, pier and beach hut lined promenade, Southwold has been described as a quintessentially British seaside town. It is indeed very British, but with upmarket accommodation, restaurants and shops, I wouldn't describe it as a typical seaside resort. Like Frinton in Essex, there is an air of gentility, with few chip shops or amusement arcades, and most visitors could definitely be described as 'middle class'.

Walking through the town I was immediately struck by the number of interesting buildings. Not just large public buildings, like the beautiful church, but the houses, shops and pubs. It is perhaps the unspoilt brick, flint and colour-washed houses that contribute most to Southwold's character. The town benefits hugely from its seven greens, around which it was rebuilt after a disastrous fire in 1659. Intended as fire breaks, they give Southwold a rare openness that makes it a pleasure to stroll around.

Approaching from the east, it was the huge 130,000 gallon capacity art deco concrete water tower that stood out on Southwold's common. Next to this is a rare survivor of a 19th century wind-powered water tower, which once had sails that drove pumps taking water from a well below. As I'd approached from the north on my previous walk it had been Southwold's lighthouse that dominated the town. Like Lowestoft's, this is set back from the shore, but rather than standing on a hill, the circular white tower sits amongst rows of houses. Built in 1890, and electrified in 1938, the lighthouse is still operational. In 2012, in advance of the decommissioning of Orford Ness Lighthouse, it was upgraded to be visible for twenty four nautical miles.

Close by is Adnam's Brewery, the hub of Southwold, with much influence around the town. Beer has been brewed on the site for at least seven hundred years. Visitors are drawn here by tours of the brewery and the new Copper House Distillery, the Cellar & Kitchen Store on the main street with its free tastings and the five Adnam's pubs dotted about the town.

George and Ernest Adman bought the Sole Bay Brewery in 1872 and it remains an independent company, manufacturing 85,000 barrels a year of cask and bottled beers. Behind the Victorian façade is one of the most energy efficient breweries in Europe, which helped the company gain a sustainable development

Queen's Award for Enterprise in 2005. For many years casks of Adnam's ale were delivered to Southwold's pubs by horse-drawn dray, a tradition that sadly ended in 2006 when a new distribution centre opened three miles outside the town. It is to Adman's great credit, that rather than move to an area with better infrastructure, the company chose to remain in Southwold, providing employment and bringing visitors to the town.

Back by the sea, I took a walk along the promenade in front of Southwold's iconic beach huts. Built in the 1960s for around £100 each, some now cost more than double this to rent for a week. The huts are prized properties, changing hands for up to £100,000. Overnight stays are not permitted, but with many containing cookers, fridges and furniture, they provide all that's needed for a refined day by the sea. In 2012 Waveney District Council came up with a novel scheme to cash in on the demand for beach huts. The 'Ladies Walk' footpath on the cliffside had been closed for several years following landslips, so to raise money for repairs it planned to build twelve new huts, to be sold at prices from £25,000.

The focal point of Southwold's seafront is Britain's only 21st century pier. Originally constructed in 1900 as a landing stage for steamships from London, as with many of our piers, a combination of storms and a series of mishaps gradually reduced its length. The T-shaped landing stage was washed away in 1934, a section removed at the outbreak of World War Two for fear the Germans should use it for invading and another hole made when it was hit by a drifting sea mine. These were repaired but storms in 1955 and 1979 reduced the weakened structure to just sixty feet.

It is perhaps typical of Southwold, that rather than allowing the pier to die, in 2001 it was rebuilt to become a high quality tourist attraction. A year later a new T-piece was added, allowing steamers to call here once more. *PS Waverly*, Britain's only remaining sea-going paddle steamer, now visits each year.

Southwold Pier is certainly a pier with a difference. There's an arcade, but no gambling machines, high quality shops and restaurants and the highly unusual 'Under–the-Pier Show' with the strangest selection of slot machines I've ever seen. For starters it's on the pier not under it.

Tim Hunkin says he's had a recurring fantasy about having his own amusement arcade since he was a teenager. As a child in the 1950s he made silly contraptions, struggling to get them to work at all. In the 1960s he had a Saturday job with Ruffler and Walker, a company building coin operated machines. He started making his own machines and when the pier reopened a small shed was found for his eccentric contraptions. Now expanded, it boasts such machines as '*Whack a Banker*' (thump the bald heads of bankers with a mallet as they emerge from their burrows), '*Autofrisk*' (where inflated rubber gloves pat you down) and '*The Chiropodist*' (into which you insert your foot to have strange things done to it). After some deliberation I chose '*The Bathyscape*', a chamber which Hunkin says was inspired by *The Blue Planet* TV series and the opportunity to poke fun at Southwold snobbery. I can report experiencing everything the machine claimed:-

Watch estate agent fish gazumping
See retired, executive fish in their luxury homes
Discover the true Robert Maxwell
Be disgusted by raw sewage
Track down the last cod
Witness canisters of nuclear waste mating

Equally eccentric is the Pier Clock. Made in 1998 by Tim Hunkin and Will Jackson, the clock was designed as a feature about water recycling, sponsored by Thames Water. Water is pumped up to the top and every half hour powers some cheeky antics. Two metal figures in a bath sit up and squirt water at each other, then two boys drop their trousers and pee, missing the toilet every time!

My wanderings concluded with an enjoyable dinner at The Red Lion, one of Southwold's oldest pubs, which of course serves the local Adman's ales. They'd said, '*you'll like Southwold*' – and so I did.

Pier Clock – Southwold

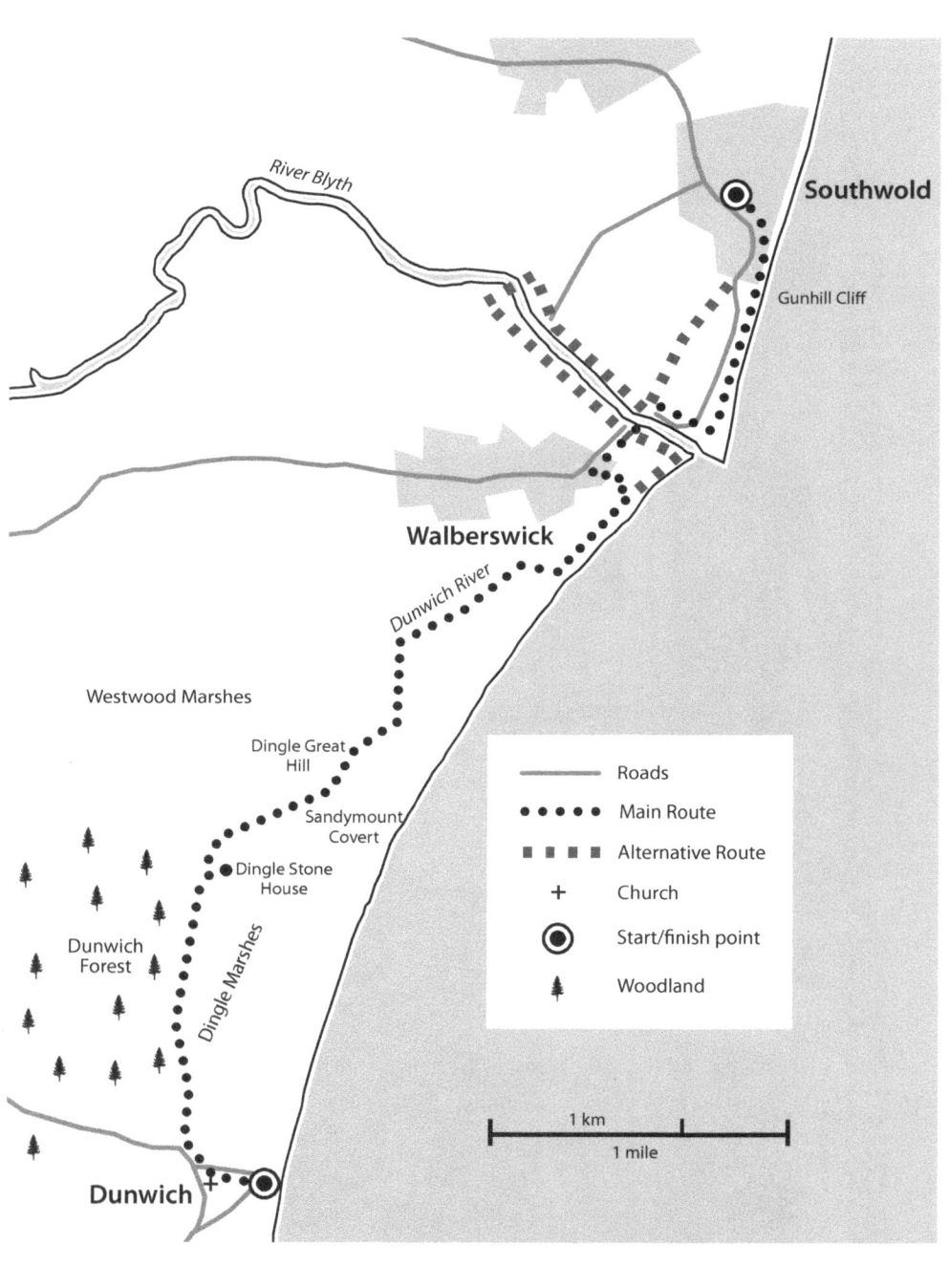

CHAPTER FOUR
SOUTHWOLD – DUNWICH

(6 Miles) 9th April

Over breakfast at Jasmine guesthouse (friendly, comfortable and cheaper than most of Southwold's somewhat expensive accommodation), I chatted to a couple from Wellingborough. It was their first visit to Suffolk. They liked the coast but found the inland scenery rather dull. Like Essex, Suffolk has some pretty villages and interesting towns, but it's where the land meets the sea that these relatively flat eastern counties hold their unique appeal.

With yesterday's misty skies replaced by a more photogenic blue, Southwold looked even better this morning; still quiet before tourists and shoppers arrived. I stopped to look inside the magnificent 15th century St Edmund church, even larger than Blythburgh's and equally beautiful. This too has an unusually light and airy interior, partly due to a Second World War bomb which narrowly missed the church but blew out most of the dull Victorian glass. The bomb destroyed houses in nearby Hollyhock square, killing several residents, and the church was hurriedly tidied for their funerals. Its 20th century glass allows us to better appreciate both the scale of the church and the beauty of its artwork, most notably three wooden screens, the central one depicting St Paul and eleven disciples (evidently Judas wasn't thought worthy of inclusion by the medieval century craftsmen).

Heading south out of the town I passed another of Southwold's lovely greens, Gun Hill at the top of the cliff. Here six 18 pound cannons stand guard across the sea. They had been captured from the Scots at the Battle of Culloden in 1746 and were presented to the town by the Duke of Cumberland. The

Germans apparently considered that these 18th century guns rendered Southwold fortified, so bombed the town in World War One. Hence the cannons were then buried and concealed again in 1939.

A pleasant walk along The Denes, an area of sand dunes by Denes Beach, took me to the mouth of the River Blyth, where the town's lifeboat is based. As at Lowestoft, the river enters the sea through a man-made cut. The Blyth used to swing south, meeting the sea nearer to Dunwich, but in 1590 a channel was dug providing easy access for fishing and trading vessels.

I'd spent some of the previous evening at Jasmine guesthouse reading their copy of *The Story of the Southwold – Walberswick Ferry* by Dani Church, and was delighted to find that the author was rowing today. We chatted briefly and I told her she'd get a mention in the book. Another lady crossing asked if I'd mention her too – because she was scared. Her daughter in a pushchair was fine, but mother was slightly embarrassed at being so anxious about a short trip in a rowing boat.

The first record of a ferry on the Blyth goes back to 1236, when on payment of one half penny, a man and his horse could be taken over the river. After the railway arrived in 1879 locals began asking for a vehicular bridge, but instead, in 1885 Ernest Adnams, and another local businessman, Henry Johnson Debney, acquired the ferry rights with a view to running a larger boat. The River Blyth Ferry Company was formed and by the following year a pontoon chain ferry was operating. Much of the £500 installation cost was recovered after just nine months, with 33,680 foot passengers, 723 'drivers with vehicles', 403 'persons and trucks' and 69 horses taken across the river, providing an income of around £300. The ferryman received less than £80 per year. Usage was such that after four years a steam engine was fitted, so the ferryman no longer had to pull the pontoon by hand. Not only did his job become easier, but he now received an annual bonus of two guineas.

Many characters operated the ferry, perhaps none less than Bob Cross, a ferryman from 1903 to 1956. With two fingers missing having turned gangrenous after a weaver fish bite, customers were amazed how he could row so skilfully with little to grip on the oar. Bob told many a story, most famously about the day two elephants rode on the chain ferry. A travelling circus due to play at Southwold had arrived at Walberswick by mistake and Bob was persuaded to carry the elephants across the water. The pair would not be parted so rode together, with the ferry weighed down to the water line. Bob would tell the story with a twinkle in his eye, but other local people say they recall seeing it, although accounts vary considerably, some claiming there were three elephants who sunk the ferry. With no photographic or news reports, whether elephants did indeed cross on the ferry will probably remain a mystery for ever.

The steam ferry continued to thrive and with 176,787 tickets issued in 1933 there was no reason to suspect that its days were numbered. It kept running after war broke out but most of its passengers were soldiers who didn't pay and with little income the service was suspended in 1940. Damage caused by the military and tides meant that the chain ferry never ran again. It was back to rowing boats.

Dani writes with great warmth of her father David Church, who was born under a table during an air raid in 1942. He started rowing the ferry aged just twelve, continuing almost until his death in 2001. Having spent so much of her childhood around the river, it seemed natural to Dani to take over responsibility, and with the help of several other rowers she keeps this popular little ferry

Southwold – Walberswick Ferry

running. As I waited on the wooden jetty I realised that the job isn't as simple as it looks. The currents are strong and rowers follow an arc to harness the water's flow, the exact route dependant on the tide. Even so it must be hard work on a Bank Holiday when queues form on both banks.

From the ferry to Dunwich I followed the Suffolk Coast Path, but with a slight diversion to look at the village of Walberswick. Here in the Parish Lantern, the village gift shop and tea room, I bought a copy of Dani's book, which I can thoroughly recommend.

Originally a small Saxon community, and for many centuries a thriving port, Walberswick now largely relies on tourism. Almost half its properties are holiday homes. It's hard to imagine that it was a busy port as recently as the early 20th century, with timber, grain, salt, cheese and of course fish landed here. The town was granted a succession of charters, the first in 1262 excepting merchants from taxes, and records show that in 1451 it had thirteen ships trading with Iceland and the Faroes.

In the 19th century the pretty village, romantic ruins of St Andrew's church, river, beach, marshes and open skies, attracted many artists, the best known probably being Charles Rennie Mackintosh and Philip Wilson Steer. Steer's paintings of the beach are said to be among the most authentically Impressionist works produced in Britain. There is still a thriving artistic community whose members exhibit regularly in the village.

Every August Walberswick hosts the British Open Crabbing Championship, a family event which raises funds for charity. According to the village's website, '*participants enjoy the delights of this simple outdoor pleasure*', although I'd wager they haven't asked the crabs.

Passing through the village, I took a footpath on the left just before The Anchor, then another left turn over a footbridge and onto the shingle beach. Black wooden fishing huts here are typical of Suffolk's coast. Although I would hear its roar across the marshes, the next half mile along typical Suffolk shingle was the last section by the sea for today. The coast path soon heads inland by a couple of pools (there's supposed to be a signpost but I didn't see it) and crosses Dunwich

Walberswick

River, which it follows for a mile or so. It was a lovely walk on grassy paths and boardwalk between water and reeds. An English Nature sign told of notable birds that nest in the reedbeds – marsh harrier, bearded tit, water rail and bittern.

Standing out amongst the vast reedbeds is Westwood Marshes Mill, a derelict tower windmill dating from the late 18th century. The three storey mill served two purposes. A cast iron scoop wheel with wooden paddles helped drain the marshes, and a pair of millstones ground corn to make feed for horses on the local estate. It operated under wind power until put out of action by soldiers using it as target practice in World War Two. The mill was repaired in the 1950s but burnt out by an arson attack in 1960. Now a listed building, one of only two remaining drainage mills on the east Suffolk marshes, it adds history and human interest to the enigmatic marshes.

With bright sunshine and very little breeze, it was quite warm walking across the marshes. Yesterday I'd worn every layer I'd bought. Today I was stopping regularly to divest myself of unwanted garments, my rucksack getting a little heavier each time.

On my right I passed Dingle Great Hill, its summit standing a whole twelve metres above the sea. It may have been an overstatement to call it a hill, and certainly an exaggeration to add the great, but it's still the highest land on the marshes. With its slight elevation and view across the flat marshes, the hill was chosen to site a World War Two Emergency Coastal Battery with two four inch guns.

The path continued into Sandymount Covert, an area of woodland which was also heavily used by the military, including a Diver Battery as defence against V1 rockets. In 1940 the Covert was an 'Emergency Platoon' area, to be manned if required by the Reserve Company of 2/4 South Lancashire Regiment. Remains of trenches and other activity can still be seen.

Walking through the woods a flash of colour caught my eye. A tiny bird with a crest of gold on its head – a goldcrest would you believe – the UK's smallest bird. As I stopped to look another joined it in the tree. I watched the pair for a few minutes as they flew from branch to branch, unperturbed by a human just a few yards away. Although not rare, I was pleased to have been so close to these attractive little birds, my sense of satisfaction boosted by being able to put a name to the species. Many more birds could be seen as I looked across to the ponds on Westwood Marshes, but it was the two goldcrests, like the curlew I'd watched at Blythborough, who I now counted as friends. It's often what you get to see close up, rather than the wider view, that makes a day special – things that you don't see from the car but are waiting for those prepared to walk.

Dingle Great Hill

From Dingle Stone House, a dressed flint house overlooking the marshes, the path became a narrow, untarmaced lane, which for a mile runs alongside Dunwich Forest. A Suffolk Wildlife Trust sign explained that as part of a partnership with the Forestry Commission, Dartmoor ponies were grazing here. Conifers were being removed and the ponies help maintain open spaces as native broad-leafed woodland matures. I sat in the woods to eat my lunch, seeing neither a pony nor person, as I looked out across Dingle Marshes.

Not having consulted the map for a while, on turning left at Bridge Farm I was slightly surprised to find I was in Dunwich. Once the second largest town in East Anglia, with 3,000 inhabitants, this is now just a small village of less than a hundred souls. Most of the town, including at least eight churches, have been consumed by the sea. The first building one sees on reaching the village is the 19th century St James church, built in 1832 as the area was then without a parish church. It looked nice enough to me but Simon Knott observes that, '*St James is about as undistinguished as it is possible to be*'.

In the churchyard is the ruin of a leper chapel. Sailors returning from far flung lands brought leprosy to the town and in the 12th century a hospital was built to care for them, well away from the main population. The leprosy chapel, one of few remaining in the country, is now all that remains.

My next stop was Dunwich's excellent museum, where a very helpful lady explained the detailed model depicting the 13th century town and showing how the coastline has moved a mile inland.

Originally settled by the Britons and Romans, it was the Saxons who first saw the potential of what was then a splendid natural harbour. Bishops were based here, the first of whom, a French monk named Felix, was despatched by the Archbishop of Canterbury in 630 AD to evangelise the people of East Anglia. The town continued to prosper under the Normans and from information in the Domesday Book it has been estimated that the population at that time was about three thousand. This included twenty four 'Franci', thought to be people of French origin who had migrated since the Conquest.

Dunwich continued to thrive in the twelfth and early thirteenth centuries. Everyday life included the rearing of sheep, pigs, and rabbits, but above all it concentrated on maritime activities. There was a busy shipbuilding industry, and ships from Dunwich were engaged in trading around the British coast and across Europe. Fishing boats brought back catches of North Sea herring and sprat, and travelled as far afield as Iceland for cod and ling. Vessels could be called upon during warfare and in 1229 Henry III requested forty ships from Dunwich, *'well equipped with all kinds of armament, good steersmen and mariners'*. After some negotiation it was agreed that Dunwich would in fact supply thirty, a contingent that made up about one eighth of the fleet that sailed from Portsmouth to carry on the wars in France. The borough was given a charter by King John, with rights over all east coast wrecks, in return for which Dunwich was required to make an annual payment – five thousand eels. I hope the King enjoyed them.

Dunwich had become one of the greatest ports on the east coast and the tenth largest place in England, with half the population of London. The town was a religious centre with large churches, monasteries, hospitals, grand public buildings and even a mint. Its citizens grew wealthy from trade, shipbuilding and fishing. However, all this began to come to an end on 1st January 1286, when for three days a terrible storm battered Dunwich, changing it for ever. The lower town was swept into the sea but this was just the start. In January 1328 another storm of monumental proportions threw up shingle and sand which completely blocked the harbour entrance – to such an extent that it was never reopened. In 1347 yet another huge storm claimed shops, windmills, churches and four hundred homes. Countless people died and only a quarter of the former town remained.

Erosion continued and by the 18th century the population had dwindled to less than three hundred. As a legacy of its previous importance Dunwich however continued to send two members to Parliament, making it one of the most notorious Rotten Boroughs. With the ancestors of the Freeman of Dunwich scattered all over England, it is said that people would travel to Dunwich for elections, going out in a boat to the point where the town hall used to be to cast their vote. By the time of the 1832 Reform Act, which abolished Rotten Boroughs, there were just thirty two voters resident in the constituency. Leeds, Birmingham and Manchester, however had not a single MP between them.

The last of the town's major buildings to fall over the cliff was All Saints church. A series of photographs in the museum show it on the cliff edge in 1904, then just the tower remaining, before the whole church had gone in 1919. All that remains of the original town is the leper chapel and ruins of a 13th century friary on the edge of the cliff.

With plenty of time before my bus, I walked past the Ship Inn and down to the beach. A few small boats were pulled up on the shingle – a meagre remnant of the town's fishing industry. With most schools still on Easter holidays, families played on the beach, while passengers from a large coach sat in the café eating fish and chips. Signs warned 'DANGER UNSTABLE CLIFFS' and fences kept people away from the base.

Erosion is ongoing, but with the shingle piled high at the top of the beach it is currently much slower. It's when the waves attack the base of the cliff that it crumbles rapidly and the natural variation in the beach's structure means that although the land recedes by an average of a metre each year, this tends to be in bursts. The lady in the museum told me that the cliff hasn't moved back for some years, but with a decision having been made not to try to protect the coast here, it is inevitable that before long the sea will be claiming more land. She said that there have been many attempts to explore the remains by divers, but poor under-water visibility makes this very hard.

In *Search for Dunwich City under the Sea* Stuart Bacon writes at length about his 1970s diving expeditions. On rare days they could see twenty feet on the sea bed, but often visibility was just a foot and sometimes the water completely black. On these days even a powerful diving lamp wouldn't illuminate a compass or depth gauge. Nevertheless the divers found several of Dunwich's churches and brought various remains to the surface, some of which are now in the museum. More recent dives using high resolution acoustic imaging have found that a great deal of the town has survived under the sea and enabled archaeologists to produce a detailed map of its layout. Using advanced 3D scanning techniques, a team led by Professor David Sear of Southampton University have identified the limits of the town, showing that it occupied an area of 1.8 square kilometres, sixty percent that of the City of London.

I'd been told to listen out for church bells by the sea. As I stood on the shingle I could hear the splashing of waves, calls of the birds and shouts of children, but nothing like a bell. According to legend, at certain states of the tide the bells of a long lost church can still be heard tolling from under the sea. It is said that fishermen wouldn't put to sea when they heard the bells, as their sound warned of an impending storm. John Day, a Master Mariner in 1856, claimed to know his position by the tolling of a bell from a submerged Dunwich church. Reputedly the peal of the phantom bells could be recognised because one of the bells was missing – just as it was when the last church was lost.

Like most legends, there are variations to the story, but a possibility that they may be based on truth. Whilst the three churches on higher ground had their bells removed before tumbling to the beach, many of the early churches to be lost were quickly inundated with no time to salvage their bells. The masonry of these early churches was very thick so they could have survived the forces of the waves for many years. It is therefore quite possible that church bells did lie intact under the sea. A bell under water however does not make a resonant ring, but just a clanging sound. It is though possible that for many years a bell could have been revealed at very low tides and heard ringing from the surface of the water. We can however discount the recognisable peel from All Saints, the last church to be lost, as all its bells were removed before it succumbed to the sea. Perhaps the fact that only a few individuals claim to have heard the submerged bells is because they are a ghostly phenomena. Or could it be related to the number of pints consumed in the Ship Inn?

Still with time to spare, I followed a path onto the cliff where Greyfriars Franciscan priory still stands. Constructed in 1290, it must have been an impressive complex, surrounded by a stone wall. The gatehouse, refectory and much of the wall remain, and thanks to grants from English Heritage and Suffolk County Council, work was in progress to preserve the wall, rebuilding some of the missing sections. Half a dozen men were busy working, some of their skills little changed from those of the medieval monks, but the music they listened to no doubt somewhat different! Also on the cliff is the grave of Jacob Forster, the last grave remaining from All Saints' cemetery. I couldn't find it.

There is just one timetabled bus a day from Dunwich, but I'd arranged a minibus ride with Coastal Accessible Transport Service (CATS), an excellent scheme where passengers book travel in advance and largely volunteer drivers follow a route arranged according to demand. As the scheme's website explains, '*CATS is a social enterprise run by the community* for *the community and combining business thinking and social values for their benefit.*' What an excellent idea. The available slot was slightly later than I'd planned for and it was touch and go whether I'd make the train at Darsham. It looked unlikely when the bus arrived several minutes late but I needn't have worried. In Lowestoft I'd had a driver who thought their foot should always be on either the brake or accelerator. The lady driving today seemed to have slightly modified that technique – plenty of accelerator and very little brake! Along with an elderly couple who appeared to be travelling just for the ride, I was whisked round the Suffolk countryside at breakneck speed and arrived a whole two minutes before the train.

Post Script

After being told of storm damage at Walberswick, almost a year to the day after I'd first walked what was one of my favourite stretches of the whole Suffolk coast, I caught a bus from Lowestoft to Southwold and once again walked to Dunwich. The river wall had been breached opposite the Harbour Inn, which had been flooded to within a foot of the 1953 level, but repairs were in progress and a temporary boardwalk laid down for walkers.

Bypassing the village of Walberswick, I turned left through the car park and along a short length of creek, then over the bridge towards the fishing huts. This route can be flooded at high tides. There was still no sign to the bridge that takes the path through the marshes, but anyone following the route should cross the bridge after about half a mile along the beach, not the one immediately after the huts.

A sign advised that the shingle bank had been breached in three places between Walberswick and Dunwich, flooding the marshes and stripping away some of the path's surface, but I found no problems at all. A Suffolk County Council sign near Dunwich saying that the path is subject to tidal flooding and asking people to avoid the route, seemed over cautious, but as with a number of sections, it may be best to avoid the highest tides.

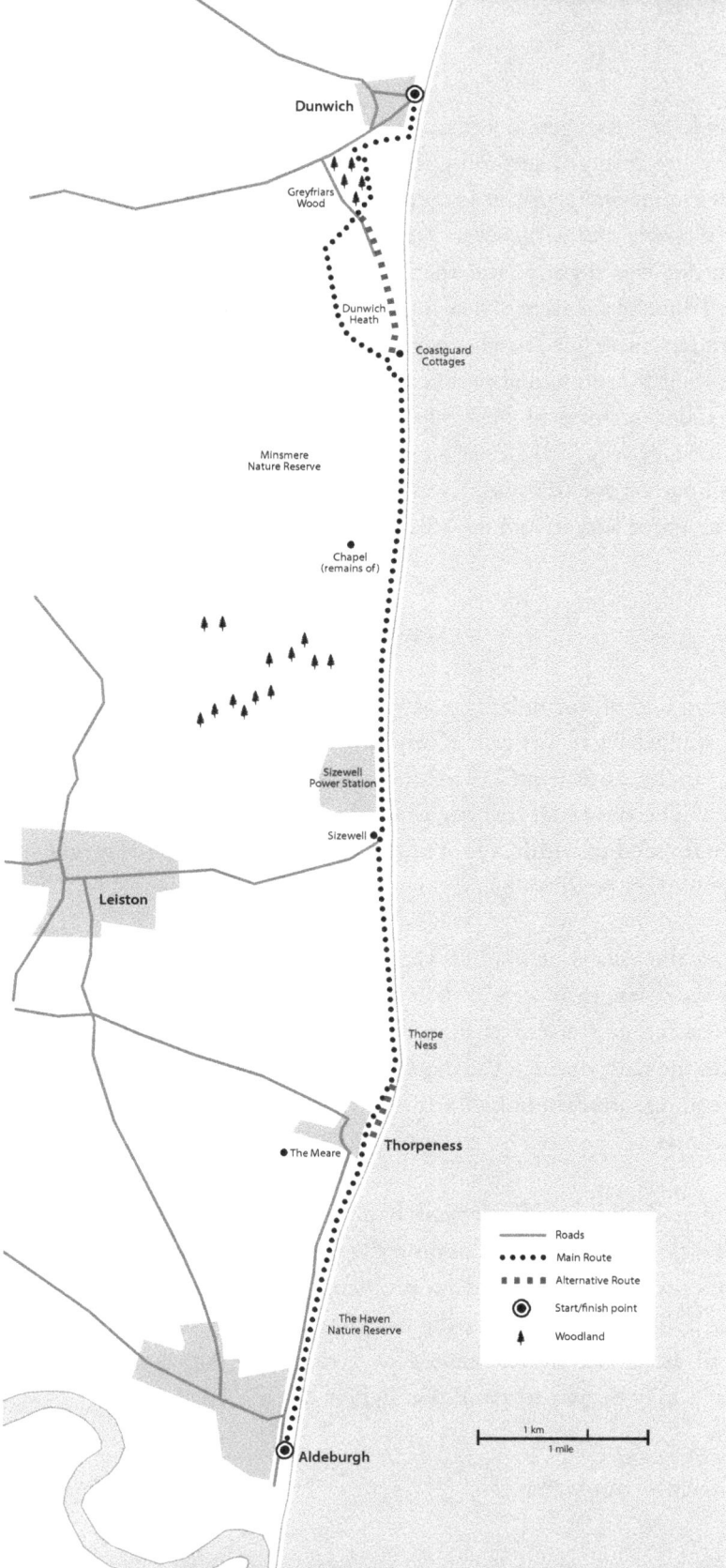

CHAPTER FIVE
DUNWICH – ALDEBURGH

(10 Miles) 13th May

Last time I'd caught the 9.00 from Liverpool Street I'd enjoyed breakfast on my way to a day's walking in Essex. This morning I was just writing a note lamenting the sad loss of restaurant cars when there was an announcement – the train had a chef on board cooking a selection of breakfast offerings. It was a trial on a couple of trains a day, so obviously my duty was to support it. Whilst not quite the refined restaurant car dining experience, a baguette stuffed with four rashers of bacon made a welcome and unexpected start to my trip.

Dunwich's one bus of the day had left half an hour before I arrived, but on alighting at Darsham my taxi was waiting. We chatted about books, Suffolk and the Southwold railway. The driver told me that a lot of locals opposed its possible reopening, as it would upset wildlife and bring too many tourists to the town. We agreed that wildlife soon gets used to the occasional passing train and questioned why a town that relies on visitors would want to keep them away – perhaps those who might come on a steam train aren't the right sort for Southwold?

Back at the Ship Inn, I rejoined the Suffolk Coast Path, which I was to be following for most of the day. It took me back onto the cliffs, where another search again failed to locate the remaining grave, past Greyfriars and into the woods. The well signed path joined a wider track known as Middle-Ditch, which was once one of the main roads into the lost town. Leaving the woods this passes a few cottages, before meeting with Westleton Road, which I followed for a short distance until turning left along the tree-lined driveway to The Dairy House. A sign advised that mobility scooters were permitted but not cycles. Beyond the house the gravel track continued through Greyfriars Wood to Minsmere Road. Here I had two options. The shortest, which was closer to the sea, was to follow the lane for a mile, then take a footpath along Minsmere Cliffs. I however chose the alternative, which was to stay on the Suffolk Coast Path across the middle of Dunwich Heath, the place I'd most wanted to see on the whole walk.

A rare area of coastal lowland heath, this is a survivor of the Suffolk Sandlings, which used to form much of the county's coast. Most have now been built on or developed for agriculture, but Dunwich Heath remains safe under the protection of the National Trust, who purchased it in 1968 with the help of a donation from H.J. Heinz Ltd. A scarce and precious habitat, the heath is home to a variety of wildlife and is one of the best places in Britain to see the rare Dartford warbler. This long-tailed warbler has suffered in the past from severe winters and its population declined to just eleven pairs in 1963, since when it has gradually recovered, increasing in both numbers and range. With 3,200 pairs it is however still at risk and protection of habitat such as at Dunwich is vital to the bird's survival.

The heath makes an ideal home to reptiles such as adders, slow-worms and common lizards, and supports insects which are unusual in both name and behaviour. Mining bees, digger wasps and ant lions all live in the ground, while emperor moths and true lover's knot (a small moth whose complex white markings are supposed to match that of the knot which symbolises a couple in love) fly above it.

Most of the heath is covered with heather and from June to September its purple and pink flowers make a wonderful sight. This is when all the pictures are taken! Although gorse gave patches of bright yellow, I have to admit that dominated by the dormant brown heather, the heath was slightly disappointing – still a lovely, tranquil place and alive with the song of birds, but lacking the colour that the photos show.

A National Trust sign marks the entrance to Dunwich Heath and Mount Pleasant Farm, the latter having been purchased by the Trust with the help of Pizza Express customers through the Neptune Coastline Campaign. It was bought to help mitigate against losses by erosion. The arable farmland is being restored to acid grassland and heather heath, providing valuable habitat that will balance losses as more of the original heath is consumed by the sea.

After half a mile the track meets a crossroads. Here I nearly went the wrong way. The sign seemed to indicate a small path between gorse bushes, but it was so narrow that I soon doubted my choice. An arrow where it met a larger path confirmed I was correct, as was a group of walking ladies who I'd caught up. We chatted briefly and they too had been relieved to find they weren't lost. They were walking the whole Suffolk Coast Path in short lengths – somewhat slowly!

Here I got my first glimpse of the 'golf ball' atop Sizewell B Power Station, three miles ahead. This was also the point to change maps and move onto my fourth Ordnance Survey sheet. Unlike Essex where they are double sided, the Suffolk maps are easy to use single sheets. No longer did I have to engage in protracted origami sessions as I attempted every possible way to re-fold it.

Dunwich Heath ends at a line of white Coastguard Cottages, which were built in 1857 and remained operational until 1909. During World War One the heath was used as a rifle range and in World War Two a radar station was set up

Dunwich Heath

together with a gun emplacement. The room that now houses an exhibition in the cottages was the command post for the guns, which later included an anti-aircraft battery. Some of the cottages are now let for holidays and the end one houses a National Trust café.

As I looked down to the sea wall and across Minsmere marshes, I was struck by the number of people walking. It was only when I'd descended the gravel path to the sea wall that I noticed every one had binoculars, cameras, or both. These were birdwatchers not ramblers. Minsmere is one of the RSPB's premier reserves and one of the most important sites for wading birds in eastern England.

More than two hundred years ago a small river estuary was closed off by a sandbank and the land reclaimed for farming. In 1940 it was flooded again as a defence against invasion and by the end of the war a perfect habitat for wading birds had been regenerated. The RSPB first leased the site in 1947, buying it thirty years later, and under their stewardship more than a hundred bird species are resident, with around a further 240 migrant visitors. Star species include marsh harrier, nightingale, avocet, bearded tit and of course, bittern. It is however not only birds who enjoy the reserve's varied habitats. Water vole, otters, adders, and one of the largest herd of red deer in England live on the reserve, and more than a thousand species of lepidoptera (butterflies and moths) have been recorded.

The coast path runs beside dunes along the edge of the reserve. A skull and crossbones sign intrigued me. What nasty things were hidden here? Closer examination showed it was on a wooden flap and lifting this revealed nothing more sinister than a clue on a childrens' smugglers trail. A short length of path was closed, with the diversion onto the beach. A few minutes struggling across shingle once again confirmed the merit of taking the varied but longer inland paths. The sea was dead calm. The constant noise today was not from waves but birds on Minsmere's lakes.

A sign pointed the way to the visitor centre. The path was dotted with twitchers with their big cameras. I took a quick look in one of the hides but felt rather inferior with my short lens. Size isn't everything though is it? Back on the path I spied a twitcher relieving himself behind a gorse bush. (Note: the two previous sentences aren't connected – I didn't look that closely!) A line of concrete blocks ran along the edge of the beach; another measure to keep out any Germans who weren't put off by the flooded marsh. A home-made sign asked for news of Dusty, a female Italian greyhound who'd gone missing last week. Where do lost dogs go I wondered – and what's the difference between and Italian and British greyhound? Maybe the former wave their paws about as they bark.

I stopped for lunch sheltered behind a huge clump of gorse, with a view across the reserve and of the equally interesting passing twitchers. One had the full camouflage gear, right down to his hat and camera. Such behaviour seems to be socially acceptable, whilst to observe trains, planes or buses is considered distinctly odd. Conversely an obsession with cars seems to be positively encouraged.

Continuing on my way, I passed the end of the reserve and everyone disappeared. Once more I had the path to myself. Across the marshes were the remains of a stone building on a slightly raised area of grass. The map told me no more than '*Chapel (remains of)*'. This was the original site of Leiston Abbey, which was built in 1182 by Ranulf de Glanville, Lord Chief Justice to Henry II, and dedicated to St Mary. With the threat of flooding on the marshy ground, in 1363 the monks moved the abbey 2½ miles inland. Most of the original was reused in the new building and just a chapel remained. It is thought that this stayed in use until the dissolution in 1537, after which it gradually decayed. A pill box and gun emplacement were inserted into the structure in the Second World War, but the ruins have now been preserved thanks to funding from English Heritage and Natural England.

For the next half hour I walked beside dunes, marsh and the bright yellow of countless gorse bushes, as Sizewell got nearer and nearer. The path took me between the power station and sea, with just a surprisingly low wooden fence surrounding the plant. Whilst I don't doubt security is tighter to enter the buildings, the perimeter boundary contrasted with Sellafield which I'd walked past the previous year. As described in *The Next Station Stop*, I'd upset a machine gun-carrying policeman by taking photos then refusing to give my name. Today I could take pictures to my heart's content.

A sign on the beach raised some worrying questions:

*Regular and routine emergency sirens and tests of
emergency equipment take place resulting in audible alarms.*

In the event of a genuine nuclear emergency you will be advised accordingly.

What is the point of the sirens if they are to be ignored? How *do* they tell you if the reactor is about to melt down? Perhaps they don't want to instil panic, so a little man sidles up to people on the beach and suggests they might like to wander off, but please don't run and make sure you look out for trip hazards as you go. Or is it the large mushroom shaped cloud above the plant that indicates it's time to leg it? The sign did go on to say that if there was a nuclear emergency you should contact local police. I'm sure they'd be pleased to be told.

Since electricity generation started here in 1966 there have been a number of incidents but the most serious potential nuclear leak, which could have caused a major disaster, was averted by a chance decision to wash some dirty clothes. On the morning of Sunday 7th January 2007, one of the contractors working on decommissioning Sizewell A was in the laundry room, when he noticed water leaking onto the floor. Investigation showed that this was coming from the pond that holds the reactor's highly radioactive spent nuclear fuel. As much

Sizewell Power Stations

as 40,000 gallons of radioactive water spilled out of a 15ft long split in a pipe, some leaking into the North Sea. The pond water level had dropped by more than a foot, yet none of the sophisticated alarms in the plant sounded in the main control room. By the time of the next scheduled safety patrol the level would have dipped far enough to expose the nuclear fuel rods, potentially causing them to overheat and catch fire, sending a plume of radioactive contamination along the coastline.

Contrasting to the rather stark concrete Sizewell A plant containing two Magnox reactors, which was shut down in 2006, Sizewell B with its white dome, is a futuristic building that looks more like you'd imagine a nuclear installation. Britain's only commercial pressurised water reactor, it generates 1191 mega watts – enough to supply 2.5 million homes, roughly the population of Suffolk and Norfolk.

With the government's decision to build a new generation of nuclear power stations, plans are well advanced for Sizewell C, a new twin reactor plant. Local opinion is decidedly mixed. Some see the jobs created and the 'clean' energy as good for Suffolk, others cite safety and environmental concerns, and claim that the risk to those living nearby has been underestimated. Emergency supplies of potassium iodide tablets are given to those living within 1½ miles of the plant, but Chernobyl and Fukushima showed that far wider areas can quickly become affected.

The biggest danger as I walked by the beach today was not from nuclear radiation, but a particularly nasty looking dog who charged up to me, circling threateningly, before eventually deciding to obey its owner's increasingly desperate calls and return to her. The praise she heaped on the brute was presumably for having chosen to merely menace a member of the public rather than actually eat them.

The tiny village of Sizewell seems to ignore its quietly humming power station. A dozen small boats sat on the shingle, stacks of lobster pots beside them. Winches lined up at the top of the beach draw the boats up the steep slope and wooden huts belong to the handful of fisherman who still work from the village.

Looking across the beach as I sat down for a while, the only signs of a power plant were two platforms in the sea from where water is drawn for cooling then released. The warmed water attracts a wide range of species making this a popular spot for sea anglers. Southwold, with its lighthouse, was still visible in the distance and on the horizon I could just pick out Gulliver back in Lowestoft.

The path runs between gorse bushes at the top of the beach, before climbing the cliff beyond the beach café and car park. Weatherboarded cottages and a concrete pill box look out to sea. On the beach a lone angler sat outside his green tent, perhaps hoping to catch a mythical three eyed fish. Chalets and caravans sit on the cliff top and a club house advertised cream teas. I could have been tempted, but like the beach café, it was closed on Mondays.

An arch takes the path under the grounds of Sizewell Hall, a Christian conference centre sitting in 32 acres of grounds. Through the hedge I could just glimpse the large house with many chimneys. This was built after the original thatched hall was burned almost to the ground in 1920. Initially a family home, it was commandeered by the army in World War Two, then served as a small private preparatory school run in a laissez-faire style by Harry Tuyn, a Dutch Quaker. A young Sheridan Morley was one of the more famous children to be educated here, but it struggled to attract enough pupils and closed in 1955, perhaps not helped by rumours of an atomic power station to be built nearby.

The Suffolk Coast path heads inland soon after Sizewell Hall, one of a number of stretches where it inexplicably leaves the sea, but I preferred to stay on the cliffs. This was a lovely stretch of coast, but with the sandy cliffs eroding and several spots where the path looked ready to slide down to the beach at the next storm, I wondered how much longer one will be able to walk here. A strong smell caused me to look inland where the cause was soon clear – a large pig farm with pigs enjoying themselves in the mud, as they do.

After Ness House, which was built in 1902 as a private museum for Menteith Ogilvie's bird collection and now houses Warden's Centre for Disabled People, the path dropped down to the base of the cliff. I was the sole person walking by this deserted beach. Between here and Thorpeness the beach route can be impassable at high tide and the water ahead was close to the cliff. Although the tide was falling I took the safer option of a path up the cliff to Thorpeness Common (see, not reckless once again). From here I got my first sight of Aldeburgh and beyond it the mysterious masts of Orford Ness.

A path across the common took me into Thorpeness – and what a strange place this is. Initially it all seemed quite normal and rather nice as I walked down North End Avenue, a cliff top road with large houses looking out across the sea. The Red House, a Georgian mansion, offers holiday lets with private access to the beach. A lovely place to stay, but at up to £4,000 per week I think we'll still have to bear approaching beaches alongside the general public. Private signs abounded but the town was deserted. I wandered round looking for the centre, or just any sign that people actually come here. There was a posh looking country club with expensive cars outside, but no sign of their owners. The houses were odd, many of them Tudor style with black wooden beams, but clearly 'mock' and not particularly old. They appeared to be occupied but their owners were either safety locked inside, or had left the town. Had there been a leak from Sizewell B and only they knew the secret sign to leave?

Then I found The Meare, a large lake with rowing boats tied up by the bank, but not one out on the open water. I'd been told to look out for the strangest building of all, a 'house in the clouds' and there across the water it was – a house at the top of a tower. A café by the lake offered quiche *'for full meal, supper or pic-nic'*. They certainly have versatile flans in Thorpeness but had all the residents gone off for the unusually hyphenated alfresco meal? Inside there were people – real people. I bought a toasted teacake (slightly burnt) and guide book (very interesting but as I was to find, not always accurate).

Until 1910, Thorpe as it was then known, was just a small agricultural and fishing hamlet, with a few cottages, a barn and an inn, but all this was to change when the wealthy landowner Glencairn Stuart Ogilvie decided to develop it as a purpose built holiday resort. Ogilvie's parents lived at Sizewell Hall, having moved from Scotland in 1859, and bought up an estate of six thousand acres along the coast. His idea was that Thorpeness would attract rich middle class families, who would of course need to be accompanied by their servants, so he built large houses. Many of these were designed to mimic historic styles, such as

Tudor, Jacobean and Dutch, so giving Thorpeness its unique look. The estate has remained in the Ogilvie's family ownership, but after Alexander Stuart, grandson of the town's founder, sadly died on the golf course in 1972, many of the buildings in Thorpeness had to be sold to pay off death duties.

Centrepiece of the town was a sixty acre lake – The Meare. This was dug by hand, mostly by local fishermen, with much of the soil removed used to form islands and landscaping around the banks. Nowhere is it more than three feet deep, making a safe boating environment for visitors. Ogilvie themed the lake around J.M. Barrie's *Peter Pan*, the author being a friend of the family, adding to the likes of Crocodile Island and The Fort, other literary references such as 'The Pirate Lair' from Robert Louis Stephenson, when naming the islands and channels. The Meare is fed by the Hundred River (not the same one as I'd crossed back at Benacre), with a sluice gate controlling the level. As well as its recreational use, the lake provides home to a wide range of birds, insects and plants, as well as coarse fish and eels which may be caught by anglers.

A railway station on the branch to Aldeburgh was opened in 1914 to bring visitors to the new resort, but the line was closed by Dr Beeching in 1966 (not the 1950s as stated in the guide book). This is now a footpath as far as Leiston, where the line to Saxmundham remains in use for trains collecting nuclear waste from Sizewell. What a shame that the last few miles couldn't be reopened

Thorpeness

and Aldeburgh put back onto the railway map, but there may be some hope. Building materials for both current power stations were brought in by rail and if Sizewell C goes ahead, part of the package to mitigate its environmental impact could be to reopen the line to Aldeburgh.

I took a short walk by the lake, heading for the strangest building in Thorpeness and one of Britain's best architectural follies – The House in the Clouds. The new resort needed a water supply and in 1923 (not 1932 as stated in the guide book) the corn mill from the nearby village of Aldringham was brought here for pumping. This fed an adjacent seventy foot tall, 50,000 gallon water tank, an arrangement which served the town well but raised the problem as to what should be done with such an ugly structure on the skyline. The solution was to clad it in weatherboarding and disguise it as a house – a cottage in the tree tops. It was though more than a cosmetic disguise, as living accommodation was built into the lower part of the tower.

In 1943 two ladies (both Miss Humphreys) were living here (or three ladies according to the guide book) when a shell aimed at a passing V1 flying bomb by a nearby artillery battery, passed through the tank. According to most sources, neither Miss Humphrey awoke from her sleep. According to the guidebook the ladies escaped the resulting deluge of water but were trapped by the lower exit door, however one had forgotten her false teeth and returned to retrieve these before rescue arrived.

After repair the tank was reduced in size to 30,000 gallons and remained in use until 1977, after which the top portion of the house was converted into further accommodation; (or if you prefer the guidebook version to every other source I could find, this happened '*after World War Two*'). The tower's six floors are now let out as self-catering accommodation and quite fittingly for a village which *Bizarre Magazine* voted '*the weirdest village in England*', it must be one of the most unusual places to take the family on holiday.

I'd strayed from the coast path (it runs through a pay & display car park) but found it again on a boardwalk heading down to the beach. From here there was no path as such and it was another stretch of finding the best walking surface on the grass, sand or shingle, at the top of the beach. The steeply shelving

Haven Beach is a fine example of vegetated shingle, where characteristic plants such as sea kale, yellow horned poppy and sea pea grow above the high tide line. A sign explained that twenty percent of the UK's vegetated shingle is in Suffolk and sections of the beach were fenced off to protect the plants and nesting skylarks.

Strangely the Suffolk Coast Path bypasses Aldeburgh, heading inland by an abandoned cottage. I was to meet up with it again tomorrow on the way to Snape Maltings. As I sat for a while on a convenient seat a golden retriever bounded up to me. I could tell at once that the dog had come just to say hello and that a bite from a walker's leg was far from his mind. This was the sort of dog where you expect the owner to be friendly too, and so he was. We chatted about Suffolk, the coast and walking. He hoped to walk the South West Path one day. He walks to this spot most days to meet his daughter off the school bus and they sit on the seat while she has a drink and tells him about the day. As the bus pulled up I vacated the seat, not wishing to intrude on father and daughter time.

From here a tarmac path runs into Aldeburgh. Standing on the beach just north of the town is one of Aldeburgh's newest and most controversial landmarks – Scallop. This four metre high steel structure was unveiled as a tribute to composer Benjamin Britten, who spent much of his life around Aldeburgh. Created by Suffolk-born artist Maggi Hambling and made by Aldeburgh craftsmen Sam and Denis Pegg, the sculpture depicts two interlocking scallop shells. The phrase '*I hear those voices that will not be drowned*', from Britten's most famous opera Peter Grimes, is pierced through the steel, to be read against the sky. Two cyclists were viewing Scallop as I approached. We chatted briefly, concurring that it was an appropriate tribute to the composer who used to walk on the beach here and launched the famous Aldeburgh Festival. They said that it had often been vandalised but I found this hard to believe in such a gentile place as Aldeburgh. It was only when I got home that I found out how controversial it was.

On the night of 3rd January 2012 someone ventured out onto the windswept beach to splash Scallop with paint and daub slogans – 'IT'S AN OLD TIN CAN' and 'HAPPY NEW YEAR'. This however wasn't an isolated attack. It

Scallop – Aldeburgh Beach

was the thirteenth time the sculpture had been defaced, although similarities in the writing suggested all may have been the work of one person. Opposition to Scallop is however far more widespread. Soon after it was unveiled a campaign was launched demanding its removal, although the almost thousand signature petition was matched by another in favour. It wasn't so much the sculpture that people objected to, but a man-made structure in the middle of the natural beach. A poll by the *East Anglian Daily Times* saw 738 people voting for it to be moved but almost three times as many in favour of it staying, and in 2004 Suffolk Coastal District Council and Aldeburgh Town Council agreed that it should remain on the beach. In 2006 it won the Marsh Award for the best public sculpture in Britain and it seems that Scallop will continue to stand in its rightful place on the shingle.

Aldeburgh is another town that has been much changed by coastal erosion and Moot Hall, which was once in the town centre, now stands by the beach. This attractive red-brick timber framed building was constructed as a town hall in the first part of the 16th century. A map of circa 1589 shows the hall in the third line of buildings back from the harbour, but by 1790 another map depicts it by the beach, with nothing but shingle between it and the sea. Once a council chamber, market, gaol and ammunition store, Moot Hall now houses the town's museum.

Construction of Moot Hall coincided with Aldeburgh's period of great prosperity, which lasted for 150 years. It was an important port and shipbuilding town. Sir Francis Drake's ships *Greyhound* and *Golden Hind* (originally named *Pelican*) were built here. After losing half the town and its harbour to the sea, Aldeburgh survived principally as a fishing village until the 19th century, when it became popular as a seaside resort. Much of its distinctive architecture derives from this period. Fishing still continues, albeit on a far smaller scale, with boats drawn up onto the shingle. It is however as an upmarket holiday and weekend break destination, with its Benjamin Britten connections, that Aldeburgh is now best known.

Before exploring further I sought out my accommodation for the night. Passing a row of identical terraced cottages with blue windows, I climbed the town steps to the cliff top roads that look over Aldeburgh, but remain safe from the sea. The rather mundane name '34 Lee Road' didn't suggest a particularly high class establishment, although the price did – typical for Aldeburgh but three

Aldeburgh Beach

times what I'd paid in Lowestoft. Now I knew why Viv and Mike at The Edingworth had told me that contractors working at Sizewell stay with them rather than in Southwold or Aldeburgh. I wasn't disappointed. This is an extremely high quality bed & breakfast, more usually frequented by couples spending a quiet weekend in Aldeburgh, perhaps taking in a concert, than lone coastal walkers. Owners Sue and Peter were most welcoming and keen to talk about the coast. Peter used to be National Trust warden for Orford Ness, so knows much about the area and offers guided walks for guests.

A bath rather than shower (although there was one of those too, and even a bidet should I have required it) provided welcome relaxation after my ten mile walk. Suitably clean and refreshed, I set out to explore. First priority was to find dinner. I'd expected more choice but on a May Monday evening the High Street was deserted. Keeping the numbers theme, I chose OneFiveTwo restaurant. I ordered cod and chips as I'd been recommended, but without the pea puree – Aldeburgh is apparently too posh to serve normal peas. The chef had done his best to make it look upmarket, carefully draping the fish across the chips, but what matters, the taste, was nothing special.

Dinner completed, I took a walk along the beach, wandering amongst fishing boats, lobster pots and huts on the shingle. Like Sizewell and Dunwich, this typifies north Suffolk beaches. Two tall stone towers stand at the top of the beach. These were once sailors' lookouts. The north lookout has been converted to holiday accommodation, while the south tower is an artists' retreat. The idea came to owner Caroline Wiseman when she spotted the For Sale sign while swimming in the sea. She bought the tower, which dates from 1830, plus its adjoining cottage, and invites artists to spend a week creating and showing their work.

At the southern end of the town is another odd building, Fort Green Mill, a four storey windmill, now without its sails and converted to residential use. Beyond here was once the fishing village of Slaughden – another of Suffolk's lost villages. Its men used to go to sea for cod, but in the end the sea came for them. In the last days fishermen had to open the front and back doors of their cottages to let the tide run through.

Sources vary as to when the last house succumbed to the unstoppable force. Some say 1926, some 1936, with most agreeing that the Mariners Inn followed soon after. Others however state that the village was lost in the 1950s. Such variation illustrates the difficulty in obtaining accurate historical information, even from less than a century ago. I contacted Aldeburgh Museum and Catherine Howard-Dobson told me, *'Unfortunately we do not have definitive date for the last building being lost to the sea. I have a newspaper account, undated, which states the Mariner's pub was demolished in 1922, but again this is not definitive. We have no exact date, but it is thought the last building went around 1935'.*

Holding Back the Tide, a project coordinated by *CoastNet* to collect stories, pictures and artefacts telling the story of East Anglian coastal change, has published an interview with Ron Ashford, the last child born in Slaughden. In its introduction it refers to Slaughden as being, *'swept away by the ravages of the North Sea by the 1950s'*. More important than inconsistent dates is the human story described by the then eighty six year old Mr Ashford:

'I was born there in 1922 and I lived there for four years, I was aged four and then a storm in 1926 washed us out. It was a very severe storm that night and I was carried out on the shoulders of one of the men that worked down on the quay and his name was George Ward. My sister, Phyllis, was taken out by another man, that worked on the river and we were taken into the town, into Aldeburgh.

My family had been washed out four times previously but on the night of 1926 the storm was so severe, I've got a picture of shingle nearly up to the second floor and my mother and I standing outside the gate and shingle all around us. After that we had to move into Aldeburgh. We had to leave the house because it was so badly damaged.'

'My father was a boat builder down on the Slaughden quay. He had two of the biggest sheds down there full of all the tools and the lathes and equipment. In 1953 the sea came over and took the lot. All the sheds, all the boats. When the men that worked on the quay looked over the end of the Brudenell on the sea wall and there wasn't a stick standing, there was nothing. Everything had been swept over into the river. And my father lost his business then and he never opened anymore 'cos he was

getting to an age where he didn't think he would start again. It was too late so I just gave him a job, keep him occupied repairing clocks.'

Just one Slaughden building now remains, a Martello tower, half a mile along the shingle spit of Orford Ness. I walked to the tower, the sun low on the horizon over the River Alde to my right and the North Sea behind the shingle beach to my left. The two stretches of water are just yards apart, but typically for the coastal geography of Suffolk, the river doesn't meet the sea for another twelve miles. It used to end at Aldeburgh and very nearly did again when the 1953 floods almost broke through the shingle, but now meanders gently past Orford, Havergate Island and almost to Shingle Street. To add to its contrary nature, once past Aldeburgh the Alde changes its name to the Ore.

The Martello Tower is the largest and most northerly in a chain of 103 fortified towers built in the early 19th century to resist a potential invasion by Napoleon. This tower is unique for its quatrefoil design, which gives it a clover-like shape when seen from above, and allows four cannons to be mounted on the roof instead of the normal one. It is yet another unusual building that's been converted into a holiday apartment for Suffolk's discerning visitors.

Beyond the tower a gate stops the public from venturing further along the mysterious Orford Ness, a site of top secret military experiments and weapons tests for much of the 20th century. A National Trust sign explains that access is not permitted – *'Fragile habitats and wildlife easily damaged and disturbed'*. The spit is one of the best preserved shingle ridges in Europe and the NT website says it may contain as much as 15% of the world's coastal vegetated shingle. As you will read in Chapter Nine, part of the southern end of the Ness can be explored with access by boat from Orford village.

As I headed back to Aldeburgh the sky ahead was black. Before I'd finished taking photos of the River Alde and its yachts, the heavens opened – not rain but a full blown hail storm. Without waterproofs I had little protection from the stinging ice, making the short walk back into Aldeburgh the least comfortable ten minutes of the whole coastal walk. I was glad to reach the comfort of 34 Lee Road.

Post Script

Remembering the eroding sandy cliffs south of Sizewell, this was another walk that needed repeating to see if the coast path had survived the storms. My wife dropped me at Dunwich, where I made a third attempt to find the last grave from All Saints church. This time I found it straight away, behind a low fence about ten yards before the pedestrian gateway to Greyfriars. Jacob Forster died aged 38 in 1796. His gravestone stands amongst bushes five yards from the cliff edge, one day to join the church and the rest of its cemetery beneath the North Sea.

At Minsmere Road, this time I turned left, following a path beside the lane. Crossing the approach road to the National Trust Coastguard Cottages (marked on OS map as a track), I approached the cottages on heather-covered cliffs, where heath truly meets the sea. At Minsmere I stopped in a hide for a while, watching half a dozen terns squabbling on a sandbank.

Jacob Forster's Grave – Dunwich

Sizewell to Thorpeness was one of my favourite sections of the whole coast and I was pleased to find that the path was no more eroded than when I'd walked here a year earlier. Like Dunwich, for the moment it seems to be protected by shingle. Several walkers bade me good afternoon as we passed and a lizard enjoying the warm sunshine scuttled off as I approached. With the tide high the beach approach to Thorpeness may not have been passable, but in any case I would recommend the path back up the cliff to the common rather than a trudge across rocks and shingle.

Sitting on the shingle at Aldeburgh we sampled the town's famous fish and chips. Now I can agree, *'good fish and chips at Aldeburgh'*.

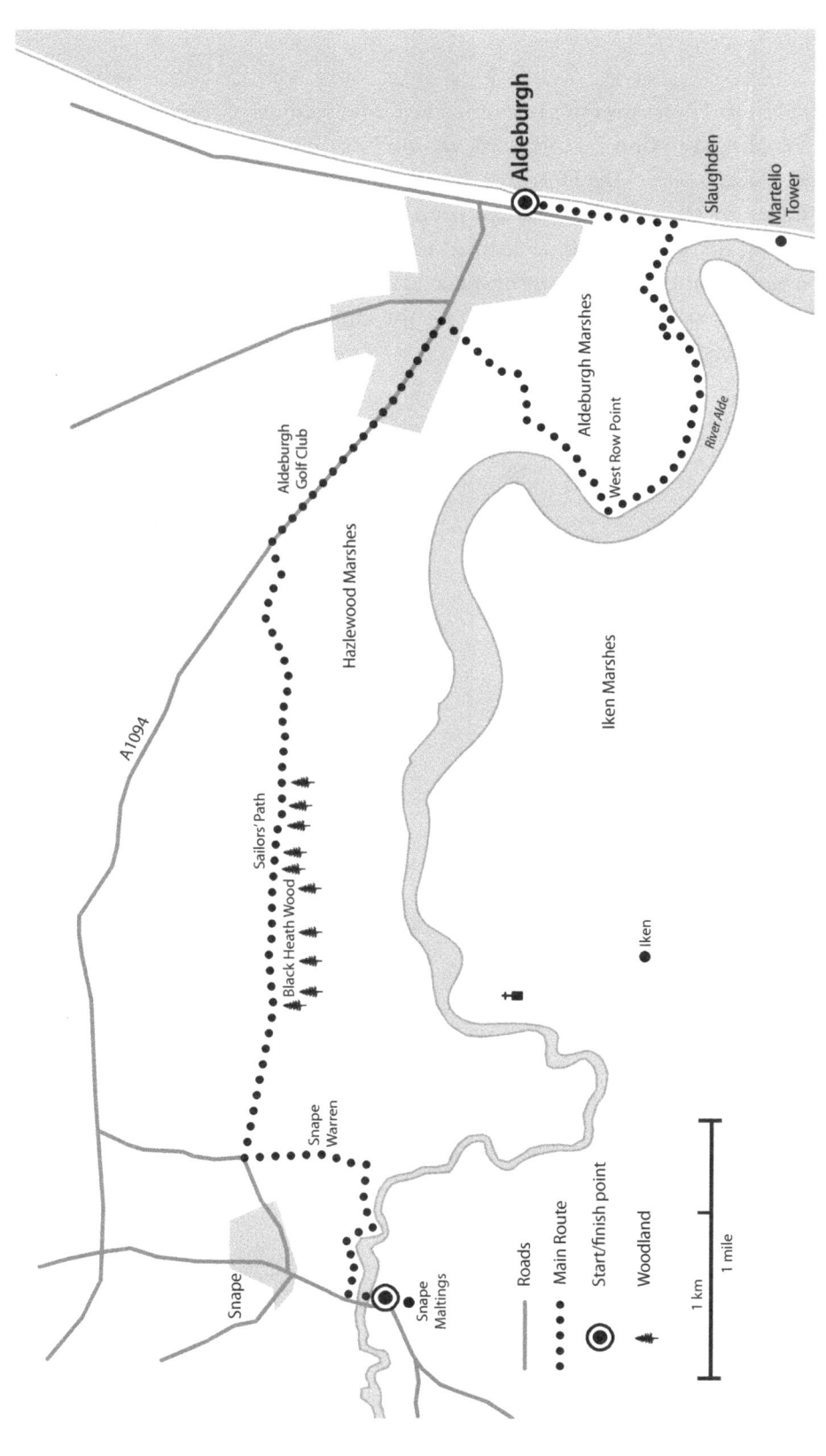

CHAPTER SIX
ALDEBURGH – SNAPE

(8 Miles) 14th May

In a rare concession to healthy eating, after yesterday's monster bacon serving on the train I declined the remarkable range of cooked breakfasts, in favour of a bowl of porridge. This though was no ordinary porridge, but a huge bowl with added apple, currants, honey and cinnamon. Excellent and healthy!

The sun was shining brightly as I left Lee Road for a last look at Aldeburgh. I decided I liked it, but not as much as Southwold. It looked a perfect day for walking but rain of monsoon proportions was forecast. The weatherman said it would be here at 2pm. My bus back from Snape Maltings was at 2.15. At least this time I'd have waterproofs with me if the rain was early or bus late.

For today's section I was to follow one of Suffolk's best known walks; the Sailors' Path from Aldeburgh to Snape Maltings. According to tradition this ancient route was used by sailors returning to Aldeburgh after unloading cargo at Snape Maltings and finding the tide too low to sail back.

The path leaves Aldeburgh on the main road, but first I planned a two mile diversion along the River Alde to the south of the town. Retracing last night's steps along the seafront I soon came to the river, where a path heads inland along the bank. Here there was a problem. The footpath was closed. An Environment Agency sign explained that as part of maintenance to the river walls, low spots were being topped up, *'to continue to protect the people and property in Aldeburgh'*. There was an orange digger in the distance but no sign of work in progress on the first part of the path. Yesterday I was very good and kept off Orford Ness. Today I was naughty again!

River Alde & Aldeburgh Martello Tower

Walking on the sea wall between marshland and river, with boats bobbing in the water, patches of salt marsh and the wooden skeleton of a wreck stuck fast in the mud, reminded me of much of my Essex coastal walking. So far Suffolk had been quite different but this was a more familiar winding river.

After about a third of a mile a path heads back across the marshes into Aldeburgh. The path on the sea wall continued without another closed sign, but now I could see the digger better. There were a couple of other vehicles and several men appeared to be working. With a long loop in the river they were half an hour's walking away, but would I be able to get past? I didn't fancy being sent back but nor did I want to miss a length of coastline. I stopped for a few minutes to consider. Should I take the path back to Aldeburgh? Did they have the authority to send me back? Could they physically stop me passing? I carried on.

Now past the boats, it was quiet – just the sound of birds and a gentle breeze. I stopped again at West Row Point where the river turns abruptly to the right. Opposite was a large barn belonging to Stanny Farm. A small dingy chugged by, towing an even smaller one. The red roof of the barn and orange top of the dingy enhanced the scene – the only bright colours amongst nature's greens, browns, blues and greys. Mankind's intervention can add to a view as much as it can spoil one.

I could see the digger more clearly now. It wasn't on the sea wall but a couple of hundred yards inland. I should be able to get by. Sections of the path had been topped with sand and clearly the work was recent, but there was nothing to impede the coastal walker. At Stanny Point my 2006 Ordnance Survey map showed Cob Island on the far side of the river, but there is now no island. It was washed away in a storm and just a marker pole remains. The river makes another ninety degree turn here but the footpath heads inland. It's not possible to walk on the Alde's banks all the way to Snape Maltings.

A sign at the bottom of steps down from the sea wall showed a map of Aldeburgh Marshes, indicating in red which footpaths were closed – all of them! As the (closed) path climbed a gentle incline through fields I bade a cheery good morning to a lady walking towards the river. She totally blanked me. The path became an earth track with contractors' vehicles parked at the edge. No doubt health and safety dictates that the public must be kept away. After walking through a farmyard, passing a garden centre and Aldeburgh Emporium antique market, I reached the main road. I had been bad again but my perambulation of Aldeburgh's marshes was complete.

Turning left onto the main road my legs slowed as I climbed the gentle hill out of Aldeburgh. Again they were telling me they wanted footpaths, but opposite the golf club there was an unexpected bonus. With no pavement this used to be a dangerous section to walk, but a new path had recently been opened along the edge of the golf course. This forms part of the Suffolk Coast Path, which meets the road here after bypassing Aldeburgh. After half a mile a wooden post with the Sailors' Path ship logo pointed to the left. From here it was a wonderful walk to Snape Maltings.

Starting as a track passing a few isolated cottages, then narrowing between hedges, the path skirts Hazlewood Marshes. Owned by Suffolk Wildlife Trust, this is one of the last wet grazing marshes on the county's coast and an important breeding site for waders such as redshank, snipe and lapwing. A grassy path took me into the woods and past a lonely house. *Suffolk Coast and*

Sculptures – Black Heath Wood

Heath Walks describes it as derelict but it looked to have been recently renovated with modern glazing units. There's no road to the house but it appeared to be being readied for habitation. I would imagine that the estate agents particulars will say something on the lines of, *'secluded property in enchanted wood – would suit family of bears, witch or lonely old lady with gullible granddaughter'.*

Coming out of the woods, the path continues on long stretches of boardwalk and little footbridges over Ham Creek Marshes; a wetland world that seemingly arrived from nowhere after the dry sandy paths. A bridge crossed a stream with trees reflected in the water: a lovely spot – so still and peaceful. The path continued alongside Black Heath Wood. Huge oaks were dotted about a green field to the right. I disturbed grazing rabbits and brown cows who stopped munching to watch me go by. This was a very English walk. I sat by a tree for lunch. Not one person passed by.

After crossing a private track the path enters the wood where two unusual terracotta towers caught my attention. Imagination suggested they may be chimneys for some secret underground installation. Two ladies walking the other way thought they were sculptures. They were right. These were two of a number of temporary sculptures erected in 2008 as part of the 'Ebb & Flow Project', which worked with local people to explore different aspects of the river. I shall leave it to the project's website to explain:

'Neolithic, Bronze, Iron, Romano, Saxon : The forested section of Sailors' Path has intriguing theatrical spaces dappled with pools of light. To heighten this experience, stacked terracotta figurative forms, referencing the pottery from Neolithic times to Anglo Saxon pre-glazed wares, stand alone alongside the path. Reminding us of the generations that have passed through the forest, the 'stacks' of pots are as they would be found in archaeological excavations, with the oldest at the bottom to the more recent at the top.'

It was a beautiful walk through the mainly birch woods, with the sun's rays illuminating young green leaves. Whilst I enjoy coastal walking, one of the delights of Suffolk was the detours inland through heaths, fields and woods.

At Snape Warren, an RSPB reserve, there were glimpses of the Alde again as it meandered inland. With the help of sheep and Exmoor ponies scrub is being cleared here to recreate the rare Suffolk Sandling heathland. As its name suggests, the land was once used for rabbit farming, a common use for the Sandlings, where acidic sandy soil gave limited opportunities for agriculture.

I could have taken a short cut through the warren but the noticeboard said 'many paths', which experience suggests I'd get lost! Instead I stayed on the main track, passing a field where brightly dressed migrant workers were busy setting up polythene tubes. There must have been twenty five or more, their laughter and chatter floating across the countryside. I'm going to get all controversial now – how sad that so many British people turn down such work, but how enriched our country is for the diversity these hard working migrants bring.

From Sailors' Path Cottages I continued along a gorse-lined lane which ended at the road into the village of Snape. Here I had a choice – take the Sandlings Walk through the village, or the Sailors' Path and Suffolk Coast Path down to the river. Essex has no official coast path and it was a luxury to have a selection of waymarked routes to follow in Suffolk – which probably explains why now almost at the end of my sixth walk, I still hadn't got lost.

A sign welcomed me to 'Warren Walks', the path running by the edge of a wood and to the bank of the Alde. The last half mile of a very varied morning's walk was along a meandering embankment with tall reedbeds on either side. The tide was down and the river mostly mud. A pair of shelducks left a trail of tiny footprints as they pecked their way across the mud. Across the river was Snape Maltings.

Built in the mid-19th century by Victorian entrepreneur Newson Garrett, Snape Maltings is an impressive complex of grade II listed buildings, which until it closed in 1965 was one of the largest barley maltings in East Anglia. Initially barley was transported from the riverside granaries by Thames barge, to be malted by breweries across England and into Europe, but soon Garrett saw an opportunity for added value. Expanding the site, he set up malthouses and began shipping malt down the River Alde.

Garrett became Mayor of Aldeburgh in 1899 and fifteen years later his daughter Elizabeth took the same post, becoming the first woman mayor in the UK.

Elizabeth Garrett Anderson was already a pioneer, leading the way for women to become doctors and setting up the New Hospital for Women in London (which later took her name), before retiring to Aldeburgh in 1902.

When the maltings owners went into liquidation it was difficult to see how the seven acres of purpose-built buildings could be put to a different use. However, matching the vision of Newson Garrett, George Gooderham, a local farmer and businessman, recognised the potential. He purchased the site and set about finding alternative uses for the buildings. By the 1960s the Aldeburgh Music Festival was outgrowing the limited space available in the town's Jubilee Hall and surrounding churches, and Benjamin Britten had started to look around for somewhere to build a concert hall. He found the largest malthouse, in its magnificent setting overlooking the river, and began negotiations with George Gooderham. After little more than a year Snape Maltings Concert Hall was ready to be opened by the Queen at the start of the 1967 Aldeburgh Festival. Two years later a disastrous fire largely destroyed the hall on the opening day of the festival, but in just twelve months the 830 seat venue had been rebuilt and the Queen was back to perform the reopening.

I crossed Snape Bridge and started to explore the complex of shops, galleries and restaurants in the old industrial buildings. Cars seemed to be everywhere. Marshals directed them where to park. Half a million people visit here each year. Most of the shops were full of people and with a rucksack on my back, every time I turned I feared knocking over a display or several old ladies. I liked the buildings and was pleased to see them put to good use, but my wife, especially if well armed with a credit card or two, would have appreciated their contents rather more.

The sky was darkening as I wandered round taking photos. Workmen were busy converting more of the buildings. Some had been recently opened as holiday apartments. More were to follow. Moored by the quay was Cygnet, a wooden sailing barge built in 1881 which used to carry farm produce along Suffolk's rivers. After being sold in 1945, two petrol engines were fitted and for some years she carried cockle shells from Foulness in Essex for sale as chicken grit. After a period working as a supply vessel to oil tankers, she was refitted as a private yacht and is now based at Snape, looking fine against the backdrop of ivy covered buildings.

'Large Interior Form' – Snape Maltings

On the lawn by the concert hall entrance was a bronze sculpture. It looked vaguely interesting, although nothing special, so I was somewhat surprised to find it was a work of Henry Moore. His friendship with Benjamin Britten and his partner the singer Peter Pears (the festival's co-founder), has led to a succession of Moore's sculptures being exhibited here. I have to admit to being a bit of a Philistine when it comes to modern art. On a recent visit to Milan I went round a Picasso exhibition wondering why the artist hadn't bothered to finish half the pictures and why most appeared to date from his infant school years. Moore's *Large Interior Form,* I am struggling to describe. There is perhaps a vague resemblance to a curved human form, with a large hole in the chest and another in the small head, but with no idea what he is trying to portray I shall once again defer to the experts.

The website *www.henrymoore.org* explains: *'Deriving from the idea of internal/external forms, a theme which Moore explored throughout his career, this work is recognisable as the internal element of Large Upright Internal/External Form and was cast separately as a sculpture in its own right. The exposed inner form stands alone and gives impetus to the idea of the internal form as a figure.'*

Does that help?

The rain started as I wandered round a small craft workshop, chatting to the ladies who were eating their lunch and hopefully disguising my limited interest in costume jewellery and hand-made childrens' clothes. As it hammered on the windows I checked my watch: five to two. The weatherman was spot on. Heading for the bus I took a quick look in the café. Goats' cheese, crayfish, basil and sun-dried tomatoes featured highly on the menu. Snape Maltings is one of Suffolk's best known tourist attractions, but it's not for me. I can see the appeal to many but give me the footpaths and sea walls any day.

I nearly missed the bus. It arrived three minutes early as I was looking the other way. A frantic wave of the arm and it halted just in time. After the obligatory circuits of a couple of deserted villages, I got off at Melton station on the outskirts of Woodbridge. The ever reliable East Suffolk train took me to Ipswich and I was home for tea (sensibly arranged and with a complete lack of basil).

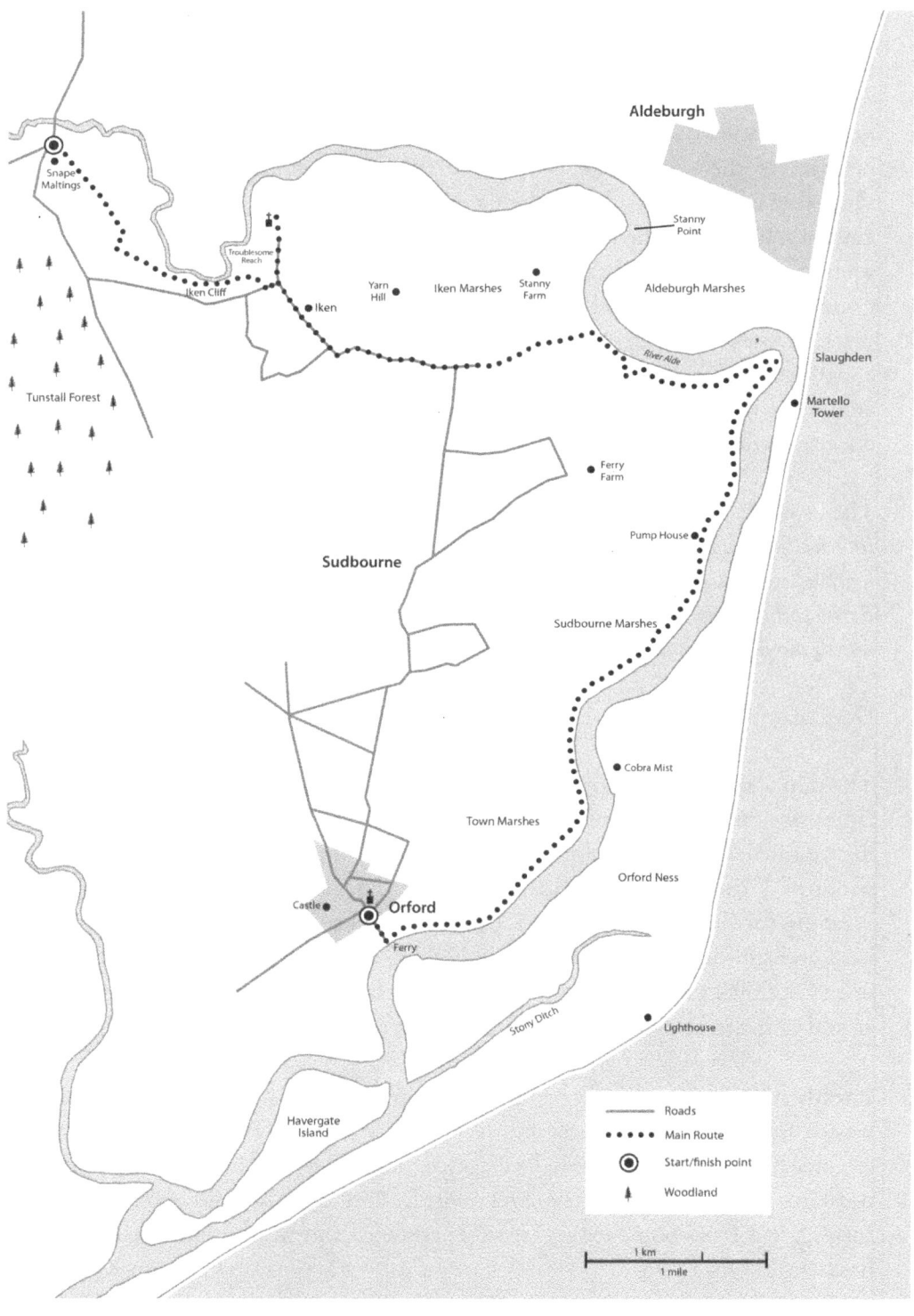

CHAPTER SEVEN
SNAPE – IKEN – ORFORD

(10 Miles) 10th June & 17th July

A combination of circumstances meant I had to change my plans to stay at Orford and had time for just a short walk today. It was though a most enjoyable stroll along the River Alde. My journey to Suffolk followed what was becoming a familiar pattern; bacon baguette on the Norwich express, change to East Suffolk Line at Ipswich and high speed bus ride along the county's lanes.

I took the opportunity to start at Snape, visiting the village I'd missed out last time. The village's website carries a message for Harry Potter fans – it has no connection with Professor Severus Snape of Hogwarts. With history going back to Roman times and positioned at the first crossing point on the Alde, Snape was once a more important settlement than Aldeburgh. Inevitably it became associated with smugglers, who needed to move their goods across the river. Their ruthlessness was illustrated by the misfortune of a Jeremiah Gardener, who in 1727 challenged a gang of smugglers and had his nose sliced off for his trouble. Had he not been able to crawl off and hide behind a hedge, poor Jeremiah would not have escaped alive. Smugglers frequented The Crown Inn, where a south facing dormer window was supposedly used to signal the all clear once the militias were safely out of the way in the bar below.

Perhaps the most attractive village sign I'd found so far, depicts a Saxon ship of the type found in nearby burial grounds, a monk from St Mary's Priory of which just a magnificent wooden barn remains, a curlew symbolising Benjamin Britten's inspiration drawn from the countryside around the Alde, and the old hump-back bridge which was demolished in the 1960s. The bridge was much loved and apparently Britten salvaged some of the bricks to build a curved wall in the garden of the Red House where he lived with Peter Pears in Aldeburgh.

With no need for a crayfish wrap or designer clothing, I walked straight through Snape Maltings, continuing along a narrow path on the river bank and disturbing a party of bird watchers. After a couple of hundred yards this reached a dead end. For the first, but probably not the last time, I'd gone the wrong way. Retracing my steps and squeezing past the twitchers once more, I returned to the Maltings, followed a boardwalk and found the correct (Suffolk Coast) path at the other end of the car park. An alternative path runs through a field past a full sized model of a horse and cart, which I thought at the time was rather naff and on reflection still do.

The path ran beside a cornfield where young shoots of maize emerged reticently from the earth, perhaps wondering where the sunshine was this year. Boardwalks took me through reedbeds alive with birdsong, passing a line of skeletal trees. I stopped to take a picture and a lady asked if I was waiting for reed bunting. We agreed a tree kept more still. A church stood on a prominentary across the water. This was my destination for today.

Marshes near Snape Maltings

The path continued to Iken Cliff, another wonderful spot on Suffolk's coast. Now a tiny settlement, Iken was once an important fishing and farming village, with its own pub. No boats fish from here now and farmland, which had been gained from draining marshes, was lost when the sea broke through in the 1953 floods. The land which slopes gently up from the river is still farmed, but this quiet spot would have been a very different scene less than two hundred years ago. Rope's Kiln, a perfectly preserved lime kiln, remains by the path, but there is little to see of the quay and warehouse, where until the 1860s the Rope family ran their corn, coal and shipping business, with sailing vessels taking goods down the Alde and on to London.

The main Suffolk Coast Path heads inland here, missing out another big section of coast, although there is an optional diversion via Orford, which I was to largely follow. This took me right down to the water's edge. It was good to be so close to the sea again. The path here can flood at high tide and yet another option is to climb steps leading up to the lane by Iken Hall. Home to Margery Spring-Rice, one of the founding members of the Aldeburgh Festival Council, Benjamin Britten named the hall as the setting of his *Let's Make an Opera* an '*Entertainment for Young People*', which was premiered at the festival.

Rope's Kiln – Iken

I stopped for lunch at a small sandy beach – an idyllic spot with little waves lapping on the sand, an occasional boat gliding by, a sailing barge moored just off the shore and Iken church across the water. Tiny marshy islands lay low in the water, providing roosts for birds who awaited the return of the mudflats, and the lunch within. I'd considered some of these islands when researching tidal islands for *No Boat Required*, but although 'dry' at low tide, the mud is too soft to permit safe access on foot. A couple with a black labrador passed by as I ate, their '*Hiya*' contrasting with the '*Good mornings*' of the more elderly walkers I'd past earlier.

The beach has been recommended for 'wild swimming', although much care is needed, with heed to be taken of both mud and tides. It is for good reason that this stretch of river was named 'Troublesome Reach' by barge sailors. An hour either side of high tide is suggested as the safe limit for swimming. Seals can be seen here, but hopefully nothing like the rather unrealistic monster shown emerging from the 'swamp' when *The Power of the Kroll*, a 1978 episode of *Doctor Who,* was filmed at Iken Cliff.

Continuing on my way, I was somewhat startled to turn a corner and find a large brown horse standing on the narrow path. Busy munching grass by the

View from Iken Beach

water, he clearly had no intention of moving, so I had to squeeze by, hoping that he didn't take offence to a walker so close behind him.

Where the path meets a lane I turned left, then left again a few yards later, towards Iken church which stands at the end of a wooded promontory that was once an island. Adjacent to the church is The Anchorage, an attractive red-brick house. A sign on the gate warned, '*Beware of dog. Enter at own risk*'. Guarding the front door was what might have been a large dog but could equally have been a medium-sized bear. The sign was superfluous. Surely no one would enter.

The churchyard is reached through a wooden gate in a tall hedge. My first impression – perfection: an ancient, partly thatched church, in a quiet, neatly tended churchyard, with a backdrop of trees, standing on a bluff above the beautiful River Alde. In the corner a man was tidying up having just finished mowing the grass. A tabby cat ambled lazily across the path. Could there be a more typically British scene?

I chatted to the man. He looks after a number of churchyards in the area but loves coming to Iken. We agreed he had a wonderful job – when the sun shone. He told me that according to a local story the body of Queen Boudica was brought back here following her defeat by the Romans. There may be some truth in this as Iken was reputedly a base of Boudica and her marauding Iceni tribes, who made good use of the commanding position on the Alde Estuary.

The gardener said I should look in the field behind the church, where I'd see Angus. Standing under a tree, Angus was a huge red Highland bull with horns plenty big enough to toss a man. Nevertheless, I think I'd still have preferred to face him than the 'bear' outside The Anchorage.

Iken is one of East Anglia's earliest Christian sites. Anglo-Saxon Chronicles for the year 654 (or possibly 653) record that the Middle Angles '*received true faith*' and that the monk Botolph (also known as Botwulf, Botulph or Botulf) began to build a minster at Icanhoh. Icanhoh, which means 'ox hill', is generally believed to be Iken. From here monks made missionary journeys across East

Anglia, but in 870 invading Danes destroyed the monastery. The site was marked with a cross, part of which may still be seen inside the church.

The church, which is dedicated to St Botolph, dates from the 11th century, when the Norman nave was built. The tower, typical of many in Suffolk, was constructed in the mid 15th century and the chancel in 1853 (replacing an earlier ruin). From the outside the church inspires by its beauty in such a wonderful setting. Inside, peace comes from simplicity, tranquillity and the thought that people have been worshipping here for a thousand years. I was glad to be the only person here. A tiny congregation still meet most weeks, their rector shared with four other churches. I picked up a newsletter which reported on Iken's annual Rogation Service that had recently been held at Stanny House Farm. It was good to read Reverend David Murdoch's letter describing the varied services held in the churches and his eagerness to encourage young families. It is that they are still living places of worship and not museums, that make our ancient churches so special, but with elderly congregations so many struggle to survive and young blood must be encouraged to continue their work.

On the 4th of April 1968, a gardener clearing the churchyard lit a bonfire. A stray spark fell on the thatched roof of St Botolph's, setting it alight. By the time the fire was extinguished the church was a burned out shell. It took twenty years for repairs to be completed, not helped by a dispute over access which meant materials had to be carried from the road by hand, but such is the spirit of Christianity in this historic place, that the setback was overcome and worship continues almost fifteen hundred years after St Botolph first landed here.

By the gate I chatted again to the man tending the grass. Tabby cat joined us and jumped onto his mower, paws poised as if to drive off. Farewells and mutual appreciation of St Botolph's shared, I wandered off. With my mind on bulls, cats, fires and a thousand years of Christian history, I wasn't paying a great deal of attention. Suddenly I looked up and found I was outside someone's front door. I'd gone through the wrong gate. This was The Anchorage – where 'bear' lives. The next ten yards were the fastest of the whole walk. He didn't spot me. Perhaps he was busy devouring a sheep or two for lunch. Had I been spied I have little doubt that the book would have finished here!

Having had to alter plans and make this a day trip, I retraced my steps to Snape Maltings. The walk back was as thoroughly enjoyable as it had been in the other direction, stopping frequently to look back at the splendid view across the Alde to the beautiful St Botolph's church, my favourite encountered so far.

As with the last walk, I had time to spare at Snape Maltings. I took another look at *Large Interior Form* and wondered again what all the fuss was about, menaced a few more old ladies with my rucksack in crowded shops, then went back in the Granary café, steered clear of basil, crayfish and dill, and enjoyed a toasted teacake sitting in the sun. (You may perhaps have noticed by now that my walks tend to be punctuated by bacon rolls and teacakes.)

Conscious of the early departure last time, I walked down to the stop in good time for the 15.15 bus, and waited. At 15.10 the day's first speck of blue sky appeared. At 15.15 the bus didn't. I waited. No bus came. The timetable showed a number to text *'for bus times'*. Reply was immediate, but simply quoted the timetable that was on the wall in front of me. What's the point? I phoned Anglian Buses. A helpful lady thought she knew the answer, but she'd have to check. She did. In term time the bus goes off for a school run, so the 15.15 doesn't run. I should have noticed the *'NS'* on the timetable. It was hardly clear. On railway timetables services that don't run every day are in red or italics to alert people to check. Now I knew the system I could see that the 16.00 wasn't going to turn up either. The next bus was 16.25. For the first time I questioned my commitment to use public transport.

* * * * *

It was the hottest day of the year as I resumed my walk to Orford – thirty two degrees in London, although thankfully a little less on the coast. My West Ham baseball cap had been replaced by a wide brimmed sunhat – more effective at protecting from the rays and at embarrassing my children, but a tempting target for the wind. I took a taxi from Melton to Iken. As we skirted Rendlesham Forest the driver told me a tale of extraterrestrial activity.

A few days after Christmas 1980, strange lights were seen apparently descending into in the forest between two RAF bases, Woodbridge and Bentwaters, both of which were used by the United States Air Force. Servicemen sent to investigate claimed to have seen an alien spacecraft. Next morning a search found burn marks and impressions in the ground. Many explanations have been put forward, ranging from a visit from extra terrestrials, Russian military activity, confusion with the flashing light of Orford Ness Lighthouse, or an elaborate hoax. My driver reckoned it was a case of the Americans having been smoking too much '*good stuff*'. For many the truth came out in 2003, when ex US security policeman Kevin Conde admitted that he and colleagues had concocted the whole thing using car headlights and a loud speaker. To others his 'confession' is just part of the establishment cover up.

The driver regaled me with tales of Suffolk smugglers, then as we passed through Tunstall Forest told me of more military activity. At the start of World War Two the forest was newly planted and large mounds of earth were built up to prevent German gliders landing here. The mounds can still be seen in the trees, a part of our country's history and as I was finding as I travelled, some of many signs of Suffolk's role in defending Britain.

With the sky blue, I took some more photos of Iken church, wandering round the back to see Angus who was enjoying the shade of a large tree. Tabby cat was nowhere to be seen and The Anchorage's 'bear' had left his gate unguarded. A sign asked for deliveries to '*call out, hoot & wait, or phone*'. This was no ordinary guard dog. A stall outside offered jam, flowers and drinks, with payment to be left in an honesty box. I dare say 'bear' keeps an eye open for anyone who might forget to pay.

The first two miles of today's walk were along lanes through the scattered village of Iken. Despite stretching for a couple of miles the village has just a handful of houses. One in five Suffolk parishes hold less than a hundred people, illustrating the sparse population in much of this largely rural county.

At Tumbleweed Cottage I exchanged greetings with a man reading a book under a tree. As I was applying the day's first coating of sun cream four elderly cyclists passed, the last commenting that it was nice in the shade. We agreed there wasn't enough. A man mending a fence at Hill Farm mopped his brow as I passed, concurring with my comment that it was too hot for such work. More than ever the weather was to be today's conversation theme.

Butterflies on the verges were enjoying the sun. Huge sprinklers irrigated crops, the sandy soil drying quickly in the heat. Glimpses of the River Alde, sparkling in sunshine, could be seen through gaps in the hedge. Also on my left was Yarn Hill, a circular wood at the top of a gentle hill, rising fourteen metres above the Alde. According to legend this is where Botolph originally tried to build his monastery, but incurred a major difficulty. Every night the stones would be moved and the workers found dead, their bodies mutilated. The legend doesn't tell how many workers he got through before deciding to give up and build it on the island of Icanho. Here he erected a seven foot tall cross, inscribed with carvings of wolves and wild dogs, to ward off evil spirits and banish the devil. Perhaps an enterprising vicar could boost church funds by marketing some of these for keeping away the double glazing salesmen.

Where the road turns sharp right I continued straight on towards Stanny Farm, along the somewhat optimistically named High Street. Opposite 'Beetlebrow', a pink cottage, a track leaves to the right. After passing a rather nice house where four ladies sat chatting in the sun, it veers right, but a small path continues ahead. This was to take me to the sea wall. The Suffolk Coast Path continues along lanes for another mile before meeting the river a little closer to Orford.

A man in a fetching red sunhat, walking an over-sized poodle, passed me, interrupting his phone conversation to say '*Morning*'. As the narrow path made its way through a rather overgrown clump of trees I received a sudden reminder of one of the drawbacks of shorts – stinging nettles. Gradually descending towards the river, the path took me alongside a field of beet. A welcome breeze brought cooling air but immediately removed my hat. I stopped to investigate a ruined building and rusty sheep crush in the corner of the field, picking up more stings for my trouble.

A wooden footbridge over the borrowdyke (the channel formed where earth was dug out to make the sea wall) took me back to the river, almost opposite West Row Point where I'd turned right two walks ago. To my left was the red roofed barn. Aldeburgh was straight ahead. Two people were walking on the wall. Maybe the paths were open again now?

View Across River Alde to Aldeburgh

From here it was sea wall for the six miles to Orford. No shelter, no pubs and no cafes! Midway along an area of salt marsh the path crossed a track heading down to a slipway. This is the Suffolk Coast Path (Orford Loop). A sign showed it heading right but the path was barely distinguishable in long grass. Back on the winding sea wall, I headed towards a promontory opposite Slaughden Quay. Half a mile ahead a couple were walking towards me. I tried to work out where we'd pass. You do these things when you walk a lot – well I do! Turning almost 180 degrees at the head of the promontory, I headed south. The couple had disappeared. I found them sitting in the long grass and getting out their lunch. We chatted for a moment. They'd walked from Orford, would have liked to have found a seat and were hot. I'd walked from Iken, was about to have lunch and was hot.

Finding a suitable spot opposite the Martello Tower, I settled down to the rather nice turkey baguette I'd bought in London. Across the river people were drinking outside the yacht club. Boats pottered on the water. A river trip chugged by. All was very different to the dark skies and hail when I'd walked on the far bank a couple of months earlier.

Continuing along the river, with Orford Ness to my left and farmland to the right, I was soon hot again. That the breeze was now insufficient to trouble my hat meant it had little cooling effect. Perhaps it would have been cooler by the open sea, the other side of Orford Ness. The steps of Sudbourne Pumping House, a small red-brick building, provided welcome shade for a few minutes.

Two sheep on the salt marsh stopped and stared as I passed. I hope they weren't aware that the salt-tolerant grasses and samphire on which they graze give meat a distinctively sweet flavour, which one day will see them served as a delicacy with new potatoes and rosemary (and perhaps a little basil should they be consumed in Suffolk?).

Sailing boats approached me from both directions. I watched to see if they greeted each other like passing rural walkers or bus drivers. They don't. Orford Ness Lighthouse came into view and across the marshes, the twin towers of Orford Castle and church, still several miles walking away. Flowers amongst the sea wall grasses attracted a host of butterflies. Admiral I recognised; many I didn't. A dark pink one fluttered alongside for a while before deciding he'd rather stay by the river than accompany me to Orford. For a minute I thought perhaps he had a family to care for, but then realised butterflies don't.

A tern circled above, squawking loudly, indignant that I'd spoiled his quiet afternoon in the sun. A whole herd of cows stopped what they were doing (eating of course), to stare at me. Walkers must be scarce here (I saw just the one couple all day), so provide rare interest for farm animals and annoyance for wildlife. The salt marsh ended opposite the Orford Ness pylons and I was right by the river, which by now had changed its name from the Alde to the Ore. The sea wall here was grazed and shorter grass made for easier walking. Opposite was the large grey 'Cobra Mist' building, once one of the many secrets of Orford Ness. Looking back the dome of Sizewell B loomed over Aldeburgh. In so many ways the Suffolk coast is a coast of contrast.

Approaching Orford four girls passed me, accompanied by Nessie, a rather naughty and very wet black labrador, who insisted on jumping in the muddy channels. We exchanged appropriate but brief conversation. Almost the first building in Orford is the Riverside Tearoom – a very welcome refuge. Decking

Cobra Mist

outside was full with elderly couples enjoying tea in the sun, but I was glad of shade inside the wooden building. Goats' cheese, caramelised onion and crayfish were all on the menu. I didn't notice any basil. My afternoon teacake (slightly burnt) and long cool drink, were much appreciated.

I soon decided that Orford was going to feature highly on my list of favourite Suffolk places. It's a picturesque village, but also very much a lived in community, with independent shops, a school and fire station. The quay seems to be one of those places that always have some kind of activity going on. A couple of men tended one of the many boats tied up on the foreshore. A little ferry deposited a handful of visitors returning from Orford Ness. Two ladies perused a notice advertising brunch and dinner cruises on the *Lady Florence*.

It was a delightful walk up Quay Street, which leads a quarter mile to the village centre. On the left is the Jolly Sailor, a pub built between the late 16th and mid 17th century, allegedly using timbers from wrecked ships. Naturally it is said to have smuggling connections. Doorways of cottages set back behind a green were festooned with flowers, and a terrace of red-brick houses adorned with ivy and climbing flowers.

I stopped at Saint Bartholomew's Church, glad to spend a few minutes out of the sun in its cool interior. The church dates from the 14th century but substantial remains of an earlier Norman building adjoin its eastern end. Whilst containing much of interest for the purists (brass figures, a fine organ screen, stained glass windows and ornate stone font), its large square interior seemed to detract from the atmosphere and this wasn't my favourite Suffolk church. St Bartholomew's stands in a large churchyard surrounded by trees. On 16th October 1987 a contract was due to be signed for the felling of eighteen trees. On the night of the 15th the worst storm to hit Southern England in three hundred years did the job for free, blowing down all eighteen of them!

At the south side of the village stands a fine 12th century castle. Down Baker's Lane, just behind the village square, is Richardson's smokehouse, a family-run business where fish, cheese and meat are slowly smoked over Suffolk oak. Close by The Butley Orford Oysterage offers a tempting range of fish and seafood caught sustainably from their two boats. Across the square independent bakers, butchers and a general store offer locally sourced products, with a wider range of fresh goods than can be found in many a larger town. What a pleasure to find genuine village shops with not a Tesco or Spar in sight.

Accommodation in Orford is limited. The three pubs have rooms, but either at a price more than I was willing to pay, or requiring a two night minimum stay. Hence I'd delayed my walk until a room was free at Ashanwell, one of only two bed and breakfast establishments in the village. Host Katharina provided a comfortable stay and friendly welcome.

An excellent dinner was enjoyed sitting in the garden of the Jolly Sailor. The cooler evening sunshine was ideal walking conditions and on completing a huge plate of ham, eggs and chips I made a snap decision – I would start tomorrow's walk today.

Back at the quay I turned right, continuing on the sea wall that I'd left three hours earlier. Out on the river a fisherman was transferring his catch from one boat to another, before rowing ashore with his afternoon's work. Like most

Suffolk coastal villages, fishing continues here in a small way, but is nothing like the industry of years gone by.

Movement on the path ahead brought me to a halt. A fat frog lolloped across and hopped into the long grass. In my favourite evening light, with the tide up and air cool, this was a lovely walk beside the Ore. A pair of noisy oystercatchers though made it clear I wasn't welcome by their sea. They live here, I was just visiting. Across the water Orford Ness's 'pagoda' laboratories oozed mystery. I passed a couple walking back to Orford. The man told me to watch out for frogs.

At Chantry Point I was opposite the end of Havergate Island, Suffolk's only island, and an important bird sanctuary (see Chapter Ten). The sound of bird song floated across the river. The evening sun shone on still pools in the saltings, accentuating its range of delicate greens and purples. I never tire of the beauty of our ever-changing salt marshes.

The path heads inland half a mile from Chantry Point, but a sign on a gate advised that there is a licensed footpath to Butley Ferry. Although not marked on the OS map, this runs for 2½ miles along the sea wall to Butley River, but from the height of the grass looked to be rarely walked. A circular walk using the Butley Ferry had been my original idea, but had to change on learning that the ferry only runs on summer weekends, when accommodation in Orford is even harder to find.

Instead, I followed a path through the agricultural land of Gedgrave Marshes, turning right for a short distance along a lane, then left onto a sandy track at Richmond Farm. Had I been continuing to Chillesford I would have stayed on this track, but with my bed for the night in Orford I took another path through fields for the mile or so back into the village. This came out at the castle, where two couples were enjoying an alfresco dinner. One of the ladies said they were waiting for boiling oil to be dropped from the ramparts above. If they were laying siege it was all very civilised.

All was well in Orford. Delicious smells pervaded from the Crown and Castle, Orford's premier (and rather expensive) inn. The Butley Orford Oysterage was full, chatter from contented diners drifting through open windows. I wandered back down to the quay, watching two girls row a tiny dingy ashore. Walking back to Ashanwell, I noticed that at Orford's garage an attendant still serves its customers with petrol. How apt for this lovely Suffolk village.

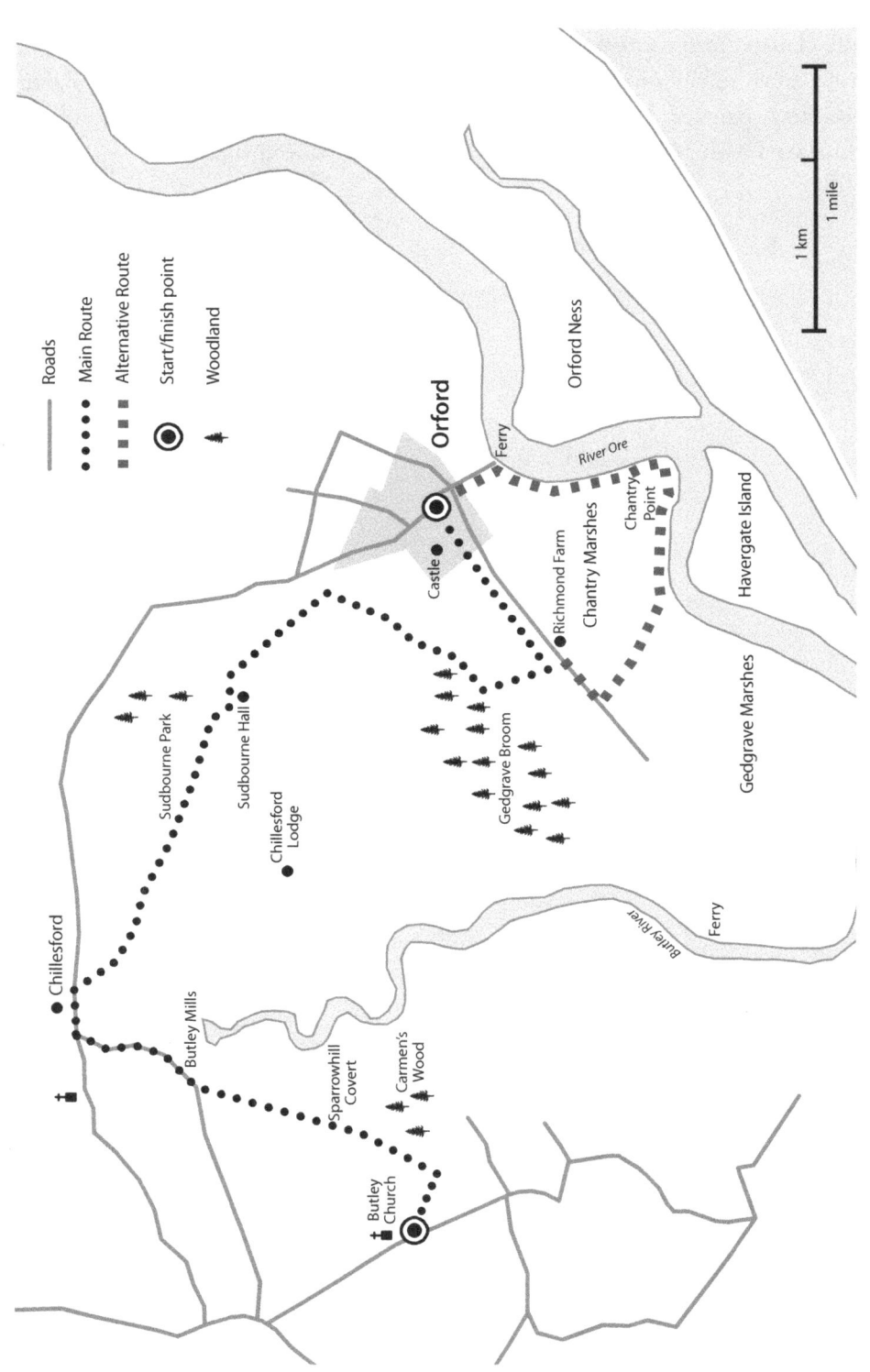

CHAPTER EIGHT
ORFORD – BUTLEY

(7 Miles) 18th July

With just a short walk today, on a mercifully cooler morning I spent another couple of hours wandering round Orford. Smoke was seeping from the blackened doors of Richardson's smokehouse. The bakery was shut for a funeral, so I looked for lunch in Orford General Store. What a wonderful shop. Incorporating a butcher, café, deli and Post Office, this is the sort of shop that most towns would be glad to have, let alone a village of six hundred permanent residents. Winner of the Countryside Alliance *Village Shop of the Year*, it provides a service not only to Orford and its visitors, but with more than thirty local suppliers, helps support the area's economy. After thoroughly perusing the deli counter, I came out with a sage, pork and apple pie, a large scotch egg and very sticky treacle tart. Lunch today would be a treat.

Across the road Orford Craft Shop wasn't yet open. It must take an age each morning to arrange the large selection of wicker baskets on the forecourt. It wasn't the crafts but the Underwater Exploration Exhibition on the floor above that I was keen to see. Returning at 10 o'clock after a walk round the churchyard, I paid my fifty pence and climbed the steep steps above the shop. The exhibition is smaller than its inclusion on the Ordnance Survey map might suggest, but most interesting, with many photos showing the local coastline and dives to the remains of Old Dunwich. I learned that in the 13th century the main car park by Orford Quay was a river inlet used by small vessels, and that the hump in the road here was installed to prevent it flooding as occurred in 1953. A photograph of the Martello Tower in Slaughden noted how much land once stood between it and the sea, and another told how seventeen metres of Covehithe Cliffs were lost in a twelve month period from 1990-91.

As I chatted to the man running the shop he introduced himself – Stuart Bacon, whose book on Old Dunwich and its underwater exploration I had very much enjoyed. He told me that with nil visibility everything had to be done by touch, including bringing up the canon that now stands outside Dunwich Museum. I mentioned his stories of freeing fishing nets caught on the ruins and he told me how dangerous this was, with the risk of getting snagged, but that he was only paid ten pounds for each net. Now aged eighty, Stuart is unable to dive, but it was a pleasure to meet him and bring some of his stories to life.

Next stop was the castle. Built by Henry II between 1165 and 1173, to protect himself against foreign invasion and uprisings by the barons of East Anglia, it served as a royal castle for 150 years. Use as both a grand residence and military stronghold continued for several centuries, but after being bought along with the Manor of Sudbourne by Sir Michael Stanhope in the 1590s, it started to fall into decline. In 1753 Orford and Sudbourne were sold to the Earl of Hereford and in 1805 his heir, the 2nd Marquis of Hereford, proposed to pull the castle down. It was only saved after the government intervened, wishing to retain the castle as a landmark for ships navigating the dangerous Whiting Sandbank.

Orford from the Castle

With changing attitudes to the preservation of historical remains, the castle's future was more secure and once maintained and furnished it was used for banquets and parties. The Second World War saw the castle defending our coast once more, with a radar post built on the south turret.

Remains of the outer buildings are now beneath earthworks (the last part of the wall collapsed *'with a tremendous crash'* on 1st July 1841) but the remarkably well preserved keep is little altered since the 12th century, and open to the public under the care of English Heritage. The view from the top was superb – to Orford Ness and the North Sea beyond, across flat Suffolk countryside and down to the village below. The dark passages, spiral staircase and battlements reminded me of the many Norman castles we enjoyed visiting on childhood holidays. As I was leaving two children had just arrived with their grandparents. Grandmother expected the visit to be educational and threatened a test at the end. Grandfather struggled with his audio guide, having to be sorted out by his young granddaughter.

During the reign of King Henry II the newly built castle featured in a local Suffolk legend – the 'Orford Merman'. At that time Orford faced the open sea and one day fisherman caught in their nets a 'wild man'. According to the writings of Ralph of Coggeshall around 1207, *'He was naked and was like a man in all his members. He was covered with hair and had a long shaggy beard'*. The merman was taken to Bartholomew de Glanville, custodian of the castle, who tried to get him to talk. Despite being hung up by his feet and tortured, the poor creature uttered not one word, although he ate almost anything, either raw or cooked. Hoping for signs of reverence, he was taken to the church, but his captors saw no change so returned him to the castle. Perhaps thinking he would be more cooperative after a swim, he was taken to the harbour and allowed into the sea, guarded by three lines of nets. The merman however dived under the nets, apparently to freedom, but after disappearing for a while returned to the nets of his own free will, before diving off once more, never to be seen again. Whilst clear in his account of the events, Ralph of Coggeshall seemed unsure as to the explanation of the merman, questioning whether he was, *'a mortal man or some fish pretending to have human form'*. Either he had a particularly vivid imagination or twelfth century fish were considerably more proficient at the art of disguise than they are now.

There are several options to continue the coast walk beyond Orford. Perhaps the best is along the sea wall as I'd started last night, then over the Butley Ferry (if running), but my rule of walking to the first fixed crossing point was to take me up the Butley River to Chillesford. This can be reached by the Suffolk Coast Path directly from Orford, or as I was to do, by a path from the castle through fields, meeting up with the track heading north at Richmond Farm. Sad to leave Orford, but knowing I'd soon be back to visit the Ness, I retraced last night's steps for a mile through fields. The sandy track then took me to the edge of Gedgrave Broom, an area of pine woodland which a sign advises is part of Chillesford Lodge Estate and *'Private'*.

Turning left at Orford Lodge, I rejoined the Suffolk Coast Path, which I was to follow for the rest of today. Running alongside wheat fields and tall woods, this was a pleasant walk. After a mile or so, and most unexpectedly, I came across a cricket ground with its wooden pavilion nestled under trees. What a place to play, where a six will land amongst the corn. Described as *'one of the prettiest in East Anglia'*, this has been home to Sudbourne Hall Cricket Club since 1893.

I'd thought of taking a diversion past Sudbourne Hall and Chillesford Lodge, to reach a footpath that runs above the River Butley into Chillesford. *'Private Residents Only'* signs at Sudbourne Park and the earlier warning from Chillesford Lodge Estate persuaded me otherwise. I really was being very good now.

Sudbourne Estate and the village of Sudbourne (two miles north) were requisitioned by the War Department in 1942 for battle-ground tank training exercises. Village houses and Sudbourne Hall were used as army accommodation, but when eventually released in 1950 the hall was in such poor condition that most of it had to be demolished. The remaining estate buildings have been converted into some rather nice homes. I turned right along a track into the woods, then left on a narrow path deeper into the trees. The track continues ahead but again walkers are barred – *'Private Farm Track. No Public Right of Way'*.

It was nice to be on a grassy path again, although this soon changed to bare earth crossing a field of onions. The Suffolk Coast Path is certainly varied walking. I met a lady with a bike. We agreed the weather was better for walking today. Only when she'd gone did I realised that she wasn't walking! Several forks in the path weren't signed, so I took what appeared to be the straight on options. At a large potato field I realised I was no longer on a path. The tower of Chillesford church was a mile or so ahead, but I had no idea which way to get there. The sun had appeared and suddenly I was rather hot. I took the obvious option and sat under a tree to eat my rather nice Orford lunch.

Suitably refreshed, and deciding that a left turn would take me to the forbidden areas of Chillesford Lodge, I opted for right along the field's edge. At the next field a tiny path emerged from the trees to my right. Opposite, and behind several yards of head high nettles, an ancient wooden finger sign showed a path to my left. Bone dry grass crunched under foot as I climbed the gentle slope to Chillesford. Turning left onto the road, I passed the village pub but only by a few yards. I was hot and inside were cool drinks. As if by magic, sixty seconds later I was at the bar.

The Froize is more restaurant than pub, but happy to serve a thirsty walker. Marrows, courgettes and squashes were for sale on the bar. The carvery looked highly appetising and with a bright yellow coach in the car park, every table was taken. I was told they come twice a year from Brentwood en route to the theatre at Southwold. The driver asked at the bar if they did sandwiches but was directed to the restaurant who would '*sort him out*'. He didn't need much encouragement!

Just above the tidal limit and stretched out along the B1084, the small village of Chillesford barely qualifies as coastal. I walked almost to the church of St Peter, which stands above the road at the east end of the village, but with time short after my diversion into The Froize, didn't climb the track to the church. On reading *Simon's Churches* I wished I had. The tower is one of only two in England to be made from coralline crag (from a quarry next door) and fossils of tiny sea creatures can be seen in the reddish rock. The old village school building was for sale. With a clock tower, six bedrooms and five acres of grounds, this traditional Victorian school will make a lovely home for someone with £750,000 to spare. I was surprised that the price wasn't even higher.

Now back on the main Suffolk Coast Path, which runs inland from Iken to Chillesford, I headed south along Mill Lane and after ten minutes reached the attractive Butley Mill. A water mill was first recorded here in 1530 and at various times water, wind, steam, diesel and electricity have been used to power mills. The current brick buildings date from the 19th century and after the mill trade ceased in 2001, were converted to another set of expensive but interesting self-catering apartments. Goods were once shipped down the river but by the late 1940s it had become too silted for commercial vessels. Climbing onto the sea wall revealed a huge expanse of reed beds – great for wildlife but not boats.

Just after the mill pond, which in World War Two was used for testing waterproofing of tanks, a wide track heads off to the left. Bone dry and sandy, it was more like walking on a beach as I ascended the slight gradient towards Low Farm. On approaching a large shed of grunting pigs an alarm sounded. No one else was around, just me and hundreds of pigs. Had I set it off or had one escaped? Two large silos by the farm were labelled, '*Pig Finishing*'. Is this why the pigs had sounded an alarm? Hopefully they've read that the other two are '*Lactating Sow*' and '*Dry Sow*', so hold food not a means of their disposal. Mind you, it must be time to get worried when Mr Piggy finds his dinner is coming from a vat marked '*finishing*'.

Back in the sun after the welcome but all too brief shade of Sparrowhill Covert, I reached a huge field of pigs. A sign at the entrance warned, '*Biosecurity do not Enter*', but the friendly wave of a farmer on his tractor confirmed it was OK to stay on the path round the edge. Butley Church, the end of today's walk, was to

Butley Mill

my right. This I reached along a path below the pig field, leaving the rest of the Butley Estuary for another day.

It was half an hour before the CATS bus was due to pick me up. Like Iken, Butley is a spread out village, and the church of St John the Baptist stands with just two cottages and an old school (now a dwelling) for company. The original village around the church was decimated by the Black Death in 1349 and Butley's population remained very low until the more labour intensive arable farming largely replaced sheep in the 19th century.

Partly thatched, this lovely church is remarkably similar to St Botolph's at Iken. I was doubly pleased to find the ancient wooden door unlocked, glad both to look round and enjoy the cool air inside, a relief from the baking sun. This too is an active church, surviving despite its isolated position and tiny population. Church Warden Malcolm McBride told me that they work hard *'to provide a place of worship that caters for both belief and historical appreciation'*. We owe a huge debt to the thousands of dedicated people around the country who give up so much time to keep our ancient churches maintained and alive as places of worship.

As I wandered round a 'bleep bleep bleep' from outside announced that my bus was here – fifteen minutes early. A gentle ride through Rendlesham Forest got me back to Melton station before we were even due to leave Butley. The East Suffolk Line train had just one coach. I got the last seat. Suffolk's rural transport was working well today.

Suffolk Link 'CATS' Bus

Police Tower

CHAPTER NINE
ORFORD NESS

(5 Miles) 24th July

We all have places that for many years we've hoped to visit, but for whatever reason not been able to. Orford Ness was one of mine. Along with Dunwich Heath, this was probably the place I was most looking forward to seeing on my Suffolk walk. I'd seen some of its strange structures from afar, but now was to explore this mysterious spit between the Ore and the North Sea.

The Ness is owned by the National Trust, whose little ferry boat provides the only public access. Tickets are limited and on busy days it can sell out. With Orford's first service bus of the day arriving at 16.50, I travelled up by car. My wife came too, keen to see some of this wonderful Suffolk coast that I'd been talking about since March. Rather than a desolate shingle spit, her preference however was for the refined shops of Aldeburgh and a swim in the sea.

Peter the ferryman took me across on the 10.20 sailing. He said they run in all weathers, only cancelling if the waves are too high to safely land at the jetty. I suppose I should have asked how we'd get back if such waves blew up during the day. The little motorboat takes up to twelve passengers, but a father with his son were the only others crossing. We were greeted on the Ness by Jack, one of four National Trust volunteers on duty today. His first job was to take our yellow tickets. These are given back to visitors as they board the return boat, and if any remain at the end of the day they know to start a search. Responding to my inevitable question and with no hint that he is probably asked the same thing every day, Jack said they very occasionally have to search for the owner of an unclaimed ticket, once finding a man fast asleep on the beach.

Our safety briefing completed (basically stick to the paths), I stayed for a while chatting to Jack, who like all the volunteers was very happy to talk to visitors. He explained that the National Trust bought Orford Ness to protect its vegetated shingle, rather than the historic buildings and secret military history. There had been much debate as to how these should be cared for and a decision was made to leave them to nature. Many of the buildings are already unsafe for visitors (although some can be entered on occasional guided tours) and in such an exposed position the ravages of coastal weather will eventually make ruins of all but the most sturdy structures. With increased interest in Cold War history it is however possible that some will be listed, in which case the Trust may need to find large sums to maintain them.

Jack told me four theories about Cobra Mist, the large concrete building that I'd seen across the river when walking from Iken. From the late 1960s this was home for the top secret 'over the horizon' radar system. The extremely costly and probably over ambitious Anglo-American project was plagued by severe 'noise' of undetermined origin and closed in June 1973. Jack's theories were that:

It didn't work.
It was jammed by Russian trawlers.
It did work but it suited the authorities to pretend it didn't.
It was never intended to work and was simply a decoy to attract Russian attention, leaving the real work undetected at another site.

Informed opinion seems to be that the whole thing was over ambitious but although not successful itself, lessons learned at Cobra Mist have contributed to the success of other early warning stations around the world. Vacated by the military, part of the building was taken over by the BBC who installed transmitters and huge aerials for its World Service. Powerful medium wave signals were beamed across Europe, but transmissions ceased after budget cuts in 2011. There has been intermittent use by Dutch radio stations, but the huge concrete building now stands virtually empty. (Unless you believe those who say it contains a captured alien spacecraft, or a 'death ray' to incapacitate Russian satellites – the answer to the Rendlesham Forest UFO?)

To modify a well known football saying, Orford Ness is a peninsular of two halves, divided by Stony Ditch, a tidal creek. Following a track beside grazing meadow and marshes, the western half was much like walking on the other side of the river. I was tempted to write mainland and had to keep reminding myself that although known by locals as 'The Island', this is a spit, cut off from the rest of Suffolk by only the gated fence at Aldeburgh. During World War Two it was joined to Orford by a pontoon bridge, although part of this was accidentally blown up when the army used explosives to clear ice in the harsh winter of 1944.

As I walked beside the ponds which have been allowed to form on the old airfield, a stoat appeared on the path ahead. He stopped, looked at me for a moment, then scurried off into the bushes. I decided that our encounter, albeit brief, qualified stoat as another friend made walking the Suffolk coast.

The airfield opened in October 1915 and was used for a whole range of experimental purposes. Two large First World War hangars have sadly been lost. One was demolished in the 1950s after a crane drove into it and the other following severe damage in the 1987 hurricane.

The National Trust have marked three safe trails across the Ness. Unexploded ordnance may lie elsewhere so it's essential to stick to the paths. The blue and green routes open only after the bird breeding season, so I was following just the red route, which takes visitors on a varied five mile exploration, passing many buildings of historic interest. I shall pick out just a few highlights and suggest that anyone wishing to learn more reads Paddy Heazell's fascinating book, *Most Secret : The Hidden History of Orford Ness*.

Orford Ness

Outside the Battery Charging Shops, which are now used by the Orford Ness Bird Ringing Group, I chatted to Helen, another Trust volunteer, who told me that today was surprisingly quiet. The Ness is closed on Mondays, and Tuesdays tend to be busy as people on a holiday like to get it in early in their week. So far less than a fifth of the maximum 150 visitors had been ferried over. She explained that the volunteers swapped posts at intervals, so I'd probably see her at the lighthouse later.

The track crosses Stony Ditch on a Bailey bridge, which was erected in 1995 close to the site of a similar bridge that was removed by the MoD in the mid 1980s. Two concrete bridges further downstream had become unsafe and were demolished in 1994. Across the creek it was a different world – a huge expanse of shingle, scattered with some distinctly odd buildings. There is one word that comes up over and over again when describing the Ness – weird.

The website *top10ten.co.uk* lists Orford Ness as number two in its list of '*top ten weird UK attractions*'. A quick internet search brought up phrases like, '*Weird and oddly compelling*', '*the weird world of Orford Ness*' and '*the whole place is seriously weird*'. I preferred the words of Belinda Hollyer:

'Arriving on Orford Ness is like entering another sensibility, or like encountering a parallel universe that turns out to be one you've always longed to inhabit. I don't think I've ever been anywhere so strange, and so hauntingly beautiful.'

The trail takes visitors across the shingle. Signs warn of the danger of straying from paths. Bits of rusting metal lie dotted about. Who knows what still lurks, ready to explode should a foolish person step out of line. Fortunately the vast majority of those who visit the Ness aren't the type to ignore such advice. My own personal risk assessments may have led to misdemeanours on the coast path, but there was no way I would put myself or Trust volunteers at risk by straying here. The shingle belongs to the plants that fight to keep a toehold as winds whip off the sea, the brown hares who dart about grazing on sparse vegetation and the birds who nest amongst the stones.

Twisted railway tracks cross the path, the remains of a narrow gauge line that ferried materials around the Ness. The 60cm gauge line was built in 1917 and operated by two petrol driven locomotives, which rather quaintly were designed to appear like steam, with a mock chimney and cylindrical motor cover. The War Office had stipulated that internal combustion was to be employed to prevent bright light from a firebox door betraying signs of the railway operating on this secret site. The line was later extended over the shingle and used to bring stone back to the airfield. During World War Two it also carried passengers, albeit unofficially, when airmen returning from an evening drinking in the Jolly Sailor would 'punt' trucks with poles back from the quay to their barracks.

New stretches of line were constructed in 1953 and 1964, to move materials required for strengthening the river wall. As recently as 1969 a further line was built to reinforce the riverbank and prevent flooding of the new Cobra Mist building. Two years later this helped to move sections from the collier *SS Kentbrook,* which had lain on the shingle for seventeen years after running aground on a spring tide and proving impossible to refloat. The ship was eventually cut up because the Americans believed it might interfere with the Cobra Mist signals.

The first building on the trail over the shingle is the Bomb Ballistics Building, the nerve centre of the experimental bombing range. Inside was a range of sophisticated equipment used to record the flight of bombs in order to enhance the aerodynamics and provide data for aircrew to improve accuracy of bombing. Dummy bombs were dropped by aircraft from RAF Martlesham, although occasionally missed the target range. On one occasion a dummy incendiary fell through the bath hut roof, landing with a huge crash in a cast iron bath next to that occupied by a member of the WAAF. Fortunately unhurt, the poor lady shot out of the hut with very little clothing on. The roof of the Ballistics Building provides a superb view of the Ness and I stayed a while, taking in the expanse of shingle. A lady joined me, a lecturer from Bristol. She had just one word for the Ness – '*weird*'.

Next stop was the lighthouse. Built as a private venture by Lord Braybroke in 1792 and taken over by Trinity House in 1837, the light had been switched off for the final time just a month before my visit. As National Trust volunteer Helen explained (we did indeed meet again at the lighthouse), the reason is

View from Bomb Ballistics Building – Orford Ness

Ordford Ness Lighthouse

clear – erosion. The lighthouse is just yards from the encroaching sea. (I know I should say metres but it just doesn't sound right). Until 1936 keepers were able to live with their families in cottages attached to the tower, but with the nature of military work being undertaken on the Ness it was decided to make the lighthouse a 'Rock' station, which meant families were not permitted. Keepers were allowed to visit Orford once a week to obtain fresh food supplies. The dangers of military activity were sadly illustrated in 1940 when a keeper was killed while beachcombing. It's thought that he either picked up or stood on something which exploded. Automated in 1965, the light was controlled from Harwich in the charge of the aptly named Keith Seaman. His prediction was that it would be lost to the sea by about 2020.

Three kilometres from the jetty (National Trust distance not mine – I'd use miles!), the lighthouse is a focal point for visitors. A family were enjoying a rather civilised picnic with plates and wine glasses. I preferred a spot a couple of hundred yards along the steeply shelving beach. Helen had told me that whilst not banned, swimming isn't encouraged due to strong currents. Five miles to the north my wife was however enjoying a swim off the safer beach at Aldeburgh.

It was hard going walking on the shingle but the path above was closed to protect sea pea (lathyrus japonicus), which survives on the fragile shingle close to the beach. It was on Orford Ness that the purple-flowering sea pea was first recorded in Britain – by John Cauis in 1570.

Public access ends at another strange building; the Police Tower. A security fence ran along the top of the beach and AWRE (Atomic Weapons Research Establishment) police used the tower to scan the beach for intruders, or anyone who might be taking too close an interest in the highly secret activities on the Ness.

Heading back inland, insofar as anywhere on the spit can really be called such, I stopped at the Black Beacon. A single storey stone building beneath a black wooden tower, this was erected in 1928 to house an experimental 'rotating loop' navigation beacon. It now houses information displays and its slit windows provide visitors with excellent views across the Ness. My chat with Clive, another Trust volunteer, was interrupted by a minor crisis. A lady had fallen on the shingle and his first aid skills were required. The volunteers all carry radios, and concerned that quite a deep cut on her arm may need stitching, he was able to arrange for the warden's Landrover to take her back to the ferry.

The final area explored on the Red Trail is perhaps the most secret of all – part of the AWRE site where atomic weapons were tested. On the right are the remains of the 'Hard Target', an impact testing facility built in 1963, with a tower used for filming the tests. Test specimens were accelerated to high speed with a rocket-propelled sledge hammer running on rails and collided with a high-density concrete target. One of the projects this facility was used for was to test time delay fuses in atomic bombs which were designed to explode on the ground rather than in the air.

Only one of the atomic weapon testing labs can be visited unescorted – Laboratory One, the largest of the six. Completed in 1956, this was used for vibration, mechanical and drop tests. Weapons such as 'Blue Danube', Britain's first atomic bomb, were lowered into a reinforced concrete pit designed to replicate the size and shape of an aircraft bomb bay. Vibration units were attached and the room sealed to allow air conditioning to manipulate temperature and humidity. To provide strength for the ten tonne crane needed to lower the bombs, the building was built on a two foot thick raft of concrete, which itself stood on sixty concrete piles driven through the shingle. The lightweight roof though was deliberately 'soft' in order to vent any accidental explosions.

Laboratory One – Atomic Weapons Testing Laboratory

A fence bars access to the main lab but the partly water-filled pit can clearly be seen. The roof is open – removed by the forces of nature, not some unfortunate explosion. Where once weapons of mass destruction were tested in great secrecy, now algae, moss and ferns colonise damp walls.

Tests were designed to ensure there would be no unplanned detonation of the bombs through vibration, environmental conditions or an accident on the runway, and although nuclear material was not present, there was a real risk of the high explosive detonating. Fortunately there were no serious mishaps but occasional alarms did occur. On one occasion a centrifuge in Laboratory Two was rotating at full speed when it began to suck up the linoleum floor covering, pulverising it with a terrifying roar and generating an impenetrable cloud of thick dust. It was with great relief that after immediately shutting down the machine, once the dust had cleared staff discovered that the source of the noise was harmless lino.

Laboratory Three holds a dark secret. In the concrete of the walls are the remains of a human skull. This was found in the shingle during building work, but rather than incur delay by informing the police or coroner, the foreman simply reburied it in the concrete mix being applied to the walls.

Conscious that an explosion through the deliberately weak roofs could scatter debris over Orford village, other designs were investigated for the final three labs. Initially it was thought that if the concrete walls and roof were thick enough they could contain an explosion without need for venting, but trials with a tenth scale model at Foulness were a complete failure, debris being scattered far and wide. Tests with an alternative design proved highly successful and led to the construction of the three 'pagoda' style labs which I'd seen across the river on my evening walk a week ago. These were built with robust walls and an enormous roof resting on strong pillars, with a window between the two where venting could occur. Debris would be directed downwards onto the shingle by the overhang. The roof was over three feet thick and loaded with a further seven feet of shingle. Had an explosion occurred the roof would have lifted then crumpled the pillars as it fell back, burying the chamber beneath and limiting the spread of blast material.

Many of the buildings could be restored but I think the National Trust is right to leave the shingle spit to nature. The sense of dereliction enhances the atmosphere in this unique finger of land. A mystical natural world dotted with fascinating, but slightly sinister remains of man's activity.

Crossing back over the Bailey bridge I was once again in a world of normality: still a place of beauty and historical interest, but without the desolation of the shingle and its strange military relics. I would have lingered longer but wanted to get back in time for a talk by Andrew Capell, the National Trust's shepherd who looks after the sheep on the marshy side of the Ness.

The sheep play a crucial role in the conservation management of the grasslands and marshes, keeping the habitat right for ground nesting birds. The height of grass is critical and sheep allow greater variation than would be achieved by mechanical cutting, with the added benefit of putting nutrients back into the soil. Andrew gave an interesting example of how such management benefits a range of species. Wasp spiders need to catch flies for food but if the grass is too long they fly above their webs; small birds eat the spiders and large birds eat small birds. Long grass means fewer spiders and hence fewer birds.

Five rare breeds are kept, grazing on the Ness in summer and on Dunwich Heath in winter. Three of the flock are black faced Norfolk Horns – Norman, Nobby and Nigel. Norman is quite a character and not afraid to throw his weight around. In the 1960s Norfolk Horns almost became extinct, with just one flock of inbred individuals remaining. With what Andrew described as rare cooperation between Norfolk and Suffolk, careful cross breeding with Suffolk Horns ensured their survival. The desperate plight of the Norfolk Horn led to an increased awareness of the need for genetic conservation amongst traditional farm animals and the consequent formation of the Rare Breed Survival Trust in 1973. Since that time no breed of domesticated livestock has become extinct.

Before a demonstration from Kite, his two year old Welsh border collie, Andrew told of us of his struggle to find an outlet for the sheep's wool. Eventually, after completing a seventeen page DEFRA form for '*Category Three Animal By-products*' he was able to sell it to local hand spinners and weavers. As he spoke there was a disturbance in the sheep. Two were fighting. No need for Andrew or Kite to get involved. Norman steamed in and sorted them out.

I'd enjoyed a wonderful day on the Ness and a little sad to leave this enchanting 'island', I boarded the ferry back to Orford Quay where I'd arranged to meet my wife. She was late. Naturally I headed for the Riverside Tearooms – toasted teacake (slightly burnt).

Update 2021
Keith Seaman was right. Orford Ness Lighthouse was demolished in July 2020. In the early 1980s it had been 90 metres from the sea but the few yards of land that I'd seen between the lighthouse and the beach had now been lost and waves were starting to erode the shingle beneath it. Protection from large 'sausages', sacks filled with shingle, had extended its life for a while but if left much longer the lighthouse would have tumbled into the sea. It was decided to use a crane to deconstruct the building and this had to be done while there was still enough shingle for it to stand on to lift its historic cap and 14 tonne lantern room. These will be incorporated into a third size memorial tower to be erected on the Orford side of the Ness. Once again the power of nature has changed the Suffolk coastline but the iconic landmark of Orford Ness Lighthouse will be sadly missed.

'October Storm'

Gullery Hide, Havergate Island

CHAPTER TEN
HAVERGATE ISLAND

(3 Miles) 1st September

Whilst Essex has more islands than any other English county, neighbouring Suffolk has just one – Havergate Island in the River Ore. A National Nature Reserve, this is owned by the RSPB and can only be visited on limited open days. A ferry takes visitors from Orford Quay, where my wife and I waited on a warm Sunday morning.

A family dangled lines for crabs, one girl screeching with delight when she pulled up two at once. A rather well attired group arrived, then wandered off to the café. Dotted about the quay more casually dressed people hung around in twos and threes, but there seemed to be more waiting than the twelve which the RSBP ferry can carry. Then the *Lady Florence* appeared from up the river, mooring at the end of the quay. I'd seen this boat several times on my walks and had just read the leaflet. Its trips with brunch, lunch or dinner to be enjoyed cruising the Ore and Alde are definitely something to add to my list of things to do 'one day'. As passengers disembarked after their brunch cruise a lady climbed aboard with bags of fresh vegetables, disappearing into the tiny galley where lunch was to be prepared. A call of 'all aboard' summoned the passengers, soon joined by the blazer wearers from the café.

Now there were twelve left waiting, all dressed in sober colours as instructed, so as not to scare the birds. As the luncheon cruisers perused menus, *October Storm*, the RSPB's little boat, appeared from down the river. Boatman Kieran called us aboard, checked names from a list, pointed out the life jackets and off we went.

Sitting low in the water, the twenty minute trip gave us a duck's eye view. It was strange to be looking up at river banks, not down from them. Soon past Orford's castle and the Ness's pagodas, we were between grazing meadows and marshes. This was the stretch of coast where I'd enjoyed an evening walk from Orford. Kieran took us to the left as the river split either side of Havergate, then stopped to point out dunlin and redshank on the mud.

John Garbutt, an RSPB volunteer, met us at the island's little jetty. Our only instructions were to stay on the paths, not climb onto the sea wall (an unexpected head popping up scares the birds off) and to be back by 3pm. The little party split, three going off on their own in search of the island's brown hares and the rest with John for a guided tour. Keen to learn more of Havergate's wildlife, we headed to the north of the island with the latter group.

First stop was the little visitor centre, from where a hide looks out across one of the lagoons that largely fill the northern part of the island. These were formed by gravel extraction in the 1930s and are now managed by the RSPB to encourage varied bird life. At considerable expense the lagoons have been profiled to varying depth, so that at any time there are areas of both water and mud. Improved water quality and more efficient sluices help fish and invertebrate populations, a key food source for migrant and breeding birds.

Standing on a mud bank was a large flock of the birds we'd most wanted to see – avocets. It was to Havergate Island that this iconic wader first returned to

Orford Ness from Havergate Island

breed in the UK. After an absence of around a hundred years, avocets were spotted on Havergate and at Minsmere in 1947, John thought possibly as a result of being disturbed by the war on the continent. Currently there were around five hundred on the island and sometimes up to a thousand can be seen.

As we peered out across the lagoon John picked out a whole variety of birds, lining up his telescope so those us of without long lenses could see close up. A group of little egrets by the far bank, golden plover congregated on the mud, a curlew stood to our right and two stock doves to the left. A redshank hurried by just in front of us. Half a dozen cormorants formed a line behind the avocets. A kestrel flew by, just yards from the hide, oblivious of ten pairs of eyes watching. This was wonderful and so much more so with a knowledgeable guide to pick out the species.

Moving on we headed to the North Hide, stopping by a patch of tall bushes. John had seen a hare here earlier. What to me were just tiny birds in a bush became real – common white throat, willow warbler and windchat. All birds that I'd no doubt seen many times on my walks, but lacking knowledge and lenses, I'd not given a second thought.

The hide revealed another expanse of mud and water. Shelduck, the UK's largest duck, was at last a bird I knew for certain. Black-headed gulls caused confusion – their heads weren't black. In summer they are dark brown but most of the year they're white. Dunlin was another bird I knew and meet on most coastal walks. Two hundred or more suddenly rose from the mud, turning as one, the flock instantly changing from black to white – what a sight.

The only disappointment was that spoonbills were nowhere to be seen. Seventeen had recently been counted on the island but they are elusive. They might have been on the Ness today. Raised platforms have been built to encourage them to nest here, but so far without success. A tall white bird with long spatulate black bills (spoons), they have started breeding in Norfolk and John thought it only a matter of time before they do here too.

As John led us back along the narrow path below the sea wall we left the group heading south and stopped by the jetty to eat lunch on the shingle beach. A tern kept us entertained, flying to and fro over the river, dropping down to the water, but never diving in. Lunch for him was proving elusive and perhaps he envied us simply opening a rucksack and unwrapping sandwiches.

We were at almost the narrowest point of the island, which stretches to only half a mile wide and is two miles long. The largest proportion of its 267 acres is taken up by the six lagoons, the rest being salt marsh, grazing marsh, vegetated shingle, mud flats and scrubland. Such ecology provides a fine mix of bird habitats and although it was the avocets who first gained the RSPB's involvement, their management of the island has helped to encourage a wide variety of species.

Havergate was first walled for land reclamation around 500 years ago and for several centuries was farmed, both arable and cattle. After the last inhabitants left at the end of the 1920s it was used for summer grazing then gravel extraction, before being taken over by the military in World War Two. It was the arrival of the avocets that ensured this little island will remain protected for wildlife, at least until such time as nature claims it back. There has already been some managed retreat and it is generally accepted that one day the walls will fail and the island erode away. Nature formed Havergate as sediment from Butley River built up over centuries and one day will take it way, a process accelerated by mankind's actions in changing climate and raising sea levels. As at Dunwich Heath, plans are in place to create replacement habitats, particularly on the remote Boyton Marshes that I was to walk past on my way to Shingle Street.

Lunch completed, we headed off in search of hares. John had told us that they can usually be spotted in an area of gorse towards the south of the island. Here we found the three ladies who'd come on the trip to see them. One beckoned us over and there in the gorse was a brown hare, sitting happily with his nose twitching as we slowly approached to within about eight yards. I've seen hares while walking but never got this near. Normally they bolt as soon as a person comes remotely close, but Havergate's are remarkably tame. The island sustains a population of around thirty, which is limited by availability of food and predation from birds of prey, plus the occasional fox who swims across the river. With numbers nationally having dramatically declined, due to changes in agricultural practice affecting its favoured grassland habits, plus shooting and coursing, the island's hares are an unusual population. We stood watching for

Hare – Havergate Island

several minutes, the hare seeming quite content under the gorse bush before he hopped off through a hedge. I had made another Suffolk coast friend.

The southern end of the island is more open with rough grass and shingle. This is the birds' breeding area. There was time for just a quick look from the hide looking towards Dove Point, the southern tip of Havergate, before returning to the jetty. Kieran was back with *October Storm*, and picked up the twelve visitors, plus John. Havergate was left to its birds and hares, perhaps as it should be. It had been a privilege to be allowed onto their island.

We arrived back at Orford just as the *Lady Florence* moored. The blazer wearing lunch cruisers returned to their four by fours in the car park. Deb and I wandered over to the Riverside Tearooms. Toasted teacakes (perfectly cooked).

Post Script

Havergate Island was badly affected by the winter storm surges. Sea walls were breached and much of the island inundated. The visitor centre and some of the hides were destroyed, and the toilet block found sitting in a tree. Fortunately a small part of the area of gorse frequented by the island's hares remained above water, but although they are strong swimmers it was thought that only ten of Havergate's twenty four animals survived the flood. They breed rapidly however and it was hoped that the population would recover.

A huge effort by the RSPB had repaired the sea walls within three months, building them lower but wider, to allow the inevitable future flooding to occur by over-topping, rather than uncontrolled breaches. The island was reopening for visitors, albeit in a reduced capacity, with limited viewing facilities. Those visiting were told that they could expect to see hares, but warned that they are more skittish and less approachable after their winter ordeal.

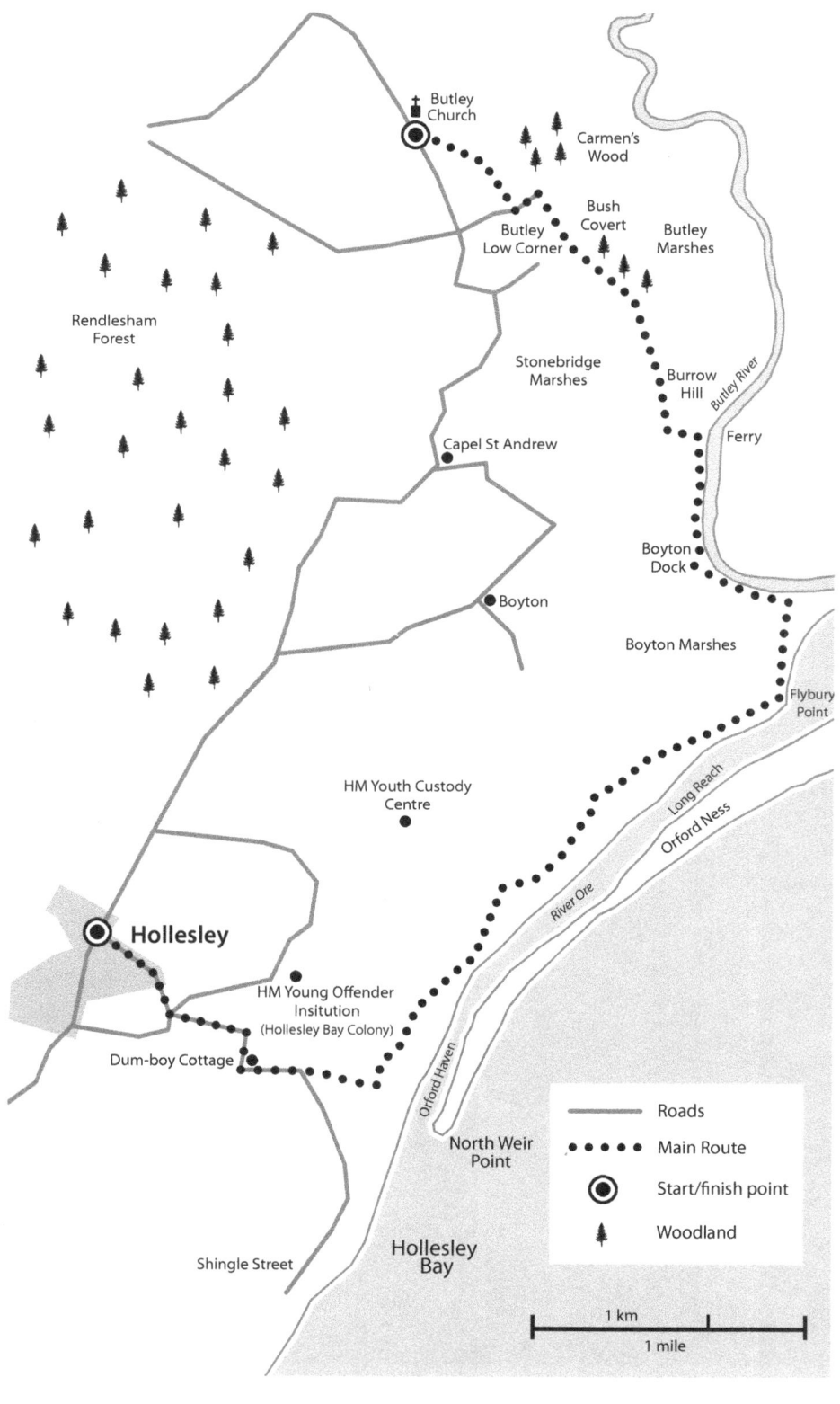

Corton Cliffs – Day One of Walk
and
Corton Cliffs – A Year later

St Andrew's Church - Covehithe
and
Southwold Pier

From top, clockwise: Mill – Westwood Marshes, Southwold Lighthouse, Juvenile Herring Gull (or is it a duck hybrid?) – Southwold and Black Headed Gull – Southwold

Beach Huts - Southwold
and
St Edmund's Church - Southwold

Greyfriars Priory - Dunwich
and
Gone Fishing - Sizewell

Minsmere and Sizewell
and
Coastguard Cottages - Dunwich

*From top, clockwise:
Thorpeness Village Sign,
House in the Clouds
and
Sizewell Beach*

*Snape Maltings
and
St Botolph Church – Iken*

*Opposite: Orford Castle
and
Orford Ness from Chantry Marshes (Orford)*

Orford Ness

*Butley River,
Hare – Havergate Island
and
St John the Baptist Church – Butley*

View to Orford from Boyton Marshes
and
Lady Florence on the River Ore

Shingle Street
and
Tide Mill – Woodbridge

Sunrise – Felixstowe – 16th October,
Sunrise – Felixstowe – 17th October
and
Felixstowe Docks and River Orwell

Levington Marina
and
Sunset over the Orwell

Swans on Loompit Lake,
Orwell Bridge
and
Stutton Mill – River Stour

CHAPTER ELEVEN
BUTLEY – HOLLESLEY

(7 Miles) 20th August

It was touch and go whether I'd be able to do the walk today. A week ago I'd hobbled into Newton Abbot Hospital, unable to put any weight on my right leg after putting my foot down a hole on Dartmoor. Diagnosis – damaged cruciate knee ligaments. Three days ago I'd only made it to West Ham's first game of the season with the aid of a crutch. A trip to the physiotherapist confirmed the problem, with advice that it was OK to walk on it, although I'm not sure that he had in mind fifteen miles along the Suffolk coast. With train and accommodation paid for, armed with a walking pole, I decided to give it a go.

My journey east had departed from tradition – no bacon baguette. The chef had recently been moved to a later train, so my walks would no longer be preceded by a freshly cooked breakfast roll. With the trip in doubt I hadn't booked the CAT's bus, so again Woodbridge Cars met me at Melton station. The taxi driver told me that he fishes from Orford Ness. A chap takes them over in a boat and they catch good numbers of codling. Apparently the shingle beach is famous for cod and some hardy souls will spend twenty four hours there, trying to snare one of the huge fish that cruise off the shore.

After two chapters which started with boat rides, it might be a good idea to remind you where we left the main walk – Butley church, after a very hot walk from Chillesford, past Butley Mills and a huge pig farm.

After another quick look in the church, I headed back up the sandy track by the pigs. The biosecurity signs had gone, but others advised anyone who might want to wander amongst the mass of grunting animals that this was Capel St Andrews

Farm Pig Unit with '*No Unauthorised Access*'. The large litters of piglets looked reasonably sweet but I'm not sure I'd want to get too close to their parents. A particularly large animal lifted his snout from the trough and stared at me as I passed. Perhaps it was a good thing I'd missed out on that baguette. I'm pretty sure the stare meant, and don't even think about bacon tomorrow either. As I stopped to take a photo three grunting, salivating pigs lumbered up to me. Was this a social visit or were they seeking revenge for all those breakfasts?

Turning right at the top of the field I was back on the Suffolk Coast Path, which on meeting a narrow lane soon turns left to Butley Low Corner. Two boys were walking up the lane with a small dog which looked friendly, right up to the moment it jumped up, put its paws on me and growled. One of the boys said sorry. I gave them a lecture on controlling their dog and how if it wasn't for my injured knee I'd have booted it over the hedge. Or did I just smile and say '*OK*'?

For a village of less than two hundred souls, Butley does well to get itself no less than eight mentions on the Ordnance Survey map. The village centre is a mile to the west of Chillesford. Butley Low Corner and Butley High Corner, half a mile to the south, both consist of just a farm with a few cottages. Had I not been minimising mileage to protect the knee, I'd have diverted to look at the gatehouse of Butley Priory, virtually all that remains of a 14th century Augustine Priory. This fine building is now let out for weddings, retreats, family reunions and other such events. French limestone and Purbeck marble used for building the priory were transported from Butley River via a canal cut by the monks.

A right turn at Butley Low Corner took me past three large empty barns. I thought of Private Fraser's *Dad's Army* tale of the '*old empty barn*' told with hushed voice and rolling eyes – – – – – – – there was nothing in it. Bearing left where the track turned sharp right, the path continued by Bush Covert. (By now you will probably have gathered that many Suffolk woods are called 'Covert'). A track at the end of the wood appeared to head down to the river. A sign warning of '*Bull in Field*' was blatantly a lie and almost made me go that way to prove it, but I stayed on the path, keen to see the view from a rare Suffolk hill.

Although rising just fifteen metres above sea level, the rounded shape of Burrow Hill dominates the marshes. It's easy to see how it was once an island and a secure home to generations of Saxon villagers. Excavations in the 1980s revealed coins, postholes for dwellings, food remains, window glass, writing implements and evidence that inhabitants could produce fine textiles. The bulk of the hill consists of sand and gravel, and when this was quarried to make local roads some two hundred skeletons were uncovered. Wooden coffins have been carbon-dated to a period around AD780. Most of the bones were male, perhaps giving credence to a legend of mass deaths in a last great battle between King Edmund's army and invading Vikings.

Climbing the grassy path up the hill brought a view worthy of a far greater summit. Ahead was the river and beyond that Havergate Island, with Orford Ness behind, then the North Sea. I wandered off the track to get a better view down to the river. What wonderful vistas; to the left up Butley River into Suffolk, ahead towards Orford and to the right the Ness. A dark-sailed barge moved slowly up the Ore. In the distance a container boat steamed by, having left Felixstowe or Harwich and heading to some unknown port. This was another little gem of the Suffolk coast.

Turning left at the foot of the hill, I was soon by the river at the little jetty from where the Butley Ferry crosses. Claimed to be the smallest licensed ferry in Europe and carrying a maximum of just four passengers fifty yards across the river, every summer weekend this little boat is rowed by local volunteers. A gentleman repairing a boat by the jetty told me he used to be the ferryman. His name was Bryan Rogers and he'd retired to Suffolk from Worcester, choosing the county for its dry weather. His retirement project was to reinstate the Butley Ferry, which hadn't run since the 1920s. With the help of a neighbour he rebuilt the jetties, then for twelve summers rowed walkers and birdwatchers across the river. Fears that when Bryan stepped down the service would cease were overcome when the Alde and Ore Association took it over.

Bryan told me that the ferry dates back to the Middle Ages when it was run by monks from Butley Abbey, who owned the local estates. Like the ferries at Southwold and Bawdsey, it was a crucial link in moving people and goods along the coast. The river banks weren't built until the 16th and 17th centuries, so it would have been a longer row, probably from a little further upstream. Later it was the military who underwrote the ferry, with a large boat rowed by

Footpath Sign – Burrow Hill

four to six hefty men carrying troops and armaments over the river. Horses had to swim behind. To be ferryman was a lucrative position, the post also giving him entitlement to wrecks on the coast, so even after paying the staff he would have been very comfortably off.

As we parted I suggested that Bryan should write a book on the ferry. His response – he wouldn't know where to start and in any case his wife would always find a hedge that needed cutting!

Quite hungry having missed my baguette this morning, I found a place on the riverbank for lunch. What an idyllic spot I thought. Then a bee stung my neck. As the pain subsided and I savoured my last mouthful of lunch, another one did the same. It had crept unseen under my shirt and stung my stomach, leaving the sting as evidence. This was an unprovoked assault. Packing up and rapidly vacating the area, I told any more bees who might be listening that I'd regretted signing that petition to save them. They weren't my friends.

Just downstream of the ferry is Boyton Dock, from where farm produce, bricks, clay and coprolite (fossilised animal dung used as fertiliser) were shipped. A red-brick warehouse still stands on the small quay, although without its roof. Until the Second World War offloaded coal would have been stored here, along with hay and straw awaiting shipment.

A small white cross at the water's edge marked what I assumed to be the point where some unfortunate person had drowned in the river. No name was shown but by the cross lay flowers and a single can of Boddingtons draft beer. Unopened, but with the ring-pull removed, I wondered if this signified a favourite tipple of the deceased, or a warning as to its role in their sad demise.

The path turned right as the Butley flowed into the Ore opposite the southern end of Havergate Island. From here the walk was very reminiscent of that from Iken to Orford. The towers of Orford church and castle were once more visible across the marshes, and beyond the island the pagodas and lighthouse rose above the shingle of Orford Ness. Three large concrete defence installations stood on Boyton Marshes, yet more reminders of the role Suffolk played in defending Britain during World War Two.

At Flybury Point the bank took another turn to the right and for the next 2½ miles I was back alongside the River Ore, with the narrowing spit of the Ness across the water. For the most part a line of salt marsh stood between the path and river, much of it now a carpet of purple flowers. An egret stood in a shallow pool. The occasional boat passed by down the river. The sun shone but with a cooling breeze this was ideal walking weather. I stopped frequently to take photos and admire the views, both close and far. At just seven miles, today's was a very gentle walk, ideal for the rambler with a dodgy knee.

Butley River

Two penal institutions appeared on my right: Warren Hill Youth Offenders Institute and Hollesley Bay Prison, often known as Hollesley Bay Colony. The prison was originally a colonial college training those who intended to emigrate, then housed unemployed men from London, who were trained for work to escape pauperism. It once had the largest prison farm in Britain but this was sold off in 2006. Up to 421 adult male Category D prisoners are held, around a hundred of whom work outside in the community. Perhaps the most famous inmate has been the disgraced Conservative politician and writer Jeffrey Archer, who ended his custodial sentence for perjury and perverting the course of justice here.

The path crossed an outlet from a pond to a channel through the salt marsh. Two signs indicated this was 'COLONY EVACUATION SLUICE'. Soon I got my first glimpse of Shingle Street, with its line of white cottages at the top of the beach. This was another place that I'd been looking forward to visiting. A gate on the bank took me into Hollesley Marshes RSBP Reserve, a grazing marsh which attracts a variety of breeding birds, wintering ducks and geese, as well as grassland insects and flowers. I passed a couple from Beccles, armed with binoculars and camera. We spoke briefly, agreeing that it was a good day for it, without defining the 'it'. Three boats were drawn up on Simpson's Saltings, a Suffolk Wildlife Trust reserve and one of the county's most important sites for its wealth of salt marsh plants. I shall raid the Trust's website for a description – *'A wonderful lonely and isolated spot with an aura of timelessness'.*

Almost opposite the end of Orford Ness a creek runs inland, reaching a road bridge. The coast path crosses the bridge before continuing around the marshes to Shingle Street, but I turned right, heading inland to Hollesley (pronounced Hoze – lee) and my stop for the night. A mile stroll up the lane took me past Dumb-Boy Cottage ('Dum-Boy' on the OS map) and the attractive Glebe House, a former rectory now converted to a retirement home. This was one of the walks where the length was constrained by availability of overnight accommodation, but with a suspect knee I was glad that I hadn't planned a long section leaving little time to savour the coast. It had actually held up remarkably well, only giving way once, when I'd crouched to take a photo.

Richmond Hill, the only B&B in the village, proved to be an excellent stopover. With Sue's friendly welcome (including a plate of rather yummy freshly cooked chocolate brownies brought to my room), a lovely bedroom and tasty breakfast, it rivalled 34 Lee Road for comfort and at little more than half the price was probably my favourite so far. Dinner was at the Shepherd and Dog, Hollesley's only pub and more of a 'local' than tourist pub. The website's recommendation to book seemed a bit optimistic – I was the only diner, but enjoyed typical English pub food, with not a hint of rocket, basil or goat's cheese.

An evening stroll round the village took me to All Saints church, which stands in a neat churchyard, its fine tower looking out across a long stretch of coast. By now my knee was telling me not to walk back down to the sea to watch the sun set and to decline Sue's offer of a bike to ride to Shingle Street, so the rest of the evening was spent reading some of her collection of Suffolk books. Bee stings apart, the gentle walk along this remote stretch of coast path had been one of the most enjoyable so far.

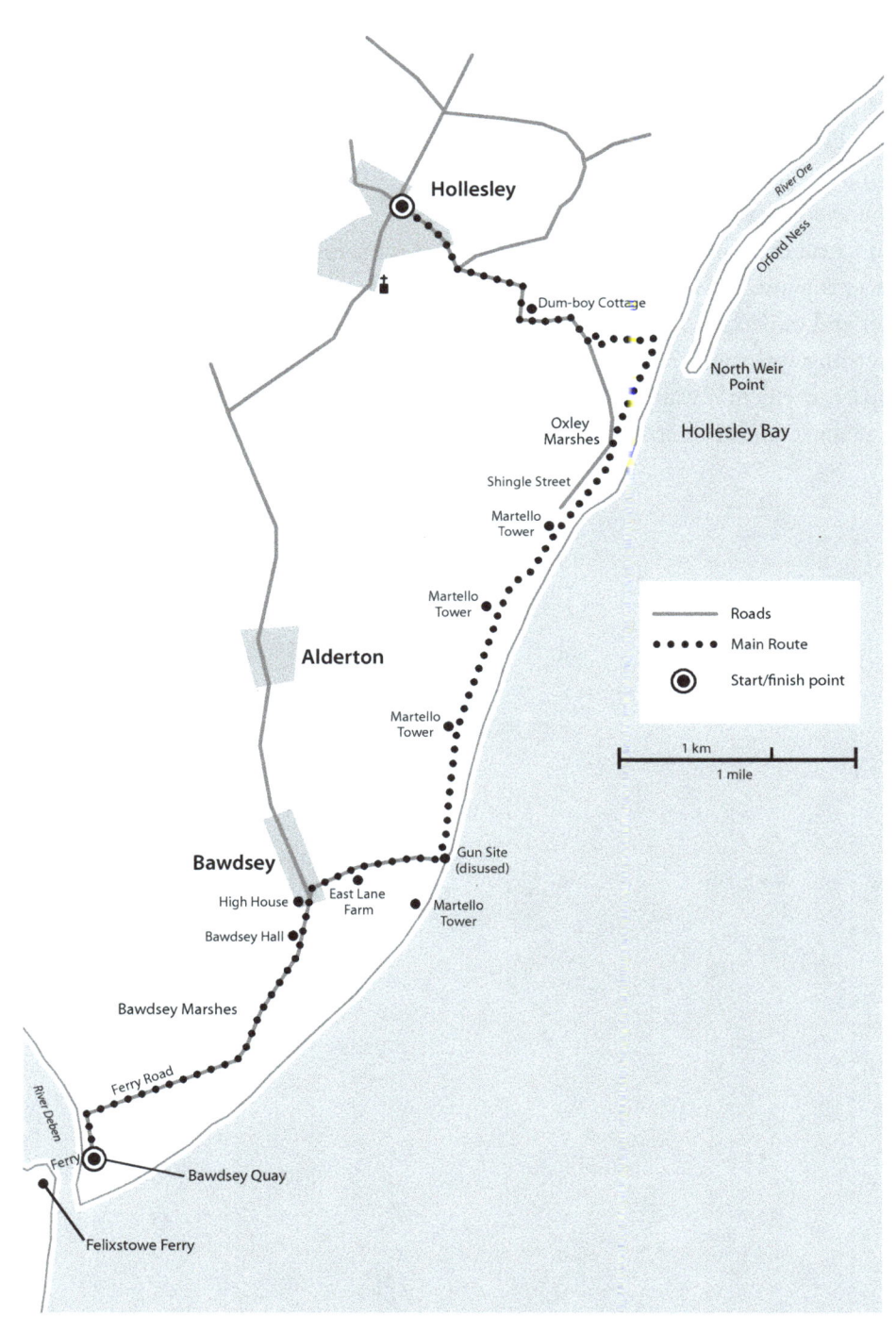

CHAPTER TWELVE
HOLLESLEY – BAWDSEY FERRY

(7 Miles) 21st August

One of the pleasures of staying in B&Bs is meeting interesting people over breakfast. It was the same in railway restaurant cars, until most train companies decided passengers didn't want to eat a proper meal as they travelled, and closed them down. This morning I shared a table with Branwen, a most interesting lady whose grandfather used to own a cottage at Shingle Street. We shared an interest in the Welsh Cambrian Coast, both having spent childhood holidays there, and she'd often walked to Ynys Gifftan, one of the little known tidal islands that I'd visited for *No Boat Required*.

I passed four people on my way to Hollesley's well stocked independent shop. All four said hello. This was another village that I liked. Not a tourist spot, not particularly picturesque, but just an ordinary, friendly, English village.

It was already hot by the time I set off back down the lane to the sea. Yesterday's wind had gone and today was going to be warm walking. Rejoining the path by the creek, I was soon opposite North Weir Point, the end of Orford Ness. With the curve of the spit, in slight haze the pagodas and lighthouse appeared to be on an island some way out to sea. For the first time since Thorpeness the coast path was back by open sea.

A man walking his dog waved a greeting from the beach. A cormorant stood on a small shingle bank, its wings stretched out drying in the sun. Two twitchers sat by the path, long lenses trained on the marsh. A sign warned that the beach was unsuitable for bathing. Branwen had told me how disappointed she'd been to see this. As a child she used to swim here, diving in from a shingle bank.

Soon I reached the line of white cottages that stand at the top of the beach, defining Shingle Street.

The hamlet is what it says; a row of cottages sheltered from the sea by a great bank of shingle. It is not an ancient settlement, the first habitation occurring in the early 1800s, at the time when the Martello Towers were built along this part of the East Coast. Fishermen, some of whom acted as pilots on the treacherous river to Aldeburgh, built cottages from driftwood. Later Coastguards moved in, taking over one of the Martello Towers when the danger of invasion had passed. The only land link with the outside world was a track to Bawdsey.

Like much of the East Coast, Shingle Street played its part in the defence of Britain in World War Two, but what happened at this isolated spot on the Suffolk coast remains a matter of much mystery. In June 1940, with just three days notice, the inhabitants were evacuated so that the beach could be mined against invasion. Some claim that two months later a German invasion force did indeed attempt to land at Shingle Street. Gary Ashford's website *www.shford.fslife.co.uk/ShingleSt* outlines the story.

It is well documented that 'Operation Sealion', the German invasion plan for Britain, was stood down after the Battle of Britain, as it relied on the Luftwaffe to gain aerial supremacy. What is less well known is that the Germans had a back up invasion plan, which involved attacking the relatively quiet and poorly fortified Suffolk coast. Perhaps this had been formulated using surveillance from the Graf Zeppelin spotted off Aldeburgh in 1938? Testimonies record a build up of German forces in French and Belgian ports during August 1940, with reports of troops dressed in captured British uniforms, presumably with the intention to confuse an un-expectant enemy. British Intelligence became aware of the unusual troop build up and at very short notice fortifications on selected parts of the East Anglian coast were enhanced. These consisted of pipelines laid into the sea, just past the low tide line. When the time came they would be pumped full of a flammable liquid (probably petrol) and set ablaze.

One Saturday in late August 1940 a flotilla of small vessels commandeered by the German army set out across the North Sea. After being picked out by RADAR a pre-emptive air strike was launched by the RAF and many of the ships destroyed.

The remainder however made for land, reaching a stretch of desolate coastline off Shingle Street. Aerial surveillance had predicted the flotilla's course and allied troops were laying in wait. At the critical moment the sea defences were activated and the sea 'set on fire'. The invaders were repelled but for many months badly burned bodies were washed up on the county's coast. For their own wholly plausible reasons both the British and German governments denied that the invasion attempt had taken place. Hitler didn't want to admit the defeat and Churchill didn't want the country panicking that the Germans were coming.

Ashford provides many statements from those who witnessed or were told first hand of unusual events that appear to corroborate the invasion story, however there are many alternative theories. Some suggest a 'friendly fire' incident which was hushed up, while others talk of rumours of an invasion flotilla being incinerated with anything between 30,000 and 80,000 dead. Many more however debunk the whole story. A BBC Suffolk investigation in 2005 found that just four dead Germans were officially acknowledged as having been washed up on the beaches, and that they came from a Heinkel bomber which crashed into the North Sea. The investigation suggested that the invasion story was simply an exaggeration of this and led to the Shingle Street myth. I'd asked Branwen over breakfast what she thought of the invasion story – not true she said. I'm inclined to agree.

What isn't in doubt is that the RAF used Shingle Street for experimental bombing and that this resulted in the loss of the hamlet's only pub, The Lifeboat Inn. There is now no pub, shop or cafe, and according to Sue at Richmond Hill, the only accommodation a lady who does bed and breakfast '*when she feels like it*'.

Walking across the shingle I could see a mysterious white line heading down the beach. My first thought was that a painted line detracted from the natural beauty, but on closer inspection I found it was made up entirely of white shells. Stretching from the cottages to the sea, it was the work of two childhood friends and artists, Lida Kindersley and Els Bottema. Both had experienced serious illness and in 2005 spent a week together at Shingle Street as they recuperated. After their first walk on the beach they sat down and arranged a ring of white shells around a plant. Each day they added shells to the growing line, a symbol of their recoveries, until it stretched to the sea. Twice a year the

Shingle Street

ladies return to repair the line, which gets damaged by weather and walkers, but also find that it has been added to by many passers by. Such natural and symbolic art seems truly at home on the stones of Shingle Beach.

If anyone wishes to experience the true atmosphere of Suffolk's coast they should go not to the goat's cheese restaurants of Southwold or Aldeburgh, but seek out this little settlement sitting at the top of a shingle beach. Sit on a shingle bank amongst the sea kale, listen to the waves and the birds, think for a moment of the people who were turned out of their houses to help defend our land, and perhaps wonder whether the Germans really chose Shingle Street as the place to invade Britain.

Walkers have a choice of paths leaving Shingle Street. The official coast path runs along shingle then at the top of the beach, but I went slightly inland by the Martello Tower, taking an easy path on the sea wall. Here I met a butterfly spotter. Armed with camera and binoculars, he asked if I'd seen any yellow butterflies. He'd been watching clouded yellows, quite a rare migrant so he told me, and wondered if I'd spied any. Sadly I hadn't, only blue ones, but I said I'd look out for them. To my perhaps impertinent query as to whether he was a butterfly spotter, he replied yes. No dressing it up as an observer or enthusiast, he was a full blown spotter. Where butterflies stand on the scale of socially acceptable spotting activities I have no idea.

By a pond opposite another Martello Tower I did spot an interesting flying creature – a huge blue dragonfly. I watched him for several minutes, wondering why these beautiful insects seem to attract little interest and whether dragonfly spotters exist, but decided that without a name he couldn't join my list of Suffolk friends. Two ladies with five dogs passed me – '*nice day*' we agreed. A lady with her son and daughter rode by on bikes, all three with a smile and greeting. I'd got used to everyone speaking on the coast paths and forgetting that such friendliness doesn't extend to towns, had recently received several blank stares when issuing greetings to dog walkers on the fields by our house.

Just before the next Martello Tower I spotted a yellow butterfly. Quite large and with light brown wing tips, it wasn't until I got home that I could confirm this was a clouded yellow. The Butterfly Conservation website advised that some are seen every year but the species are famous for occasional mass migrations, which '*are fondly and long remembered as Clouded Yellow Years*'. They have been shown to over-winter in the South of England, but as both the larvae and pupae are easily killed by damp and frosts, most individuals perish. I watched my new butterfly friend for a few minutes as he fluttered amidst flowers on the bank, then left him to enjoy the sunshine while I continued south.

The OS map shows the path returning to the beach before reaching a long narrow lagoon, but a much easier path carried on along the sea wall. An egret stood alone in the lagoon, pristine white and ungainly on its spindly legs. As

Martello Tower South of Shingle Street

the path dropped down to the top of the beach I was once more by the open sea, but this was to be short lived. This is another stretch of coast where erosion is rapid and the path was soon to head inland. I took what would be my last opportunity for many miles to sit on the shingle, picking a spot by the water's edge to eat the pork pie I'd bought in Hollesley. The lighthouse and pagodas of Orford Ness were still just visible on the horizon, now looking even more like offshore islands.

The path continued on a low cliff above newly fenced off sea defences. The beach that the map shows the Suffolk Coast Path crossing has gone and signs warn, '*Multi Hazard Area – Keep off Beach*'. Map makers cannot keep up with this changing coastline.

Ahead on the headland is yet another Martello Tower. By a corner of the largest of four rectangular ponds a large World War Two pill box looks out to sea. Just inland stands a concrete watchtower, which was used to spot German planes. Soldiers in the tower would signal to the gun battery to open fire. This must have been considered a strategic point in the defence of our coast.

World War Two Watch Tower – Bawdsey

With no coastal path, I headed inland along East Lane to Bawdsey, turning left by the primary school and onto Ferry Road. Here I found a lovely house – the aptly named High House Farm. Symmetrical, with five windows on the upper two storeys, and four plus a central blue front door on the lower, identical chimney stacks at each end both with three pots, and surrounded by a low walled garden with flowers and an old oak tree, this was just how one imagines a country house. The house reflected in a pond, a family of moorhens on the water and an old style post box by the fence added to the scene of rural Britishness.

Just down the road is Bawdsey Hall, an 18th century hunting lodge, which now offers high quality bed & breakfast accommodation. Soon after here the Suffolk Coast Path heads back to the beach, but a sign advised this was closed following erosion. I recalled the late Spud Talbot-Ponsonby's experience on this section as she walked the coast of Britain with her dog, writing in *Two Feet Four Paws*, *'In an attempt to avoid road walking I decided to stick to the shingle beach once north of the River Deben. It was a terrible mistake and one I fruitlessly vowed never to make again. My boots disappeared between small stones and Tess's paws were splayed out at all angles'.* With a suspect knee, erosion or not, there was no question that I'd stay on the road to Bawdsey Quay.

This took me past Bawdsey Manor, another highly significant place in our military history. The magnificent mansion in 150 acres of parkland overlooking the Deben estuary, was built by Sir William Cuthbert Quilter in Victorian Gothic style. Quilter made his fortune as a London stockbroker and after marrying a Suffolk lady, turned his attention to the area around the Deben, buying up 8,000 acres of land. Completion of Bawdsey Manor took almost twenty years, the last addition being the White Tower for Christmas reunions with his grandchildren, which was finished in 1904. A story claims that the reason for the manor's nine towers is that for every million pounds he made another tower was added. Quilter ruled the household with a typical mix of Victorian authority and generosity. Young people were to speak only when spoken to and anyone caught malingering was likely to be sacked, but he was generous to those in need, creating jobs where they weren't needed, and even providing a steam boat for the Deben ferry.

In 1936 the Government bought Bawdsey Manor for top secret military research. It was here that RADAR was developed. Sir Robert Watson-Watt had been working on the idea of radio detection and ranging on Orford Ness, and with total secrecy his team moved to Bawdsey. Development continued here and Bawdsey became the prototype for the chain of twenty five radar stations that by the outbreak of war were operational on the south and east coasts of Britain.

The manor remained in MoD hands as a training school, before being sold to the Toettcher family in 1994. Now a venue for conferences and weddings, as well as a private home, the manor and its beautiful gardens are open for pre-booked tours a few days each year. To my growing list of 'things I must do one day' I shall add the five hour tour, which includes lunch, the Magic Ear Exhibition in the Transmitter Block and a walk on the most unusual artificial Pulhamite Cliff. Those wishing to see just the radar exhibition may visit on around a dozen open days each year.

A plethora of private signs warn off anyone considering a short cut through the Manor's grounds but soon I could see white sails on my next river estuary – the Deben. For a while I'd been hearing a loud noise ahead and soon the source was apparent – a young boy of no more than eight or nine cruising up and down on a motorbike. *'Awesome noise'* he said to his Mum as I passed. It is perhaps fortunate that I resisted the temptation to comment.

After miles of largely deserted coastline it was quite a shock to turn a corner and find a packed beach at Bawdsey Quay, a picturesque spot almost at the mouth of the Deben. Young children were playing on the sand, while older ones messed around with small boats and their fathers with bigger boats. Grandparents sat on chairs at the top of the beach and whole families dangled crab lines from the jetty. Yachts bobbed about in the water and the little ferry plied to and fro. What a contrast of colour and activity to all that deserted salt marsh and shingle. A sign beyond the quay confirmed that the Suffolk Coast Path was indeed closed.

My next walk was to take me up the Deben to Woodbridge but the easiest way home today was to cross the river and take a train from Felixstowe. The busy little ferry boat took me to Felixstowe Ferry, about which you will have to wait a few chapters to read more. I can though let on that I enjoyed a perfectly cooked teacake in the Ferry Café. The young lady serving reminded that I was

Felixstowe – Bawdsey Ferry

getting closer to Essex – butter was pronounced without the 't's. You wouldn't get that in Southwold or Aldeburgh!

It's a three mile walk into Felixstowe but I caught a bus. In fact the walk had been planned around the timetable. Felixstowe Ferry has a bus service for two days a week, just six weeks of the year – an open top tourist route from Ipswich. A pleasant if rather windy ride took me to Felixstowe's unusual railway station. The once grand terminus station has been converted to shops, most of the platforms are now a car park and trains stop at what was formerly the tip of a single platform. Thirty or so passengers stood waiting patiently but as departure time came and went, no train arrived. There was no announcement and nobody to ask, but high up by the roof I spotted an information screen. '*15.28 – Cancelled*', was the extent of its information. The Help Point wasn't much better. Pressing the button put me through to a National Rail man in India who confirmed that the train was indeed cancelled. His accent however was so strong that I simply couldn't decipher his attempts to explain why. It was left to me to tell the waiting passengers that their train wasn't coming. With much muttering and tutting we all dispersed. The platform was busy when we came back for the next train an hour later and it was quite a squeeze to get everyone in the single coach.

Some credit though to Greater Anglia. I wrote to complain, not about the cancellation (these are sometimes unavoidable) but the poor provision of information at Felixstowe. Rather than the standard reply that most company's customer service departments send, I received a full refund and personal letter dealing with all the points raised. A contrast to Virgin Trains, who once sent me an apology and compensation voucher after I'd sent them a letter of praise!

Bawdsey Quay

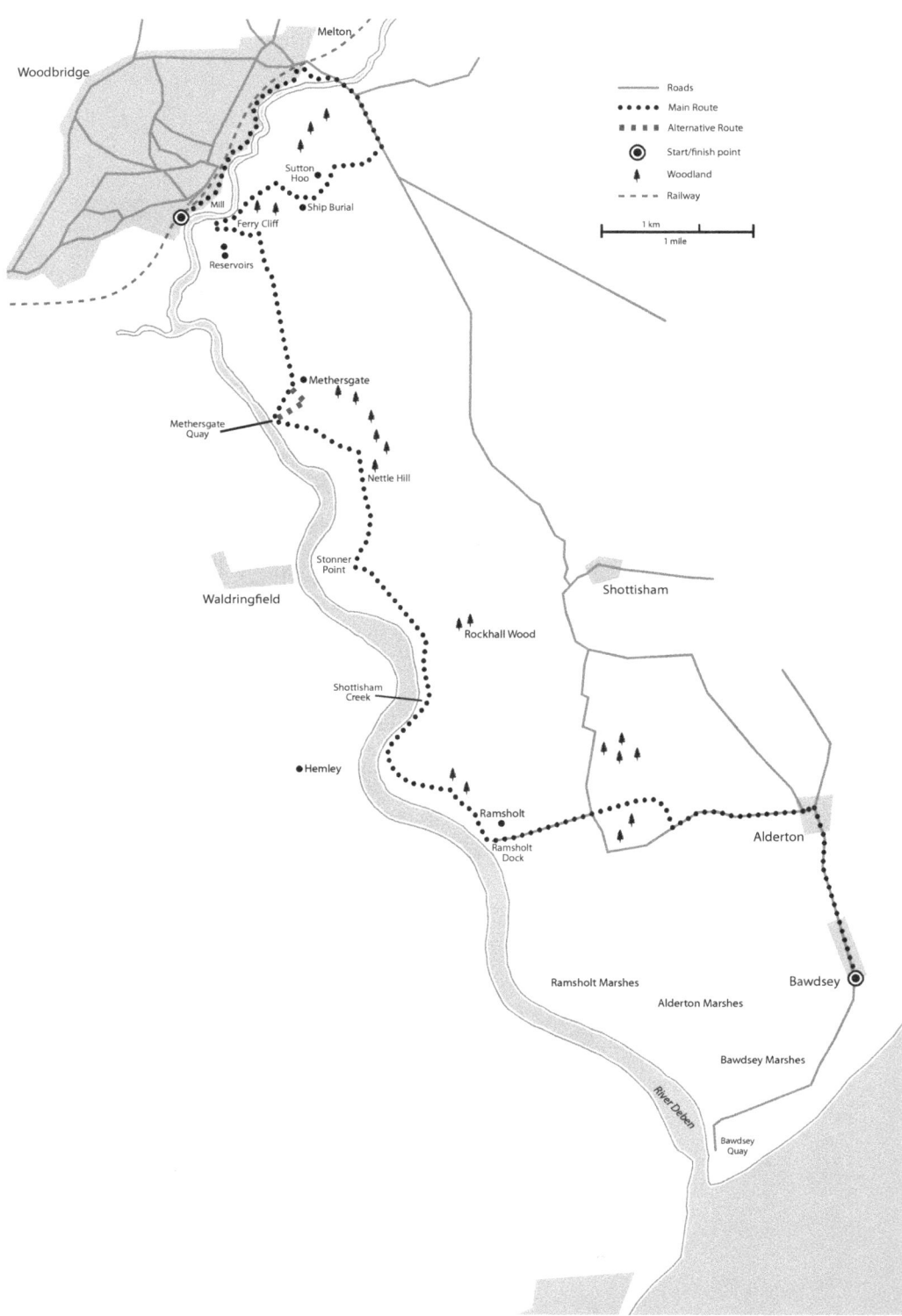

CHAPTER THIRTEEN
BAWDSEY – WOODBRIDGE

(13 Miles) 12th September

My day started at 6.35 as the early morning train from Lowestoft pulled into Woodbridge. Not that I was on the train. I was tucked up nice and warm in the Station House Guest House, fast asleep until a train stopped just yards from my bedroom window. With the longest walk so far, I'd come up the night before to make an early start. I hadn't envisaged quite so early but part of the character of this friendly guesthouse is to look out onto the station platform. It was however the view of the sun rising over the River Deben that got me to dress and head outside with a camera. With misty sunlight over the water and the town's famous tide mill, it was well worth leaving my warm bed.

Woodbridge Sunrise

Carla who served breakfast in the Whistle Stop Café downstairs, told me I'd love the walk along the Deben. Her grandfather had a boat at Waldringfield and they'd often looked across the water at walkers on the path. Just as arranged, the CAT bus arrived on the dot of 9.30 and once we'd overtaken an elderly couple on a tricycle tandem towing two dogs in a cage, gave me the usual high speed ride through Suffolk lanes.

My original plan had been to travel via Felixstowe and the ferry, but there's no path shown on the first three miles of the Deben's north bank. Enquiries had failed to find anyone who'd walked it and checking as I'd walked into Bawdsey Quay last time showed no sign of a path on the sea wall. Had the distance been shorter I'd have given it a try, but should it be blocked after a couple of miles, retracing steps and diversion inland would have made a twenty mile walk. Reluctantly therefore I was to start in Bawdsey village and walk three miles to the river at Ramsholt. The bus dropped me just down from the school, linking with my last walk where I'd come in from the sea and taken the road to Bawdsey Quay.

First stop of the day was St Mary's Church, an attractive building set in a wooded churchyard. It has an unfortunate history. The once grand medieval building became derelict after the Reformation and a new smaller church was built in the ruins, probably in the late 17th century. In the 1820s the tower was considered to be in danger of collapse, so to prevent roof tiles being broken by falling masonry they were replaced by thatch. Unfortunately, on Guy Fawkes Night in 1841 a group of youths decided to set off fireworks from the top of the tower, which set light to the thatch, completely gutting the church. Around two thirds of the tower was then removed and the current Victorian building constructed inside the original walls.

I walked along The Street (a road name that I'd found in many Suffolk and north Essex villages) past well kept cottages and gardens. Across the fields were occasional glimpses of the sea to the east and Orford Ness Lighthouse further north. I'd recently heard that this may be demolished on safety grounds. How wrong that seems. Nature should be left to claim it when she feels the time is right. In contrast to other Suffolk villages, Bawdsey has actually moved away from the sea. In Saxon times it was an island in the

Alderton Village Sign

mouth of the Deben and in the Middle Ages a sand causeway connected it to the mainland.

Alderton, the next village, is almost joined to Bawdsey. Its sign was one of the most attractive I'd seen so far. An old gentleman was sitting on the pavement outside his house. *'Nice day'* we concurred. *'So far'* he added. Indeed it was nice – perfect for walking, with a bright sun but big fluffy white clouds for it to hide behind when the gentle breeze wasn't enough to cool a walker. I hoped it would remain so considerate all day.

Cutting off a corner, I turned left into the churchyard just before the Swan Inn, a 16th century pub with inevitable smuggling connections. St Andrew's church immediately strikes one as a little odd. It has just a stump of a tower. For many years the tower had crumbled, before falling to the ground in 1821. The collapse occurred during a morning service, so it is perhaps fortunate that the only casualty was a cow, who I understand was not attending worship and met her demise outside.

Leaving the churchyard by the main entrance, I turned immediately left where a sign indicated Ramsholt was a further two miles. With two diversions into churches progress was slow this morning. It was a most pleasant walk along the quiet lane, passing Grange Farm and an absolutely enormous haystack. A footpath headed off to the right beside Heath Cottage, a rather isolated white weatherboard house. The sandy track took me across typical Suffolk bracken covered heathland. Now quite warm, once out of sight of the road I swapped trousers for shorts. A pair of buzzards circled slowly on thermals. Two small brown birds flew out of a bush. I wished I could have identified them. The path narrowed, running through the edge of Zoe's Wood (I hope Zoe didn't mind), then alongside open fields. To the left were glimpses of the Deben with a host of masts off Bawdsey Quay. This was perfect walking.

The path rejoined the lane at Dock Road, which took me down a gentle hill to Ramsholt Quay, a lovely spot on the river. Once a flourishing village and important barge halt, the first quay on the north bank up river from Bawdsey, this now consists of just a few cottages, a pub and isolated church. For hundreds of years a ferry ran to Kirton Creek, ceasing within living memory. The pub, which looks out across the river, was known as Ferry House. Now named the Ramsholt Arms and recently reopened under new ownership, it looked a lovely place to dine.

I wandered along the quay where a sign advised crabbing was not permitted, although both the pub and *Visit-Woodbridge* websites specifically suggest it. With the Ramsholt Arms not yet open, I drank my own water sitting on a seat by the quay, enjoying this peaceful spot on the quiet river. The only other person here changed into wellingtons and rowed his tiny boat over the still water to a yacht moored across the river.

Ramsholt Arms

Going back a few hundred years the scene at Ramsholt would have been one of activity, as sailing barges brought coal and supplies up the river, taking away sugar beet, vegetables, bricks and coprolite, to be shipped all over the country. A generation ago it was quiet but I'm told that on summer weekends Ramsholt is now packed with visitors. As a resident of the county, Simon Knott's words on how the Suffolk coast is changing, speak with more feeling than any I could write as a mere visitor, and I'm grateful to him for allowing them to be reproduced below.

'It hasn't always been so. Twenty years ago you could come here on a sunny day and enjoy the silence of the shoreline as you sat behind your pint of Adnams. It was considered by those who knew of it one of the best kept secrets in the county. And then came the 1990s, and Suffolk was 'discovered'. It is hard to remember now just how unfashionable it had been before. As recently as 1986, Michael Palin could make a comedy film, East of Ipswich, about going on holiday with his parents in the years after the War to Southwold. Southwold! Who would ever want to visit such a backwater, let alone go on holiday there!

Nowadays, it is hard to pick up a colour supplement without finding an article about some actor, or designer, or investment banker who has a holiday cottage near the mouth of the Deben or the Blyth. Foodie articles focus on Suffolk produce and Suffolk restaurants. House prices have rocketed; it simply isn't possible for young locals to live here any more. A beach hut recently exchanged hands in Southwold for about the same as my house in the middle of Ipswich is worth.

Quiet havens where you took your mum for lunch when she visited are becoming overwhelmed with yachting types up from London for the weekend. Does this sound snobbish? I'm sorry. But you might as well be in Stratford upon Avon or suburban Cambridge. I am seeing my lovely Suffolk destroyed, and it seriously pisses me off.'

Undoubtedly the county has changed, but as I was finding there are still plenty of peaceful places on the coast, although sometimes to miss the crowds you have to avoid busy days.

River Deben Towards Bawdsey from Ramsholt

From Ramsholt the next four miles were a wonderful walk along the river bank, diverting inland every so often through woods or along the edge of a field. The picturesque All Saints Church, with its round tower, stood alone on the hillside. It is remarkable that in a village with just a handful of houses services are still held here twice a month. In the 19th century the Norman building was a derelict ruin and had fallen out of use, but restoration began in the 1950s, with the long rotted away thatched roof replaced with tiles. These small churches, beautifully restored and maintained, and remaining active despite tiny populations, are a real feature of the Suffolk coast.

The path rose above the river at Ramsholt Cliff, running through a wood where a notice requested people to stay on the path as this is a *'wildlife haven'*. It is in fact one of Suffolk's many SSSIs (Site of Special Scientific Interest) and historically important for its sedimentological and palaeontological features, including well preserved fossils of rarely found barnacles, coral and molluscs.

As the path took me alongside a field of asparagus I thought, how apt for Suffolk – and wondered where they grow the basil. Turning to the left just before Sluice Cottage, a Grade II listed house dating from the 17th century, I was back by the water, a wooden bridge taking me over Shottisham Creek.

Soon I stopped for lunch, choosing a lonely spot just before a large area of salt marsh separated path from river. I sat for almost an hour, seeing just two boats pass – quite a large trimaran and a somewhat slower single-sailed dingy.

Sitting in the sun in such a lovely spot I thought how fortunate I am to be able to do this. The main aim of starting my own business twenty three years ago had been freedom, and now I was able to enjoy walking, confident in the abilities of those left in charge of the glue factory. Suddenly I was conscious of a fizzing sound. It took a moment before I realised the source – and by then half a can of Coke had emptied itself onto the grass. Bother!

Suitably refreshed, I continued the walk along the banks of the picturesque River Deben, bearing right at Stonner Point opposite Waldringfield, my destination for tomorrow. Wooden steps took the path through woods on Nettle Hill. In a few places it was a little overgrown but generally the well maintained path made for easy walking. Yet few walk here. Not only did I see no one until I got almost to Woodbridge, but there were hardly any footprints in the mud.

Just before Methersgate Quay the path stopped. I made my way across the salt marsh but this might not be possible in winter or at very high tides. The alternative was to squeeze through a gap in the hedge and along the fence by a cottage. A ridiculously large sign on the quay offered the cottage for rent. By the quay I met a man who was cutting marsh samphire – to accompany the fish pie they were having for dinner. He showed me sea purslane growing on the marsh and said you can eat that too.

It's not possible to walk on the next two miles of river bank and the path headed inland. Ignoring a footpath sign to the right, to cut off a corner I stayed on the track that passes Apple House. A sign at the top said 'PRIVATE PLEASE USE FOOTPATH'. Oh well! By Methersgate Hall I encountered a rare problem of lack of signage, but my instinct to turn left along the edge of a field parallel to the river proved correct. A gate into the next field suggested this was a walking route, but again there was no sign. I assumed that a gas canister on the field with plastic pipe attached was a bird scarer and not some kind of sinister explosive device. The loud bang it made just after I passed certainly scared me and it was several seconds before I had returned inside my skin.

Now on a clear path, I crossed the private road to Haddon Hall and track to Ferry Farm. Here signs pointed back to the footpath I'd traversed and forward through a gap in the hedge. This took me to a grassy meadow, but no path. I headed for the corner of Deben Wood. A map was essential for this section of walk. Woodbridge came into sight across the river, St Mary's Church prominent above the houses. The sun sparkled on two reservoirs to my left. Following a narrow path around the edge of the wood, which soon became a grassy track, I could pick out the Station House and even my bedroom window. There were though still several miles walking to get back across the river.

The path took me down the hill, coming out opposite the tide mill, by a little wooden hut next to the river. This was the waiting hut for the rowing boat ferry that until the 1970s ran from Woodbridge. The Whisstocks Project, a campaign set up by the Woodbridge Riverside Trust to bring the town's Whisstocks boatyard into community use, has a long term aim to reinstate the ferry service. A feasibility study has been carried out and although expensive maintenance would be required to hards on both sides, a service running only at high tides would be fairly easy to start.

The map showed a path running upstream by the riverside but all I could find were tall reeds right down to the water's edge. There was no way anyone could walk by the river here. It had all been going so well, but now it seemed the map was wrong and I'd have to divert back inland. In times of crisis turning to food always seems a good idea. I sat in the isolated little hut and ate my Kit Kat.

Less than a hundred yards back up the hill was another gap in the hedge. Steps led down to the river. I take it all back, I'd found the path. I plead guilty to consumption of a Kit Kat under false pretences. The narrow path made a delightful riverside walk through the woods under the National Trust owned Ferry Cliff. With little wooden bridges, the well maintained route was an easy walk, but without the ferry few people come here.

Leaving the river, the path took me past marshes to Sutton Hoo Farm and ended at a lane. Here I studied a National Trust map, albeit with some difficulty as it was oriented at ninety degrees to mine. Either left or right would have taken me on towards Woodbridge, but I chose right, to visit one of the most remarkable archaeological sites in Britain. Bearing left by Little Sutton Hoo, a house that had recently changed hands for just over a million pounds, I headed up a gentle slope between the delightfully named Top Hat Wood and Rabbit Field. A right turn took me to a viewing platform from where I looked out on ancient burial grounds.

In the late 1930s Sutton Hoo house and estate belonged to Mrs Edith May Pretty. Keen to learn more of the cluster of ancient burial mounds which her house overlooked, in the summer of 1937 she approached Ipswich Corporation Museum, who agreed to release its archaeologist, Basil Brown. The following summer Brown opened three of the bracken and gorse covered mounds, discovering that they had already been looted, but finding ornaments, remains of iron weapons and traces of a buried boat. Returning in 1938 at Mrs Petty's suggestion, and with the help of her gardener and gamekeeper, Brown dug a trench through the largest mound. Within a short time he found iron ship-rivets in the sandy soil, which he carefully left in position, and following their pattern began to uncover the rising stem of a huge ship. The wood had rotted away, leaving an impression of the planks, like a fossil cast. With skill and patience Brown revealed the outline of the ship, some 27 metres long, then deep within the vessel reached the grave itself. Clearly this was a hugely significant find and on the advice of Charles Phillips from Cambridge University, the British Museum was contacted.

In June 1939 Phillips took charge of further excavation, unearthing a breathtaking array of treasures – fine Celtic enamels, silver bowls, armour, weapons, fragments of clothes, thirty seven gold coins and most impressive of all, large gold ornaments of early Anglo-Saxon workmanship. Inlaid with bright red garnets, these came out of the ground as bright as the day they were buried. It was amongst the finest graves ever excavated in Europe. Secrecy was essential and a police guard was mounted, but eventually the story was leaked to the press. With war looming the team had to work quickly, but by September most of the recording was completed and the ship's impression protected with bracken and turf. Within a few days Britain was at war with Germany, and the artefacts, which a Treasure Trove Inquest decided belonged to Mrs Petty, entrusted to the British Museum to be safely stored on Platform Two of Aldwych station on the London Underground.

A path through an avenue of trees took me past the Edwardian Tranmer House to the National Trust reception, café and exhibition. The lady at reception told me that she is one of the volunteers who maintain the Ferry Cliff footpath and agreed that it's a shame more people don't walk it. To my suggestion that they should reopen the ferry she replied, '*Watch this space*'. Discussions were at an early stage but it was quite possible that before too long visitors would be able to get off the train at Woodbridge, take the high tide ferry across the Deben and walk through the woods to Sutton Hoo. What an excellent day out and what marketing opportunities for both the Trust and East Suffolk Railway Line.

Highlight of the exhibition is a life-sized reconstruction of a section of the ship and furnished burial chamber. I'd made the mistake of asking the volunteer guide where the actual ship was, presuming that it had either been removed for preservation or reburied. As he probably has to dozens of times a day, he explained how the wood had long ago decayed, leaving just its impression in the soil.

The archaeologists had found no trace of a skeleton when the chamber was unearthed, and for some time it was thought that the man had been lost in battle or at sea, so this was a monument rather than grave. More recently traces of phosphate found in the soil suggest that a body had lain here and it is believed that this had simply dissolved away in the acid soil. The size of the ship and magnificence of the treasures suggest that this was the grave of a great military leader, probably a king. Most likely it was King Raedwald of East Anglia, who died around AD616, whose ship was carried up the hill and buried with such honour, lying undisturbed for thirteen centuries.

Before leaving I took a quick look in Tranmer House, Mrs Pretty's home, which stands majestically on the hill overlooking the burial grounds. Built in 1910, it has been left as it was in the 1930s and unusually the National Trust encourages a hands-on approach. Visitors may sit on the chaise longue, read 1930s magazines, play music on a gramophone and imagine the life of Edith Pretty, to whom the nation owes a debt for both her vision and generosity. Sutton Hoo had been one of the most interesting stops on my walk so far and I was fortunate that no diversion was needed, my 'coastal path' running right through it.

From the driveway I turned left onto the road heading back into Woodbridge. The noise of traffic was an unwelcome contrast to the peaceful river I'd walked along earlier, but I was soon to be back by the Deben. Wilford Bridge, the first fixed crossing point and close to the tidal limit, took me to the outskirts of Melton. A path by the bridge headed along the river bank, but this didn't compare with my walk earlier. The surface was gravel, the wall metal and the sound of birds replaced by constant roar of cars. Soon I was at the spot I'd walked down to several times while waiting for trains and buses at Melton.

An old established settlement, mentioned in the Domesday Book, Melton is now joined to Woodbridge just a mile away, its separate identity not helped by the lack of a village centre. The railway station closed in 1955 but was reopened by public demand in 1984, and seems to get reasonable use. The station buildings contain an excellent butchers shop.

In the 1765 a 'House of Industry' was built in Melton at a cost of £9,200. Despite its grand name, the H-shaped red-brick building was a workhouse, where the destitute were employed spinning wool, albeit in better conditions than many other such establishments. It however failed to produce enough money to pay back the building costs, the net income from the inmates' labour in 1774 being just £237 15s 6d. The unusually high standard of living and medical care it provided contributed to financial difficulties and eventual closure in 1826.

Suffolk County Council bought the buildings and it was reopened as the 'Suffolk County Asylum for Pauper Lunatics'. In 1917 the name was changed to 'St Audry's Hospital for Mental Diseases' with patient numbers peaking at 1,200 in 1935. After closing in 1993 the buildings were converted to residential accommodation.

Commercial navigation of the Deben was extended from Woodbridge to Melton in 1840, with the construction of a new quay. It remains navigable at high tide but a feature of this stretch of river is a succession of wrecks lying in the mud. A survey conducted in 2000 by Robert Simper of Ramsholt, found the wreckage of lifeboats, inshore fishing boats, an 83ft Thames sailing barge reputed to have taken part in the 1940 Dunkirk Evacuation, a Bailey bridge converted to a houseboat, cargo craft and a dredger. Local opinion is divided as to whether they are eyesores that should be removed, or part of the river's history and character that should stay. I would be firmly in the latter camp.

At last I was passing other people – a succession of dog walkers, runners and cyclists. This though, as several blank looks told me, isn't a 'greeting' section of path. The dog owners of Suffolk probably have a warning out – watch out for strange man with shorts and rucksack who says inappropriate hellos on the county's footpaths. The final section was the least scenic, running inland behind houses and boatyards, before emerging at the town's iconic tide mill. I took more photos with the low sun shining on the mill and reflecting in the still river, a contrast to my misty shots this morning.

For more than eight hundred years man has harnessed the Deben's tides to drive millstones producing flour and animal feed. The first recorded mill here was in 1170 and the current three storey building dates back to 1793. Before the main oak shaft broke and the mill closed in 1957, it was the last commercially working tide mill in the UK. After standing derelict for some years it was purchased by Mrs Jean Gardner and following a programme of restoration, opened to the public in 1975. More recent restoration, including a new water wheel and main shaft, has brought it back into use as a fully working tide mill. The original reservoir is now a marina but when tides permit a new half acre reservoir allows the five metre English oak waterwheel to turn machinery, grinding grain to flour. A symbol of Woodbridge, the white Suffolk boarding-clad mill makes a fine sight on the bank of the Deben, and when the wheels turn must bring the town's history back to life. A return to see the mill working is yet another to add to my 'one day' list.

A most enjoyable day was rounded off with an excellent Chinese meal in the Golden Panda. I'd been woken by the train at 6.30 this morning. Tonight, just as I was ready to fall asleep there was a commotion outside. I looked out the window. On the platform were about thirty young people, presumably returning to Ipswich after an evening in Woodbridge's pubs. Bang on time the train arrived at 22.18. For the next eight hours all would be quiet once more.

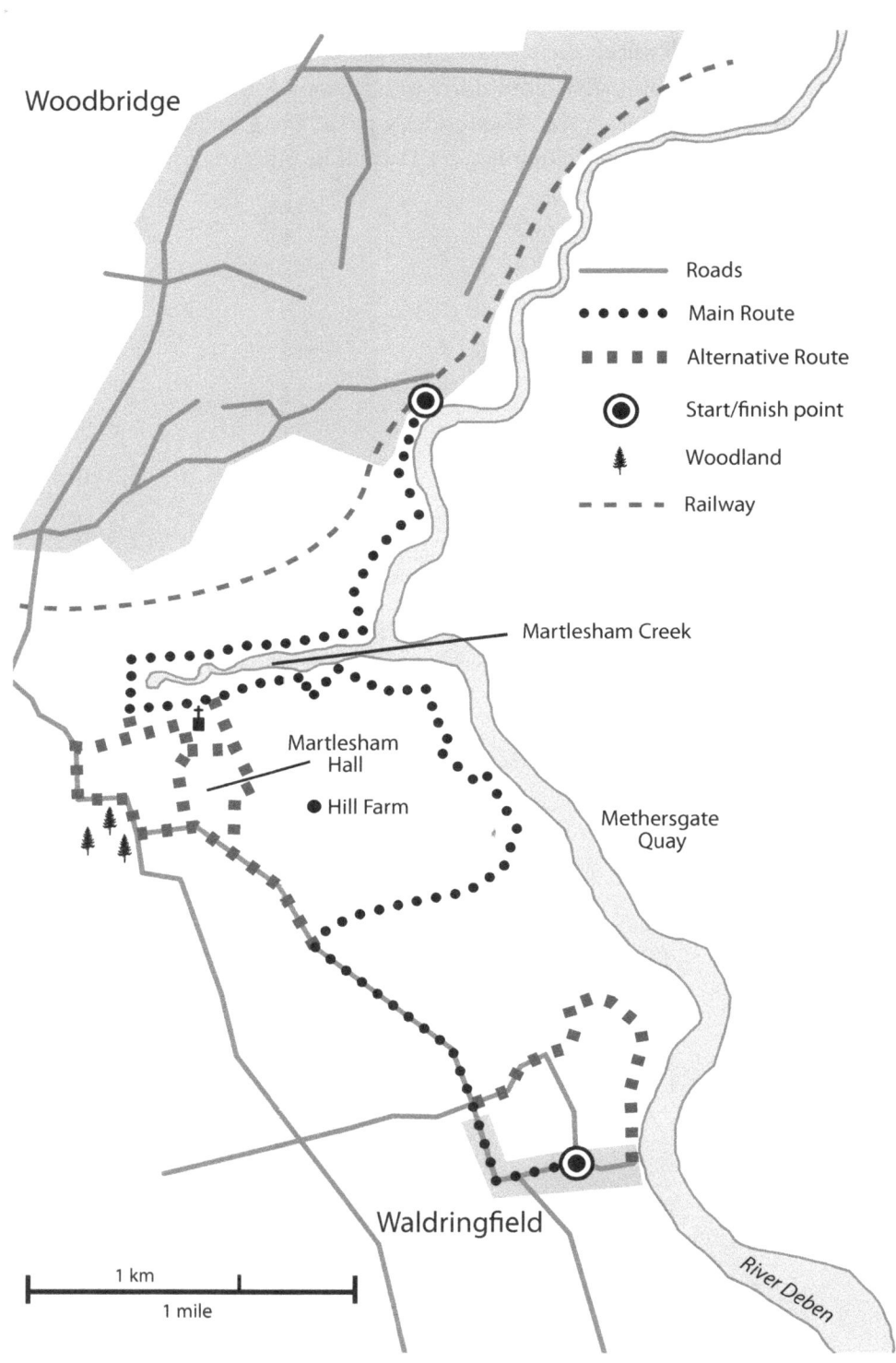

CHAPTER FOURTEEN
WOODBRIDGE – WALDRINGFIELD

(6 Miles) 13th September

Remarkably I'd now completed thirteen walks without getting wet. The ten minutes of hail in Aldeburgh had been uncomfortable but I'd managed to walk a hundred miles without rain. One of those nasty black clouds on last night's weather map had suggested that today I wouldn't be so fortunate. Pulling the curtains after been awoken once more by the 6.35 to Ipswich, revealed a dismal scene. Rain pouring down over the grey river. The hill where yesterday I'd looked down to a sunny Woodbridge, cloaked in thick cloud. No early morning photos today but another hour under warm covers.

Woodbridge Station (and my bedroom!)

I spent a while exploring Woodbridge. Recorded in the Domesday Book as part of Loes Hundred, much of the town was granted to the powerful Bigod family who built Framlingham Castle. From the Middle Ages it was a port, with boat-building, sail and rope making industries. The waterfront remains active, but now with a marina and varied selection of houseboats. Big enough to support a good range of shops, schools, a cinema and theatre, with good transport links, but far enough from Ipswich to be independent, Woodbridge looks a nice place to live. Tourism is important but it gives the impression of being a thriving country town that doesn't rely solely on visitors. Judging by the antique shops, galleries and fashion boutiques, those who do visit have money to spend.

At the top of the town are the picturesque Market Hill and Elizabethan Shire Hall, which originally housed court rooms on the upper floor and a corn market below. Standing in the centre of the square, the hall has been much altered over the centuries, but continued to serve as a Magistrates' Court until quite recently. Purchased by the Town Council in 1987 and renovated in 2004, it is now an administration centre.

Steps off the square lead to St. Mary's Parish Church. Defying the weatherman, the sun was now shining brightly and I stopped to talk to a man tending the churchyard. Dennis was wearing a Brighton Marathon T-shirt and told me he runs all over the world. He also walks the Suffolk coast, not my measly ten mile

Shire Hall – Woodbridge

wanders, but thirty or forty miles a day. As we chatted a couple of chickens shuffled by. These Dennis informed me were likely to be the subject of a legal battle as their owner refused to keep them out of the churchyard. I've been scanning the internet for several months looking for news of the court hearing, 'The Church of England versus Woodbridge poultry owner with hole in fence', but so far the closest reference Google has found is a review for Church's Chicken fast food outlet in Woodbridge Avenue, Harvey, Illinois.

Dennis told me that he often ran to Waldringfield and that I'd enjoy my walk there. First I took a look inside St Mary's, which like almost every Suffolk church I'd passed is kept unlocked for visitors. Funded by rich merchants in the 14th century, it is a fine building. The interior however I felt matched neither the splendour of Blythburgh and Southwold, or the intimacy and atmosphere of Iken and Butley. Not that I didn't like it and apologies to anyone who may be offended, but it was the exterior and setting that I found most memorable about St Mary's. As I'd seen from across the river yesterday, its tall tower rises above town, looking down on the trees and houses which surround the narrow churchyard. I'd walked through typical English villages but this is one of our classic historic small country towns.

Back at the quay, I turned right to follow the river wall to Waldringfield – or so I thought. After passing refreshment huts, a yacht club and model boating pool, the path leaves Woodbridge and sets off on its winding route to the sea. It was surprisingly busy, a succession of dog walkers, mothers with prams and visitors with rucksacks passing by. A popular stroll for locals, this is part of two paths; The Sandlings Way which I'd met every so often on my travels since Southwold and the Fynn Valley Walk which links Woodbridge with Westerfield.

At the steps down to Kingstone Marsh Sluice a man with a ladder appeared to be talking to himself. I stopped to enquire what he was doing and his mate appeared on the mud below. They were from the Environment Agency and checking the flap on the outlet as, *'we don't want Woodbridge to flood'*. We agreed it was messy work but they didn't mind as it was *'natural mess'*. I asked if it was OK to take a photo. A deal was proposed. If I got his lifejacket from the wheelbarrow on the path I could take a picture. Fair enough.

Suffolk Mud – River Deben

At Kyson Point the path runs along a short length of beach. This may not be passable at very high tides, when a diversion via Broom Heath is required. To the right is Kyson Hill, a grassy hill surrounded by wooded belts, which slopes down to the saltings. Donated to the National Trust in 1934, when it became its first Suffolk property, the hill has been a popular walk for generations of Woodbridge residents.

The path turns sharp right, heading up the mile long Martlesham Creek, but a notice advised it was closed. As at Aldeburgh, maintenance was being carried out and I had a decision to make. As at Aldeburgh I decided to give it a go. Passing two ladies walking with five dogs suggested that I could at least make it to the head of the creek, where a path runs up to the road. A big orange digger however cast doubt as to whether continuing on the river wall towards Waldringfield would be possible.

The picturesque little creek with abundant birdlife reminded me of the many I'd followed on my Essex walk. Bare earth on the bank crossing the head of the creek showed work was in progress but a large temporary fence had been removed. I walked swiftly across, studiously avoiding looking at the man in the digger. Again my persistence had avoided a long diversion. Again I had been a little bit naughty.

On returning home a look at The River Deben Association website explained the work. A mile of river wall was being strengthened and raised. Work started on Monday 11th September and was expected to last about six weeks. Whilst construction was taking place the footpath would be closed with no diversion. To save cost and the environmental impact of lorries, the clay for the works was being dug from the adjacent farmland. Before work started the contractor undertook protection measures for the many voles and lizards living along this stretch of river, plus one of Britain's rarest snails, the narrow-mouth whorl snail, Vertigo angustior, which is only found at nine sites in the UK.

A lagoon in the corner of the creek teemed with shoals of fish swimming just below the surface. Every so often one jumped out to look at the illicit walker on the bank. Turning left over a little footbridge the path took me through Sluice Wood, then a boatyard, before returning to the river wall. I stopped for an early lunch, sitting on some rather cold metal steps by a little inlet, looking across to Kyson Point and watching three swans swim gently around in the still water.

A few yards further on a path ran inland; part of the Martlesham Circular Walk. Immediately after this the river wall footpath deteriorated. My notes recorded that it was the most overgrown path so far and that few people must walk it. I climbed down from the wall to walk on the edge of an area of salt marsh, an 'Anglian Wildfowlers' Association Conservation Area' – 'No Shooting Allowed'. Beyond here the path was totally blocked with gorse, brambles and small trees. Progress was slow, alternating between the overgrown river wall and muddy marsh below. The latter was far from easy, not entirely safe and at high tide wouldn't have been possible at all. This is not a route I'd recommend anyone to follow. Surely Dennis from Woodbridge doesn't run this way to Waldringfield. Yesterday I'd decided to write to Suffolk County Council praising their upkeep of footpaths. My praise would now be tempered by experience of this path, that's clearly marked on the map, but no longer exists.

Opposite Methersgate Quay was the answer. The river wall had been breached and there was no way through to Waldringfield. I had two options. To turn back and fight my way through the vegetation and salt marsh, adding to the scratches and mud on my legs, or head inland around the large marshy inlet. I chose the latter but there was no path marked on the map here and mature trees growing on the wall suggested there never has been. The only way forward was to gingerly make my way along the slope of the wall, hoping not to slip and land in the mud below. Eventually reaching the head of the inlet, I had another decision to make; ignore the private sign and continue in similar manner hoping that eventually the path would materialise, or find a way inland. On safety rather than trespass grounds, I chose the latter. Tractor tracks beside two narrow lakes implied there must be a way to the road. More fishes jumped out the water to glimpse the now rather muddy walker. Mosquitoes seized the opportunity of a rare passing human to feast on his flesh. This wasn't the best bit of Suffolk walking!

Eventually a track took me up the hill, coming out on the road by Howe's Farm. For once I was glad to be on hard tarmac. The following week I emailed Suffolk County Council. Within an hour a reply arrived from Annette Robinson, the Council's 'East Area Rights of Way Manager'. She explained that the river wall footpath was breached in the 1950s, making the path unusable. There should be signs to warn walkers, but as these had obviously gone missing she would organise replacements. Most helpfully, she warned me that there is another breach in the wall east of Waldringfield, so my next walk would also need a diversion inland.

The next week another email arrived – from Martin Williams, Rights of Way Officer (East), which explained that, *'due to the legal mechanisms surrounding public rights of way, the route continues to be shown on the legal maps.'* The same explanation applies for the mysterious paths marked on the map crossing the Blyth and Alde estuaries. I'd encountered similar problems in Essex (although with a far less helpful response from the County Council), so a coastal walker is well advised not to rely on paths on the Ordnance Survey map actually existing. My suggestion is to seek local advice, or better still purchase a book describing a walk along the county's entire coast!

It was a pleasant walk to the village, a couple of miles along the quiet Waldringfield Lane. I could have turned left, back down to the river at the crossroads by The Old School House, but with my adventures on the marshes time was getting tight for the bus. Plus I had doubts over the river wall footpath, although I now believe that this does exist as far as Manor House, making a circular walk from the village.

Turning left by the village school I found the bus stop and a welcome seat. Just as I sat down the rain started. It hadn't stopped when I got home that evening. Once again I'd been remarkably fortunate with the weather, if not the footpaths. Beestons' Number 179 arrived on time. I was the only passenger – the driver seemed quite surprised to even have one. With half an hour until the train at Felixstowe there was time for a quick toasted teacake in the River of Life Café. Perfectly cooked and with big juicy currants, it was the best yet.

Post Script

Having read reports of breaches to the river wall in Martlesham Creek, on a sunny May morning I returned to Woodbridge, to check on the creek and find an alternative route to Waldringfield that didn't involve risking life and limb.

A sturdy wooden fence across the path at the start of Martlesham Creek didn't bode well, but there were no signs and well trodden earth suggested that plenty of people had walked round the fence. Indeed I past several walkers by the creek. Several small and one large breach had been temporarily repaired and were easily crossed. Another fence (no signs) could be bypassed and the path across the head of the creek was now officially open.

A network of paths gives many options for the next section and Wilfred George's *Footpath Map of Woodbridge*, which I'd bought earlier in the excellent Woodbridge Books, provides a useful guide. As before, I turned left over the footbridge into the woods at the head of the creek, following the path through the boatyard and onto the river wall. Towards the end of the creek another wooden fence blocked the way, this time with signs explaining that the path was closed. This was not just the 1953 breach that had forced me inland back in September, but three more from the recent tidal surge. A new earth wall was being constructed a couple of hundred yards inland, returning to the sea grazing land which man had claimed many centuries ago.

New River Wall, Martlesham Creek

The path heading away from the river that I'd hoped to take was closed – blocked by the new wall – and just in case anyone had fancied trying to use it a wooden footbridge over the borrowdyke had been moved. I retraced my steps to the point the path emerges from the wood by the creek and took a wider path up the hill. At a crossroads of paths I made the first of two mistakes today. A turn to the left, then very soon to the right, would have taken me across fields to Lumber Wood and Waldringfield Road. Instead I turned right, passing the most attractive Martlesham Hall and briefly diverting into the secluded St Mary's Church. Quite dark inside, the east window stands out with a striking depiction of the crucifixion.

Continuing on Church Lane, I passed steps through the woods which are the most direct path up from the creek. After two left turns it was only when the Sandlings Way met the lane that I realised I'd made an unnecessary mile diversion on roads. Following that path back to Martlesham Hall showed where I'd gone wrong. The Sandlings Way crosses Church Lane then runs parallel at the edge of a field, passing within yards of Martlesham Hall. Unfortunately there's no sign to the path from the lane, so I'd missed it. I should have taken the track signed 'Hall Farm'.

Retracing steps for the second time today, I followed the Sandlings Way as far as a footpath crossroads, turned left, then right at Lumber Wood, coming out again on what the OS map calls Waldringfield Lane and Wilfred George marks as Woodbridge Road.

With much confusion and many options I should perhaps suggest just two routes for anyone walking this way. The simplest is to follow the Sandlings Way uphill from the head of the Creek, with short diversions to look at St Mary's church and Martlesham Hall should you wish. Alternatively follow the creek past the boatyard, turn right up the hill, continue to Lumber Wood and meet the road slightly further towards Waldringfield.

There's no alternative to the road for the next mile or so, however having been recently designated a 'Quiet Lane' along with a number of other rural routes in this part of Suffolk, traffic should be considerate of walkers.

Turning left down Fishpond Road by the Old School House (1864), I headed back to the river to find out whether the last final half mile of Deben wall is walkable into Waldringfield. The wall had been overtopped, flooding riverside homes, but the path was now open and made a lovely walk alongside salt marsh with views to the far bank that I'd enjoyed walking so much back in September.

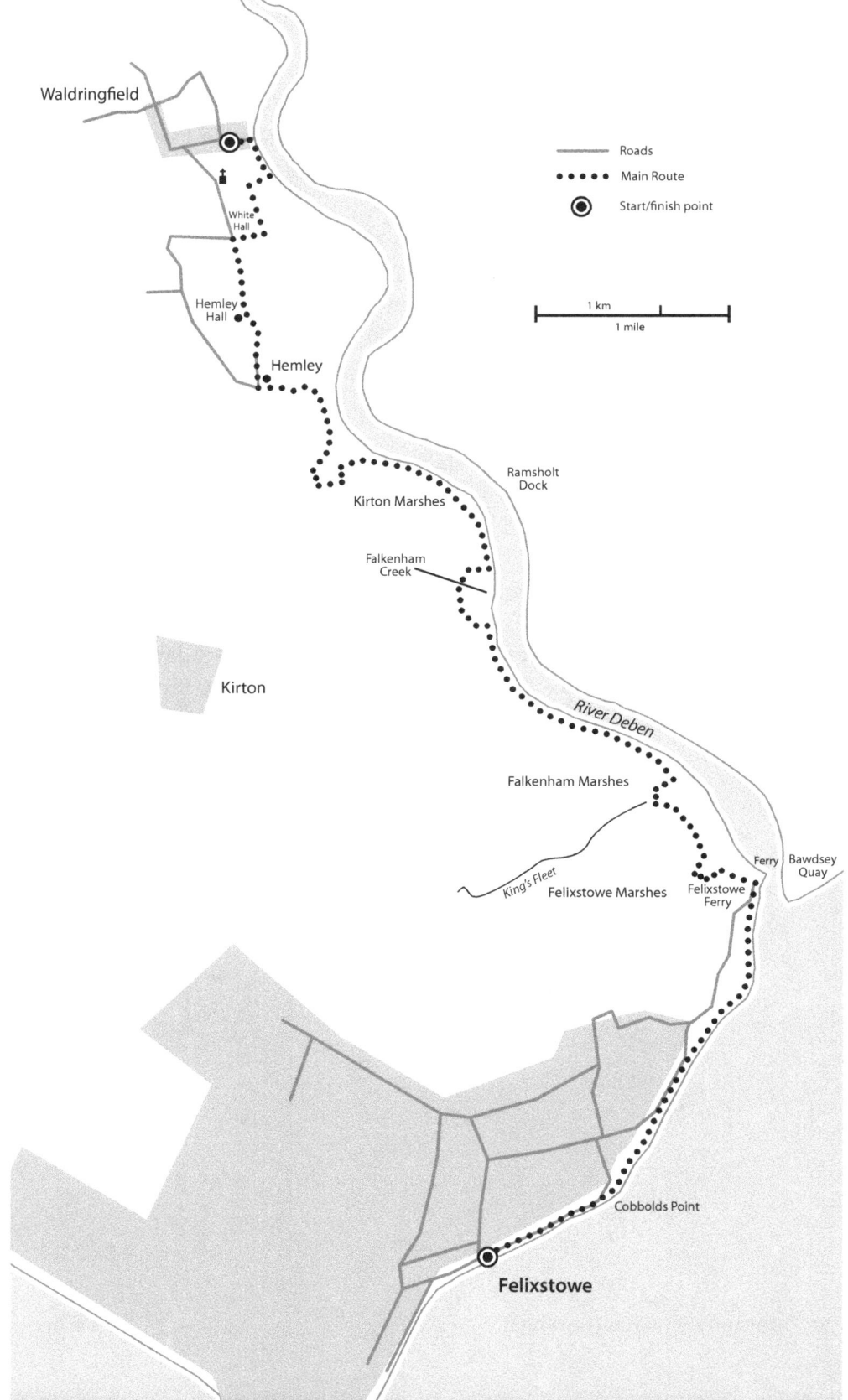

CHAPTER FIFTEEN
WALDRINGFIELD – FELIXSTOWE

(10 Miles) 16th October

Pulling the curtains in the Norfolk Guest House revealed the sun rising over Felixstowe beach. Once again I dressed hurriedly and scampered out to take photos. For me this was really quite uncharacteristic behaviour. My wife isn't far from the truth when she says the only time I'll get up early is to travel to West Ham games. It was though well worth leaving warm bedclothes to watch the sun rise over a misty North Sea, and how different to Woodbridge's mud. The Suffolk coast is truly a coast of variety.

Tripadvisor had promised a warm welcome at the Norfolk and I wasn't to be disappointed. Nowadays most guest houses offer a good level of comfort, service and breakfasts, but it is the extras that separate the excellent from the good. Here Rob and Dee excelled. Breakfast provided the interesting company of a gentleman who works on the railway in the docks, shunting trucks for the thirty trains which arrive or leave here every day. We talked of walking, coast and railways. His interests included modelling and he told me how obsessive some enthusiasts are, complaining if a model doesn't have exactly the right number of rivets as the real engine. Then, without a hint of irony, went on to bemoan those who run their model railways but don't operate the signals correctly.

Rain was forecast and Dee's offer to dry my clothes when I got back didn't bode well, but it was still dry as I set out along the seafront into Felixstowe centre. I was fortunate to find that Greggs had no baguettes as The Sandwich Shop next door provided a better and cheaper selection, with personal service from a charming man who lives on the Shotley Peninsular. He walks on the coast and said that if I came back for my lunch again tomorrow he'd try to find the answer to my question about accommodation at Shotley, a potential difficulty for my final few walks.

The bus to Waldringfield provided a little confusion. First I had to catch the 173 to Martlesham, then change to the 174. Traveline had told me that the 173 left from outside Nat West Bank at 10.02. The timetable on the stop showed 10.32. A lady waiting with me said she'd rung Ipswich Buses and been told 10.02. I phoned them and got the answer. The council are responsible for timetables on bus stops and this one was out of date. The bus would arrive at 10.02. Indeed it did. The driver suggested I changed at Tesco, where the same bus would return in thirty minutes, this time as a 174. And so it did. I doubled the number of passengers.

A half mile walk along Cliff Road took me back to the Deben by the Maybush, a popular waterfront pub. Originally a farmhouse, it was first licensed around 1745. Until the mid 19th century, Waldringfield, like many of the villages I'd walked through, was a scattered settlement. In 1850 few of the 140 inhabitants ventured even as far as Ipswich or Woodbridge, and having its own farms, shop, inn and craftsmen, the village was almost self-supporting. Most men worked on the farms while the women looked after their homes. Beer was made at a little brewery (now The Old Maltings opposite the Maybush), by John Hill, who grew his own barley and sold the ale at a shilling a gallon.

Felixstowe Pier at Sunrise

Then industry came to the village. From 1860 coprolite was dug from pits in the fields, washed and sifted on the beach, then shipped by barge to be processed in Ipswich. Towards the end of the 19th century a cement-making industry appeared, using mud from the river mixed with chalk shipped in from the Medway. With twelve kilns spewing out clouds of dirty brown smoke, it must have seemed more like an industrial town than a little village in rural Suffolk. Waldringfield anchorage accommodated a fleet of Thames barges and the quay would have been a hive of activity as up to a hundred boats were loaded and unloaded each week.

The cement kilns were demolished in 1912 and the village returned to its former pastoral life. As the Deben was gradually taken over by pleasure sailors, the picturesque setting of Waldringfield attracted visitors, with new homes springing up to house those wanting to live here. Large enough to keep its own school and community, but without the commercialisation of tourism, the village seems to have found a nice balance.

A footpath runs along the sandy beach, where a family were throwing crab lines into the river while Nobby their labrador swam in the river. The beach would have looked very different in World War Two, when barbed wire and iron spikes were laid and a 'dummy' fleet constructed out of poles and canvas. Lit up at night, this helped give the enemy a false impression of our naval strength in East Anglia.

The Maybush – Waldringfield

Prominent on the foreshore is Waldringfield Sailing Club, which formed in 1921 and now has around 650 members, 80 of whom live in the village. After a line of beach huts, the path reached an area of salt marsh. The OS map shows a path running beside the marsh and after about a mile crossing Early Creek. There was no path and no sign, but forewarned by the helpful people at Suffolk Council, I knew that this was another section where the wall had been breached. Hence I headed inland on a path that runs through a little wood and by a very pretty pond, where a length of blue rope hung from a tree over the water. Was this used for ducking witches or kids auditioning for *You've Been Framed* I wondered?

Turning sharp left, the path took me through a cornfield where just stubble remained from the summer's crop, then across a field of sugar beet which looked ready for harvest. This takes place between September and Christmas, when the beet's sugar content is at its highest. Another right turn at White Hall took me further inland. Currently empty, this Grade II listed 18th century farm house was up for sale. Reached by a private driveway and surrounded by countryside, it would make a lovely home for someone looking for views and isolation – provided they had the £1.25 million asking price.

As I stood looking at the house wondering what tales it could tell, a conker landed at my feet. Autumn had truly arrived. Walking down the driveway I met a barrier. A tree had fallen blocking the way. From the other side was the sound of laughter. Then an elderly lady emerged through the leaves, followed by five more. Greetings were exchanged. They were doing a circular walk from the Maybush. We agreed that it was a good thing none of us had been on the path when the tree fell. It would have given us a nasty bump.

Meeting the lane at Plum Tree Cottage, the path turned sharp left (this was a path of right angle turns) running for a mile along the side of the gentle hill, with views down the misty Deben to Ramsholt, Bawdsey Quay and the North Sea. At Hemley Hall I felt the first spots of rain. Path soon became lane, passing old coprolite pits and an attractive line of cottages. By Hemley church it was pouring. I sought refuge inside.

Formerly a port and centre of salt manufacture, the village now consists of just a few scattered houses, Hemley Hall and All Saints church. Despite the tiny population services are still held here regularly. The church was largely rebuilt in 1889 having fallen into disrepair and its main historical interest is a stone font dating from the mid 13th century or even earlier. Inside it is quite plain with no stained glass – but dry. With its Tudor red-brick tower, outside the church was attractive – but wet! With no shelter until the café at Felixstowe Ferry five miles ahead, I sat in the timber framed porch to eat my lunch. I hope no one minded.

After donning waterproofs and popping back into the church to put another pound in the pot as payment for shelter, I set off towards the river. A notice advised that Footpath 61 was closed before Felixstowe Ferry until 29th November and there was no diversion. That was five miles away. I'd deal with the problem when I got there.

The charmingly named Eelsfoot Cottage was the last building for some miles. This black weatherboard cottage is let as a holiday home. What a lovely place to stay in an isolated spot so close to the river, and at a price far below similar standards of accommodation in Southwold or Aldeburgh. I managed to make contact with Patrick Bowden Smith, whose family have owned the cottage and adjacent farm for a hundred years.

He told me that Eelsfoot was the last remaining of two rows of cottages that used to run down both sides of the road. Its design is most unusual, being based on an upturned Thames barge, which was covered with river mud, on top of which Patrick put the weatherboarding. He extended the cottage using sweet chestnut from trees blown down in the wood by Kirton Creek in the great storm of 1987. Digging out the foundations revealed the flint base of an earlier building, suggesting that this is an ancient site. The cottage had once been home to the Marsh Keeper, the man who controlled the sluices along the river bank. He would probably have made money catching eels, which is perhaps where its unusual name came from.

At the river wall a sign advised there was no through route back towards Waldringfield as the footpath had been lost to erosion. Patrick told me that like the breach I'd encountered west of Waldringfield, the land here was inundated in the Great Flood of 1953. Before then his family used to keep a dairy on the land, but once the seawater came in it soon changed to saltings. He built an inner sea wall thirty years ago, but the tide now reaches almost to the top, and he reckons the level has risen six to eight inches since he put the wall up. The old well in the cottage garden also illustrates how sea levels are rising, with the once fresh water now brackish as the river seeps in. Eelsfoot Cottage has never flooded, not even in 1953, but like so much of the East Coast, it will be increasingly vulnerable as mankind continues to affect the Earth's climate, raising sea levels and bringing more severe storms.

I turned to the right where a clear path ran alongside the delicate colours of autumn salt marsh. The rain had virtually stopped and all was well with the world. The path took me around Kirton Creek, a backwater in the truest sense of the term. This is a remote and sparsely populated corner of Suffolk. The remains of a quay and a very dilapidated wooden boat on the mud showed signs that it was once a busier place. Now it is enjoyed just by birds whose tracks criss-crossed the mud. With the tide low just a narrow channel wound its way through the brown mud. Four shelducks pottered. An egret, who I'd watched statuesque as I walked round the embankment, flew off as I got close. He really didn't need to. I didn't intend any harm. Next I disturbed a roe deer who bounded off across the field, disappearing into trees, and no doubt like the egret cursing the walker who'd disturbed his afternoon.

Ignoring a notice that sections of the path were to be closed for a short period seven years ago, I was soon back on the main river wall opposite Ramsholt; deserted on a damp October afternoon. To my right the cranes of Felixstowe poked up above Falkenham Wood. By Falkenham Creek the rain had returned. The next couple of miles were wild. A strong wind blew rain into my face and whipped up waves on the Deben. Two men held fishing rods on a dingy midstream in the river. Were they mad to go fishing in such weather, or was I mad to be walking?

With no let up in the wind and rain, I pressed on at a good pace thinking of the warm Ferry Cafe and a toasted teacake. Would I have it with jam or just dripping with butter? At Kings Fleet another sign told me that Footpath 61 was closed. Again I ignored it and pressed on.

Fishing Boat in the Rain

In Medieval times this area of marshes was a large basin off the Deben, with the river reaching almost two miles inland of the current wall. The outline of the basin can be roughly traced by the five metre contour on the OS map. This sheltered anchorage was known as Goseford, and was one of the most important ports on the East Coast. In 1337 Edward III claimed the throne of France and thus began the Hundred Years War. Suffolk's ports became important gathering places for ships bound for the continent and Edward used this stretch of sheltered water to prepare vessels for war. As the river changed and larger ships required deeper anchorages Goseford fell out of use, but the remaining narrow strip of water that runs more than a mile inland is still called King's Fleet.

A sign at the little creek that leads up to Felixstowe Ferry said the path was closed – but it was five years old. This was the section of Footpath 61 that two earlier signs had told me was closed until 29th November this year. The path was open and there was no work being done. For the third time on my coastal walk I had ignored 'footpath closed' signs and found the path to be quite passable.

Felixstowe Ferry was very different from the busy place I'd walked through in August. Houseboats and the obligatory wooden wreck sat on the mud, but there was no one about. I headed for the Ferry Café, a prefabricated American house which was bought at a cost of £130 and put on the shingle in 1955. It was shut. No teacakes today and nowhere to dry out. The wet fish shop was open but with no customers. I walked along the quay and looked across to Bawdsey. It was totally deserted. Not a soul. What a contrast to the colour and activity two months ago.

There has been a settlement here since early times and recorded buildings date back to 1043, when a fisherman's hut sold fish on the site of the Ferry Boat Inn. Until the early part of the 19th century this little collection of houses, huts and boats was called simply Felixstowe, the much larger town which now bears the name being known as the Waltons.

I headed south on the sea wall towards Felixstowe. With a fierce wind whipping off the open sea this was wilder still. Not one player had ventured out onto the golf course to my right. Behind me Bawdsey Manor looked out across the river. I passed two Martello Towers but the only other person to have ventured from the warmth of their houses seemed to be a lone kite surfer speeding to and fro across a sandbank.

Taking advantage of a brief lull in the rain, I sat on a wet seat and ate the emergency Kit Kat I keep in my bag – for days when there are no teacakes to be found. The rain didn't stop for long and as the concrete path continued in front of windswept beach huts I knew I'd be making use of Dee's drying services at the Norfolk. An equally wet man walking a Scottie dog passed me. We exchanged looks. No words were necessary.

The path stopped abruptly at a fence. I had the choice of going inland up a flight of steps known as Jacob's Ladder, or continuing along the beach which a sign warned was impassable at high tide. It seemed fairly well down so I continued on sand and shingle, climbing wooden steps over the groynes. At low tide it's possible to spot the seaweed covered remains of a Roman fort on the beach.

At Cobbolds Point there was a new promenade, opened in 2012 as part of a ten million pound sea defence scheme. Eighteen new rock groynes were built using

50,000 tonnes of granite from Larvik Quarry in Norway, with a further 23,000 tonnes of rock positioned in front of the walkway to keep the sea at bay. Above the promenade is Crammer House, a red-brick and mock-Tudor house built in 1885 for the Cobbold family. The Grade II listed building is now divided into flats and private signs abounded.

Close by used to be Beach House, where Wallis Simpson had stayed during the 1936 abdication crisis. Her divorce was being heard in Ipswich and she needed to stay in the country to establish a residential qualification to marry King Edward VIII. She didn't like Felixstowe, complaining that, *'the only sounds were the melancholy boom of the sea breaking on the deserted beach and the rustling of wind around shuttered cottages'*. I don't think she'd have enjoyed my walks! Despite its historical interest the house was demolished in 1994.

Looking from the beach this morning, on the skyline a large building with a central tower had loomed out of the mist. Now I was walking beneath it and could see that the tower held a clock. This impressive building opened in 1903 as the Balmoral Hotel, soon changed to the Felix Hotel, *'the* place to stay', in Felixstowe. Steps led from fine terraced gardens to the beach. After the hotel closed in 1951 it was bought for office and conference accommodation by Fisons, who renamed it Harvest House and presented the gardens to the town. Thankfully Fisons' application to demolish the building in 1974 was refused as it was listed and it now contains luxury retirement apartments.

The pier also survived an attempt to demolish it, with permission refused in 2004, but only the shore end with amusements and cafes remains open. Originally half a mile long, with an electric tram running to the end, the pier opened in 1905 and was a stopping point for the 'Belle' paddle steamers operating between London and Great Yarmouth. It was sectioned for defence reasons in World War Two and the seaward end demolished in 1949. When in 2012 a hole suddenly appeared in the floor after a pillar shifted in the shingle, things didn't look good for its future. However, following the success of Southwold, plans have been approved for a new pier to include a multi-million pound entertainment and conference venue with restaurants and retail units.

Felixstowe had been a big surprise to me. I'd expected a dull town dominated by its port, but it is in fact a historic and attractive seaside resort, which happens to have the largest container port in Britain at one end. The beach was clean and the long expanse of sand and shingle broken only by the many lines of rocky groynes. The late Victorian and early Edwardian seafront houses had character, many with verandas looking across the beach. Careful regulation and conservation areas protect the architecture, although Dee had told me this meant that to keep out drafts in winter they have to seal the balcony windows in The Norfolk.

The rain stopped just before I got back. Within an hour my clothes were dried and I was heading into town for dinner. China Garden proved a good choice – an excellent duck with orange sauce. Initially I was the only diner, but a mother and daughter soon came in and chose a table close to mine. If they didn't want me to hear their conversation they should have been a bit quieter! Now I know all about mother's hysterical phone call, daughter's problems at work, and just what they think about the father who left them. When mother ordered a second bottle of wine, '*to celebrate their love and friendship for each other*', I didn't know whether to laugh, cry or vomit!

Felixstowe Pier

Felixstowe Ferry

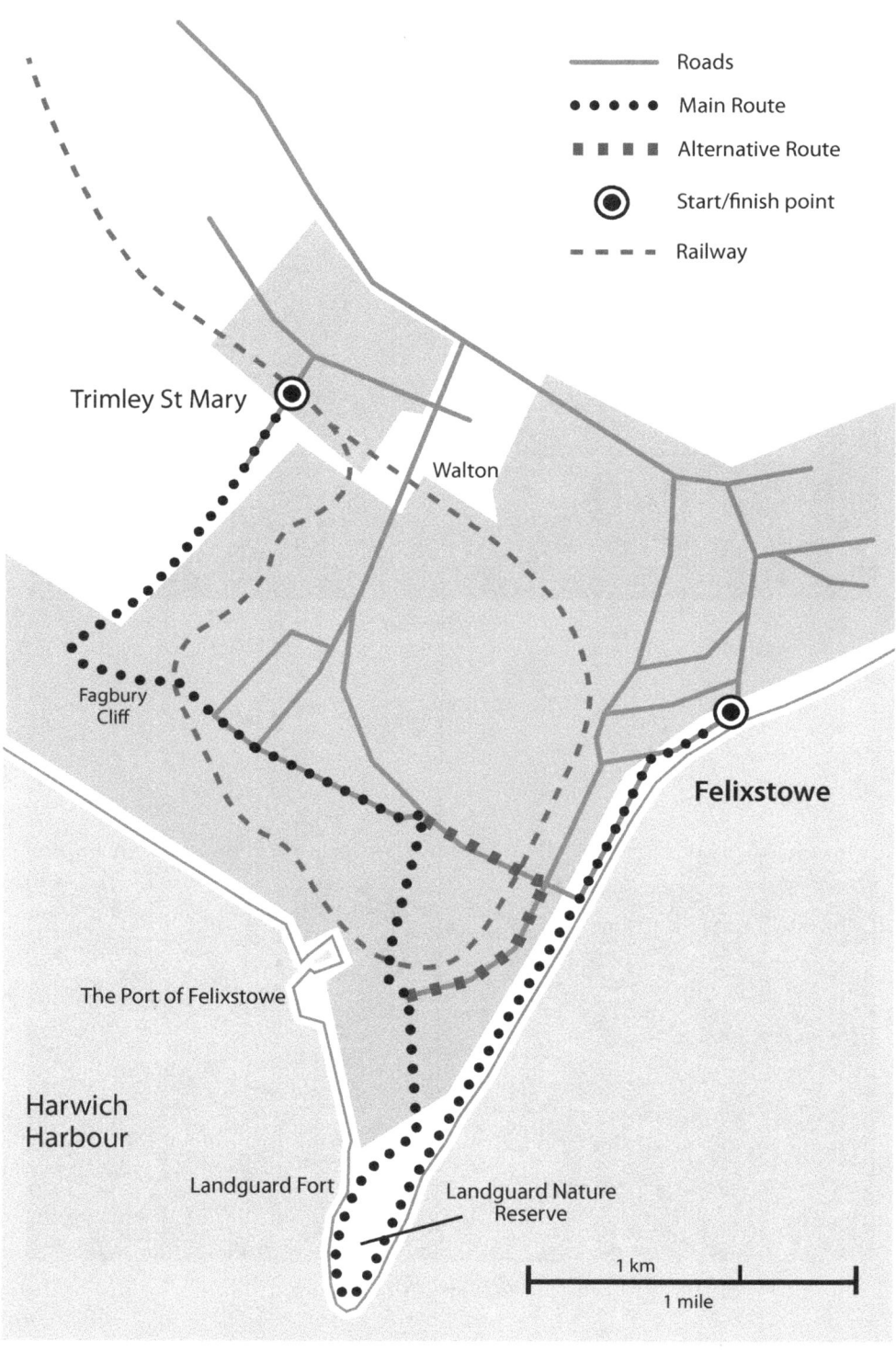

CHAPTER SIXTEEN
FELIXSTOWE – TRIMLEY

(7 Miles) 17th October

Once again at 7am I was on the beach watching the sun rise over the North Sea. With none of yesterday's mist it was a spectacular sunrise, silhouetting container ships as they steamed by. And again we talked trains over breakfast. It had been a hectic night in the docks with freight trains delayed by a derailment near London. Before leaving I chatted once more to Rob and Dee, urging Rob to press on with the book he was writing. It will be an interesting story telling the history of the guesthouse and some of the more unusual people who've stayed there; most notably an escaped prisoner from Hollesley who they wondered why had arrived with his clothes still in their shop wrappers.

Returning to The Sandwich Shop to buy lunch, the man serving told me he'd checked and there was no accommodation in Shotley. With shorter daylight hours curtailing walking time, I'd need to find an alterative plan for my final walks. It was good to see that Felixstowe still has a selection of traditional shops and that unlike many towns one can still buy fresh meat, hardware, fabrics and books on the High Street.

Returning to the seafront, I turned right towards Landguard Point, two miles along the beach. The first mile was on a paved promenade, passing beach huts, cafes and amusements. In warm sunshine dog walkers and elderly couples were out in force. One of the problems of walking in spring and autumn is our variable weather. Yesterday I'd been glad of clothing to keep out cold and rain. Today I was rapidly shedding layers until my bag was full, eventually carrying a jacket which wouldn't squeeze in.

Felixstowe Seafront

A white art deco building with four towers offered a *'Magical Golf Adventure'*. My occasional forays onto a golf course tend to provide adventure but little in the way of magic. This was Manning & Sons amusement park, which was originally opened by Billy Butlin in 1933 and run by the Manning family since 1946. Its claim to be *'The most established landmark on Felixstowe's coastline'* could perhaps be disputed by the pier (1905), four Martello Towers (1804 – 1812) or Landguard Fort (1539).

The Stour and Orwell Walk runs along the seafront but heads inland down Beach Station Road, missing Landguard Point, one of the highlights of the two rivers. With the way forward barred by Suffolk Sands Holiday Park, I continued on the sandy beach; not easy walking on what was now a very warm morning. Who would have thought that in mid October I'd have regretted not packing shorts? Sitting down on a rock for a few minutes I discovered a set of keys in my pocket – Norfolk Guesthouse keys. Bother!

A path across Landguard Nature Reserve made for much easier walking. This 81 acre shingle spit is designated as an SSSI for the rarity of its vegetated shingle habitat, and a Scheduled Ancient Monument because of the historic military significance of the site's fortifications spanning four hundred years. Botanically the most notable feature of the reserve is the vegetation that has evolved to grow on shingle beaches where the soil is virtually non existent and few nutrients are available. Plants such as sea rocket store water in their swollen leaves and others like the sea kale grow tap roots up to two metres long to reach the fresh water far below the surface.

The coastline is like a highway for migrating birds, many stopping off for a rest and to feed, including unusual and scarce species attracted in to land by the bright lights that illuminate the docks. An old military building houses an observatory which overlooks the reserve. Migratory birds are recorded and ringed as they pass by. Moths are also recorded and over nine hundred have been identified, some of whom fly here all the way from Germany.

At Landguard Point I was just a mile from Essex and landmarks in Harwich across the water reminded me of the walk along my home county's coast. I had reached what for many is the end of the Suffolk coast. The Suffolk Coast Path finishes here and long distance walkers tend to take the summer-only ferry across Harwich Harbour, a deep pool of water where the Orwell and Stour meet. I still however had these two rivers to walk before finally reaching Essex.

The Point's strategic importance is illustrated by the many military remains and buildings; Victorian gun plinths, 19th century accommodation, Second World War concrete blocks, and Landguard Fort, one of Britain's best preserved coastal forts, which defended the coast for almost 450 years. Standing tall above all this military history is a modern radar tower, which guides ships into the twin ports of Felixstowe and Harwich.

As I sat on the shingle for an early lunch a vast container ship, the *Cosco Fortune,* slipped slowly out to sea. At 366 metres long, 142,000 tonnes and with capacity for 13,000 containers, this is a huge vessel. As I wrote this chapter seventeen days later, a ship spotting website (yes they exist) told me that the ship was now in Suez, en route to Singapore.

By the docks a new visitor centre and café was busy. It had only been open for six months but had already become a popular place to eat and drink while watching the port's activity. It was all rather different to the closed, wet and deserted Felixstowe Ferry I'd walked through yesterday. I stopped for a while, watching cranes unload the *MSC Laurence,* which *shipspotting.com* told me had come from Ningbo and was now in Gioia Tauro. (I'll admit to having to look up where both are – China and Southern Italy).

The only safe deep water landing place between the Thames and Humber,

Felixstowe Docks

Felixstowe is the UK's busiest container port. Officially opened in 1887, its history is however far from one of continuous success. Construction of a large roller mill to take Canadian grain in 1904 marked the beginning of the end of many East Anglian windmills, but the First World War brought a change to military use. Harwich basin became a base for motor torpedo boats and later for minesweepers. A fleet including thirty battleships and cruisers was based at Harwich, using Felixstowe as a coaling station. After being badly hit by the depression, the next World War revived the port, which was used by both the Navy and RAF, the latter as a flying boat and air sea rescue base.

Again the port declined after the war and by the 1950s all that remained was a single, crumbling wooden jetty and a hinterland scattered with military huts. Then Gordon Parker, an East Anglian corn merchant, set about reviving it. By 1957 several weekly cargo services were docking here and exclusion from the 1960 National Dock Labour Scheme meant that when other ports were crippled by strikes, Felixstowe kept working. In 1961 the government blocked the town council's attempt to buy much of the port's land for a rubbish dump and with new jetties it continued to expand. In 1967 Britain's first container terminal was set up here and a new road constructed in 1973 enabled vehicles to bypass the town centre. With nine berths Felixstowe now welcomes four thousand ships per year, carrying 40% of the UK's containers and linking with 365 ports around the world.

Landguard Fort

Ever since Henry VIII personally inspected the sheltered haven, an artillery fort on Landguard Point has guarded the port of Harwich. One of Britain's best preserved coastal defences, Landguard Fort is managed by a trust whose dedicated volunteers are supported by English Heritage. I spent a most interesting hour wandering round the extensive fortifications, mostly dating from the mid 18th century, but with major changes made in Victorian times.

Landguard Fort holds a unique place in the history of Britain and her military. It was here that the Royal Marines fought their first land battle, repelling the last attempted invasion of England. In the summer of 1667 England was at war with the Dutch – well it made a change from the French. Having raided the Medway Dockyards, capturing and burning English ships, the Dutch navy sailed up the east coast, heading for Harwich.

Led by Colonel Thomas Dolman, two thousand men came ashore at what is now known as Cobbolds Point in Felixstowe. A group of Dutch Marines climbed up the cliff and defeated the Suffolk Militia. The rest set off towards the Landguard Fort. Armed with long pikes and muskets, and carrying ladders, they dragged their small cannons across the shingle. The English, under the command of Captain Nathaniel Darell, were heavily outnumbered, but the fort's defenders were experienced musketeers.

The Dutch formed up on the beach awaiting the command to attack. Soon after 4 o'clock in the afternoon a hail of shot hit the northern wall. One landed on the catwalk wounding three men. The Dutch ladders were put up and as the first marines moved towards the thick stone walls, Darell's whistle gave the signal to open fire. Marksmen chose their targets wisely. As each man fired he handed the weapon to a man behind him, receiving a charged musket in return.

Grenadiers strode along the catwalk listening for the thud of a new ladder going up against the wall. As each Dutch head came over the parapet, the grenadier ducked the downward curve of a cutlass and hurled his grenade to the foot of the ladder. With a slash of his sword, Dolman signalled his troops forward, but a marksman had the Dutch Colonel in his sights and he fell to the ground. As Captain Darell leaned forward, checking that the dead Dutch officer was Dolman, a shot smashed into his shoulder but realising it wasn't fatal he continued to lead his men. With Dolman dead the invaders appetite for fighting faded and soon the Dutch retreated. With one killed and four wounded the English had repelled the enemy.

Signs on a tall spiked fence advised that the port was a restricted area, so a diversion was to be needed. Quite how much of a diversion was yet to be seen. At Tilbury in Essex I'd nonchalantly walked past the security gate and spent a couple of hours wandering around the port. Following a path along the nature reserve, then joining View Point Road and passing Custom House, I soon reached the A154. Here I had a choice – turn right and follow the main road around the docks, or left and try to get to the footpath that the OS map shows running alongside the railway inside the port. You won't be surprised that I chose the latter.

Unlocked gates allowed me to use a foot crossing over the railway line. I must have been too busy reading the police sign that advised that the next gate was locked at night, to see the other one that said no unauthorised persons were allowed through. I was in the dock, albeit not the terminals within the tall spiked fence. Finding the path wasn't so easy. The layout didn't seem to match my map at all. Cars and lorries drove by but no one seemed to walk here. No one challenged me as I passed the dock's police station. Following the road I came to a roundabout, where a sign indicated straight on for the exit and left for Trimley Terminal. Left was the direction which I wanted to be heading, but conscious of having failed to find a way out at Tilbury and having to return to the entrance, I chose the safer option.

I stopped to buy a drink at a petrol station. The man serving assumed I'd come off a ship and was heading for London. He wanted to know if I'd been to Norway and how much beer cost there. Vehicles were being stopped at the exit checkpoint but I walked straight through without a challenge. I hadn't managed to find the path, quite possibly because it doesn't exist, but my illicit shortcut through the docks had saved a mile of main road walking.

The next half mile along the noisy Walton Avenue was not pleasant walking. I trusted the map which showed the Stour and Orwell Walk running along Fagbury Road, although there was no sign and it seemed to be heading into a dead end industrial area. It was right though. A foot crossing over the dock railway leads to a path through woods up Fagbury Cliff. Several trains were lined up on the tracks and apparently it can be a long wait to cross if one is trundling by.

At last I was back in the countryside, albeit with the background roar of lorries and docks. A viewpoint looks out across the port and over the water to Essex. Slightly to the right was the Shotley Peninsular, where I'd be completing my coastal walk in somewhat cooler weather than today. Had I been continuing down the Orwell I would have turned left towards Trimley Marshes, but that would be the next walk. Instead I carried on for a mile along a track through an avenue of trees, reaching a lane that led to Trimley station. The first stop after Felixstowe, this was a sad site. Posters told of a campaign to save the station building but such was its dilapidated state, I fear they may have left it too late.

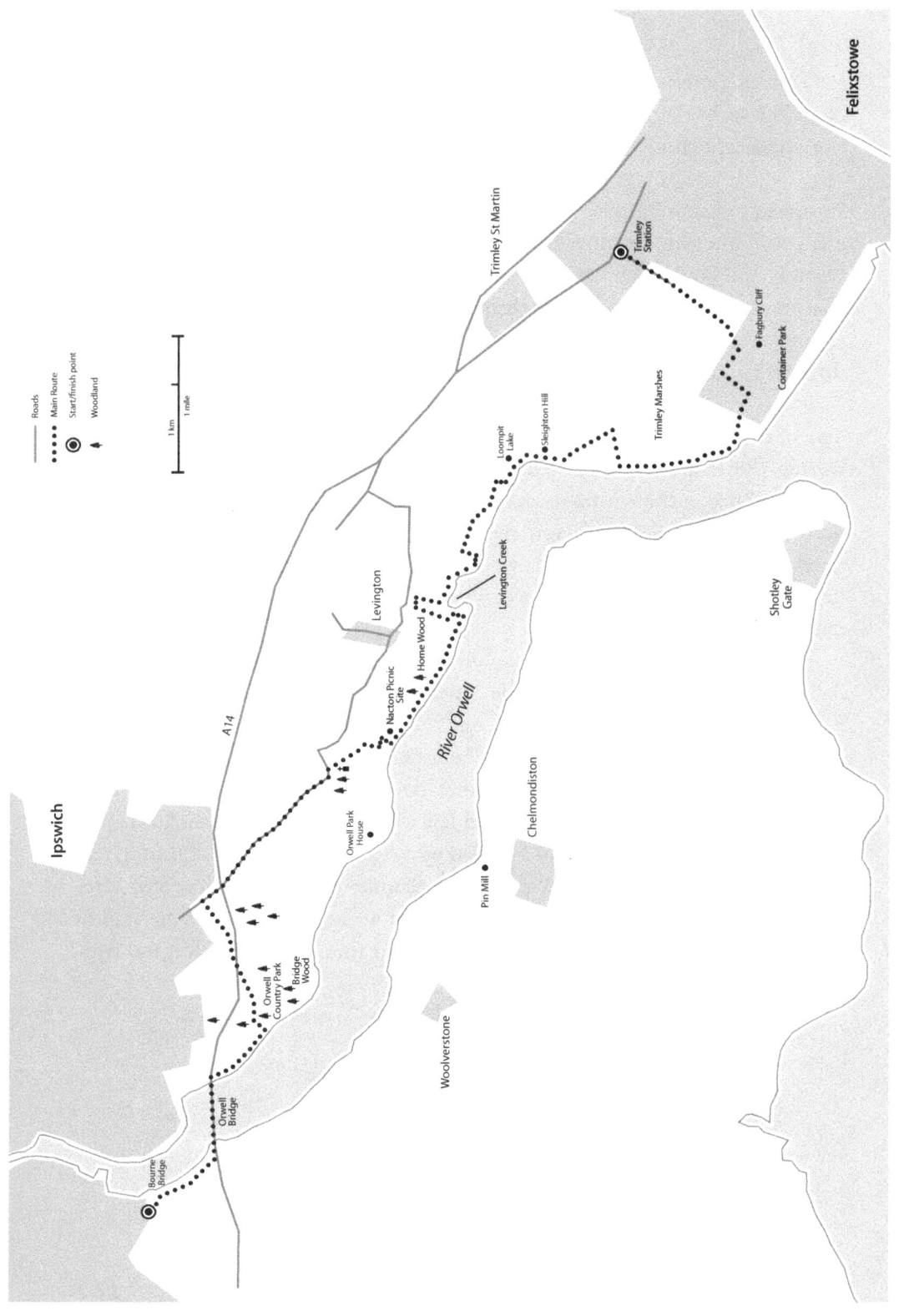

CHAPTER SEVENTEEN
TRIMLEY – IPSWICH

(12 Miles) 13th November

Today was just as sunny as the day I'd left Trimley a month before – but about fifteen degrees colder! Fields had been white with frost as I'd travelled up from London and I set off wearing many layers. This was the first walk straight from a railway station and one of few not to need a bus at either end.

At the end of the lane two men were unloading bikes from cars. They were heading to the bird reserve and said they'd soon catch me up. Four sets of couples with assorted dogs on the path down to the river all agreed it was a nice day. The cyclists whizzed by enjoying the gentle slope. They'd said it was a nicer ride down than up! Leaving the path that climbs up to Fagbury Cliff, I turned right towards Trimley Marshes. I was back on the Stour and Orwell Walk, but soon left it again, taking a path on the left into the reserve which is owned by the Suffolk Wildlife Trust.

In 1984 a bill put before Parliament asked permission to extend the Port of Felixstowe into the Orwell Estuary. Four years of arguments followed, with conservation organisations objecting because the development would mean the loss of a large area of inter-tidal mud, an important winter food source for wading birds. Eventually a scheme was agreed which would include some benefits to wildlife, with the Port providing 205 acres of land and funding the creation of a reserve on Trimley Marshes. Fields which had been intensively farmed with crops that left few opportunities for birds, mammals, insects or flowers, were transformed into wetland with a diverse range of wildlife habitats.

Careful management of water levels by Suffolk Wildlife Trust ensures that wet conditions can be maintained for over-wintering wildfowl, and breeding waders. The reserve is particularly noted for redshank, avocet, oystercatcher, little grebe and gadwall, but a remarkable total of 249 bird species have been recorded here. Amongst the less likely species listed are budgerigar, cockatiel and Pacific swift. The last of these made its unexpected appearance in June 2013, five years after it had last been seen in Britain. Such was the excitement at this extremely rare visitor which normally lives in Asia, that police had to be called to deal with the number of twitchers descending on the reserve.

My face broke a cobweb as I climbed steps to a viewing platform, suggesting that I was the first visitor of the day. A peaceful view across the marshes contrasted with the rumbles, bumps and bangs from the docks behind me. Three men were thinning trees by the path. Wednesday was volunteer day. Approaching the river huge cranes loomed over the track, more contrasts of the Suffolk coast.

Two bikes lay by the river wall and at the water's edge my cycling friends poked about in mud with buckets and spades. A sign asked people to keep off Shingle Island, a small area of shingle separated from the mainland by a short causeway. It's an extremely important area for roosting and ground-nesting birds. Continuing on the somewhat muddy path on the river wall (there was an easier track below the wall but I preferred to see the water), I soon reached the Visitor Centre. Unstaffed, but with excellent information displays, it would provide useful shelter to anyone doing this section of walk on a wet day. The next shelter is several miles away.

Back on the river wall I looked across to the reserve's lagoons. A lone heron stood upright on a tiny islet. Half a dozen small yachts sailed serenely down the river. An oystercatcher pottered on the mud by the remains of an old quay. Ahead, to left and to right, the scene was of rural tranquillity. Behind me the docks continued to rumble and bang.

In 2001 the sea wall was deliberately breached to create new inter-tidal habitat for wading birds and the path now runs around what at low tide was a huge expanse of mud. The skeletons of three trees killed by the salt water stood eerily on newly formed salt marsh at the edge of the mud.

I stopped to eat the rather mediocre ham baguette I'd bought this morning at Stratford station. As I looked out over the mud in bright sunshine I made another Suffolk friend – a small tortoiseshell butterfly who settled on my leg. Three times he flew off as I reached for my camera, and three times returned to the same spot on my jeans. I wondered if it was the light colour or warmth that had attracted to sit here, or perhaps he was just friendly. He was only a common butterfly but this little encounter with nature was a highlight of my day.

As I set off once more along the river wall an orange boat of the Harwich Port Pilot chugged downstream. Harwich Haven Authority employs thirty pilots, assisting ships using the ports of Harwich, Felixstowe, Ipswich and Mistley, or onwards to the Thames, Medway and Crouch. At Sleighton Hill the path climbed through trees, reaching a superb viewpoint looking out across the river. A tree clung to the edge of the cliff, its roots exposed. How much longer until it drops onto the sandy beach below?

The next little stretch was one of the highlights of my Suffolk walk – the causeway between the beautiful Loompit Lake and the River Orwell. Surrounded by trees on three sides, the dark, still waters of the lake contrasted with the ever-moving river. A pair of swans alternately dipped their heads into the water, for some time thwarting my efforts to get a photo until I eventually got the reflection shot I wanted, enhanced by the ripples of movement. I asked a man fishing what he was after – *'Trout. I know they're there, it's just a question of getting them out'*.

Loompit Lake and Causeway

A couple walking their three dogs stopped to chat. They were involved with the Woodbridge RSPB Group and very familiar with the county's coast and birds. We agreed that this was a lovely spot. They recommended a new RSPB book, *Suffolk's Wildlife Coast*, which isn't widely available but Browsers Bookshop in Woodbridge supplied me with a copy by post.

The 34 acre Loompit Lake was formed when the river wall was breached in the 1953 floods. Now just the narrow walkway separates river from lake; two very different wildlife habitats. Should this be breached the freshwater fish, plants, birds and insects would be lost, with the lake soon becoming salt marsh. Both are valuable, but for the inhabitants of Loompit Lake it is a fine line between survival and disaster.

In the woods on Stratton Cliff a man with an impressive looking camera stopped to talk. We concurred that it was a good day for photography. He told me that he'd been taking shots of ladybirds on a barbeque by the marina. Finding the barbeque (commemorating the Queen's Golden Jubilee) I spent a while observing a remarkable number of several types of ladybird.

With 550 high quality berths Levington Marina claims to be '*The East Coast's Leading Marina*'. A mass of masts pointed skywards, a red lightship in their midst, yet fifty years ago this was marshland. *Harbouring the Dream* by Martin Treadway tells the remarkable story of how the vision of one man and the hard work of many, led to the creation of Suffolk Yacht Harbour. On a cold winter morning in 1961, Michael Spear, a chartered surveyor, was carrying out a valuation on the thousand acre estate of Mr James Stennet, which had recently been inherited by his son Charles. The estate included sixty acres of saltings, formed in 1942 when a freak tide had breached the ancient river wall constructed by Napoleonic prisoners of war. As Messrs Spear and Stennet viewed the flooded area, considering the land's value and whether it could be put to gainful use, an idea was formed. Nine years later *Merry Heart* became the first boat to enter the newly opened forty berth Suffolk Yacht Harbour.

With much dredging and piling the marina grew but lacked a crucial facility – a clubhouse where yachtsmen could meet, relax and exchange stories. In 1975 a redundant lightship was purchased from Trinity House. Built in Glasgow in

1932, the ship was originally the *Mid Barrow LV87* before ending her career as the Cromer Light Vessel. The interior formed a perfect clubhouse but something was lacking – the lightvessel had no light. Two years later Michael Spear was passing through Norwich when he spied *TS Lord Nelson*, another former Trinity Lightvessel, complete with light. Thinking that for its use as a Sea Cadet training vessel a clear deck would allow more room for manoeuvres, Spear suggested doing the cadets 'a favour' by removing it free of charge. Their commanding officers were pleased to oblige, not least because the more enthusiastic boys had been climbing on the light to peer into bedroom windows of an adjacent hotel!

The path runs through trees above the marina, crosses the access road and enters a boatyard. Of the various nautical businesses 'Mr Stainless' promised the most – apparently he *'works wonders with stainless steel'*. The route wasn't clear but a straight line through the boatyard came to a line of trees, behind which the path continues after a sharp left turn. This took me round Levington Creek, a popular spot for birdwatchers. The remains of what was thought to be a Viking ship were found in the mud here and may have been one of the Danish fleet which raided Ipswich in 991AD and later fought the Saxons at the Battle of Maldon (a remarkable story which I recount in *Essex Coast Walk*.) The creek was used for commercial barge traffic until the 1920s and like many of the county's backwaters, not all the trade was strictly legitimate. In 1817 smugglers were caught carrying forty eight tubs of sprits aboard a boat called *Daisy*.

It had been my original intention to stop at Levington's Ship Inn for lunch, but after reading some excellent internet reviews I found that it had in fact closed six months ago, although hopefully not permanently. Hence I missed out this quiet village, once a winner of The Calor Village of the Year competition.

Back by the main river I sat for a while on a little beach surrounded by thousands of tiny shells. It's strange how shells accumulate on some beaches while others barely have any. The next mile was easy walking beside the water, then rising slightly through the trees of Home Wood. At Nacton picnic site I stopped for a snack, sitting on a seat dedicated to Carol Ann Jones. Born in 1960, the same year as me, she passed away in 2011. '*This is where she found peace in this world*' said the dedication. Only the sound of birds and distant shouts of children disturbed the quiet of the peaceful riverside.

Just back from the river is the magnificent Broke Hall, a red-brick country house built by James Wyatt in 1792. Its sixteen acres of grounds were designed by Humphry Repton, considered to be the last great English landscape designer of the 18th century and who produced designs for the grounds of many of England's foremost country houses. The house was originally the seat of the Broke family, whose number included Admiral Philip Broke who commanded *HMS Shannon*, a thirty eight gun frigate noted for her capture of the *USS Chesapeake* in the summer of 1813. It is now divided into apartments.

There's no public access to the two miles of river beyond Nacton, so the Stour and Orwell Walk diverts inland. The OS map shows a series of tracks passing Park Farm and Goldsmith's Covert, but the grounds of Orwell Park House (a 17th century mansion which is now a preparatory school) are private, so the walk continues on roads with no view of the river.

A lane took me uphill alongside a brick wall, from behind which came the enthusiastic shouts of a boys rugby match. Staying on the road at the entrance to the picnic site (ignoring the bridleway ahead) took me past Orwell Park School, a rather posh affair. It was their boys playing rugby above the river. A dome on one of the school's towers houses the seventh largest privately owned telescope in Britain; not the sort of thing found on your average comprehensive.

The Georgian building was originally owned by Admiral Edward Vernon, whose enduring claim to fame was not for the battles he fought, but his inadvertent contribution to sailors' health. In 1740 he ordered that the daily rum ration should be diluted, with lemon or lime juice usually added to cut down on the water's foulness. Although they didn't know the reason at the time, thanks to this daily dose of vitamin C Admiral Vernon's sailors were healthier than the rest of the navy. In 1747 James Lind proved that scurvy could be prevented by supplementing the diet with citrus fruit and the rest of the Royal Navy rapidly followed Vernon's lead, supposedly calling the new drink 'grog' after Vernon's nickname 'Old Grog', attributed to his habitual wearing of a grogram coat.

Next to the school is St Martin's Church, which with dull grey rendering wasn't the prettiest I'd seen on my walks. It was locked. The scattered village of Nacton used to be served by Orwell railway station, but this closed in 1959 when diesel trains were introduced and the little-used stop sacrificed as part of the acceleration that allowed a single train to work an hourly service on the Felixstowe branch.

Turning left at a T junction, the next 1½ miles were along Ipswich Road, with frequent need to step onto the verge as cars whooshed past. Aware that I still had several miles to walk and only an hour or so of daylight, I made a good pace. Most of today's walk had been with the background of noise from Felixstowe Docks or A14 traffic – the Orwell may match the Deben for beauty but not always for peacefulness. Now approaching this busy road the distant rumble became a roar. Surely more of the unending succession of lorries should be put on the railways. The Ipswich Road took me under the A14, but crossing the busy slip roads either side wasn't easy. Some diversions inland had added to the enjoyment of my walks, but not this one. What a shame that two miles of the Orwell riverside are barred to walkers. I fully concur with Griff Chamberlain whose excellent website *http://griffmonster-walks.blogspot.co.uk/* describes a wide variety of walks focussing primarily on Suffolk and Norfolk:

"It is unfortunate that there is no access along the river bank by Orwell Park House as this necessitates a long trudge up a rather busy country road to Ransomes Europark, an industrial complex by the side of the A14. This is a hazardous walk as there is no pavement and the straight road results in lots of speeding cars. It did leave me thinking that the landowners of Orwell Park House, which these days is a rather posh prep school, must be pretty mean to not allow walkers to navigate around the edge of their land. There may be other reasons but judging by the many Private signs on that side of the road, they certainly didn't want Joe public on their land!"

But it shouldn't be like this. In 2007 the then Environment Secretary David Milliband promised that within a decade one of the world's longest public footpaths would be created along the entire 2,800 miles of England's coast. Six years later, after just twenty miles of new paths had been completed (fast tracked for the Olympic sailing at Weymouth), Conservative Environment Minister Richard Benyon hinted at cost cutting, describing it as a '*sledgehammer to crack a nut*'. According to BBC Countryfile later that year, the £50 million budget had been cut to £4.5 million. Meanwhile Wales had completed its path in four years and found the income generated for local business was far exceeding the cost of the path.

I had reached the outskirts of Ipswich. I'd deliberated long and hard about what to do about Suffolk's county town. By the rules of my walk I should take the A14 across the Orwell Bridge, but did I want to miss what is an historic town, and as a tidal port, must count as part of the coast? My decision was to walk over the bridge but spend another day in Ipswich.

A few hundred yards along the A1189 a road heads left into the 200 acre Orwell Country Park. Opened to the public in 1995, the park provides a variety of woodland and shoreline walks. After a mile or so a bridge took me over the A14, after which the road ends at a car park and a network of paths spread through Bridge Wood. To the left a path runs down to the river and along the shore by Alnesbourne Golf Club and the remains of Alnesbourne Priory, a small Augustine monastic house now incorporated into the clubhouse. I however continued along the well signed route that took me to back to the river half a mile or so from the Orwell Bridge.

The sun was setting and I walked quickly along the beach, keen to get over the bridge while there was still some light. Rejoining the path as it passes under the bridge, I stopped to take photos against the reddening sky. Driving over one doesn't really appreciate the scale of this 18 span, 1287 metre crossing, which rises 39 metres above the Orwell, but standing by one of the immense concrete pillars gives a real sense of its scale. Opened in 1982, the main span of 190 metres was then the longest pre-stressed concrete span in the world. Now it doesn't even make the top ten, nine of which have been built in China and Norway since 1997. The nineteen sets of pillars support two hollow concrete box girders, which as well as carrying the road surface, provide access for services, including a 711mm water main from Alton Water reservoir. Ingenious springs allow the bridge to expand by up to two feet in hot weather.

Construction of the bridge was not without its mishaps. In September 1980 a skip truck slipped over the edge of a lagoon and in August 1981 a crane collapsed in the mud. Whilst these incidents were without serious injury, two lives were sadly lost during construction work. To show that the team of 300

Orwell Bridge

workers were not simply there to build, but to add something to the community, one December pier six was adorned with a huge Christmas tree made using scraps of steel, decorated in lights and lifted in place by a crane.

Anyone preferring not to brave the crossing can walk into the centre of Ipswich largely on paths through parkland, but just beyond the bridge I took a path that climbs steeply to the A14. Not a lover of heights, I have to admit that it was with some trepidation that I set out along the walkway. A sign warned walkers not to cross in windy weather. A Samaritans' phone provides hope for desperate people, on what is known locally as the suicide bridge from the number of people who have sadly ended their lives here. The wall is not much more than a metre high and climbable, with the outcome certain. The local Conservative MP had recently called for action to prevent the tragedies, but some of his constituents suggested that the answer lies not in a higher wall but in better mental health care.

I had noticed little wind by the river today but once high above the water a steady breeze blew across the bridge. Every passing lorry, and there were many, brought a whoosh of air. I wouldn't have wanted to be up here in even

Warning Sign, Orwell Bridge

moderately windy weather. An illogical fear that I would fall over the edge kept me away from the wall, so I plodded up the slope staying by the low barrier at the carriageway edge, looking resolutely ahead – not down! To my left, as the sun disappeared clouds changed shape and colour every minute. To my right was the town of Ipswich and its docks. Far below was the river, but I knew that to stop and look down and would send my legs all wobbly.

The fifteen minute crossing wasn't my favourite bit of Suffolk's coastal walk. The constant traffic and a sense that this isn't really a place for walkers doesn't encourage lingering. If they took away all the lorries and cars it would make a nice pedestrian bridge! I crossed on the northern side. It was only after getting home that I read that the Stour and Orwell Walk follows the southern footway. I should have climbed the steps before going under the bridge. Signs tell pedestrians not to cross the carriageway and with no let up in the stream of vehicles roaring past this wasn't an instruction I was going to disobey.

The way down from the south side is half a mile or so from the river bank, but a metal gate and some steps seem to serve as an unofficial route off the north side of the bridge. A very steep path runs down the hillside to a track which links to the B1456. With no accommodation towards Shotley, I headed a mile up the river. The road was busy and with it now dark, not particularly safe for walkers. I'd felt it was too dark to walk on the river wall (a good decision as I was to find out tomorrow), but an embankment alongside the road provided a safe, if rather muddy alternative. The only obstruction here was a lone swan who loomed out of the dark and hissed furiously at me as I passed. I suspect the hissing meant that yes it is true, swans can break a man's arm, but like the various pigs, horses and dogs I'd encountered on my walks, he decided not to inflict harm. Only the bees of Butley River had chosen to hurt me.

My accommodation for the night was the Premier Inn. I can safely say that I was the muddiest guest! Surprisingly it was actually the cheapest night of my walk, a benefit of having booked a month ahead. I'd expected to be writing of a purely functional and soulless hotel, but was pleasantly surprised. Katie on reception was welcoming and friendly, telling me she likes the evening shift as there's time to talk to people. The waitress who served my excellent dinner in the Oyster Reach was interested in walking and loved the Orwell. As ever, it is the staff who turn an ordinary stay into a good one.

I was only a mile or so from the centre of Ipswich but didn't venture far on what was now a very cold evening. Just a wander over Bourne Bridge which crosses the Belstead Brook as it flows into the Orwell. Ipswich was to wait for another day.

Post Script

Returning on a sunny May weekend, I was to see rather more people today. On Stratton Cliff I made friends with another butterfly. Again a small tortoiseshell, but this time rather than sit on my trousers he flew between dandelions, stopping to feast on each flower for long enough to allow me to take photos. Although still one of our most widespread butterflies, small tortoiseshells are declining in number, possibly due to a parasitic fly which is common in mainland Europe and as a result of global warming has increasing presence here.

At Loompit Lake I chatted to Robin Biddle, a local birdwatcher, who told me that he's seen 220 species in the square mile around the lake. There were fewer this year though, as in the winter storms a surge tide had over-topped the causeway, inundating the lake with four feet of sea water. Fortunately they'd been able to drain it in two days, and the trout, being reasonably tolerant of salt, had survived. Other species had been less fortunate and with less food, fewer birds were nesting. Usually there are countless mallard chicks and around fifty goslings, but this year not one duck had bred. There were only fifteen goslings, most of whom swam past as we talked – a brood of seven with their brent geese parents and five with their Canada goose mother.

We tend to think of climate change as it affects humans or polar bears, but the influence of mankind on our planet has far reaching consequences for creatures large and small all around the globe.

Cormorants have been nesting at Loompit for many years (causing some conflict with anglers who resent the trout they take) and fortunately don't seem to have been affected by the sea water incursion. Robin told me to look for the colony in the northern corner of the lake, and what a remarkable sight it was. Around eighty birds, most perched on branches of dead trees splattered white with their droppings, some circling the lake and every few minutes one flying back with a beak full of nesting materials. It wasn't just twigs they were carrying but branches with leaves, some longer than the birds themselves. What a privilege it was to sit for half an hour and watch them.

I was to have one more wildlife treat today. By a small lake at the entrance to Levington Creek another bird watcher invited me to look through his telescope. At the edge of the water was a greenshank, not a rare bird but one that he doesn't see that often. Two redshanks close by were more common. An egret landed on the water and above a distant line of poplar trees two crows mobbed a buzzard. He'd seen a cuckoo over the gorse and told me that roe deer live nearby. There is so much wildlife to see in our countryside but sometimes you have to stop, be still and wait.

I'd been told that breaches in the river wall at Levington Creek had closed the path, so my main reason for coming back today was to see if it was passable or find another route. An out of date sign about a closure for maintenance last year was to be ignored, but two more near the top of the creek advised that the path was closed due to breaches. The metal fence however had been swung back and people had clearly walked on. I did the same, soon reaching the first of several breaches, about twenty yards long. All had been repaired, although with more work still to be done to properly reinstate the path. Alternatively a simple diversion runs into Levington village then back to the main river wall.

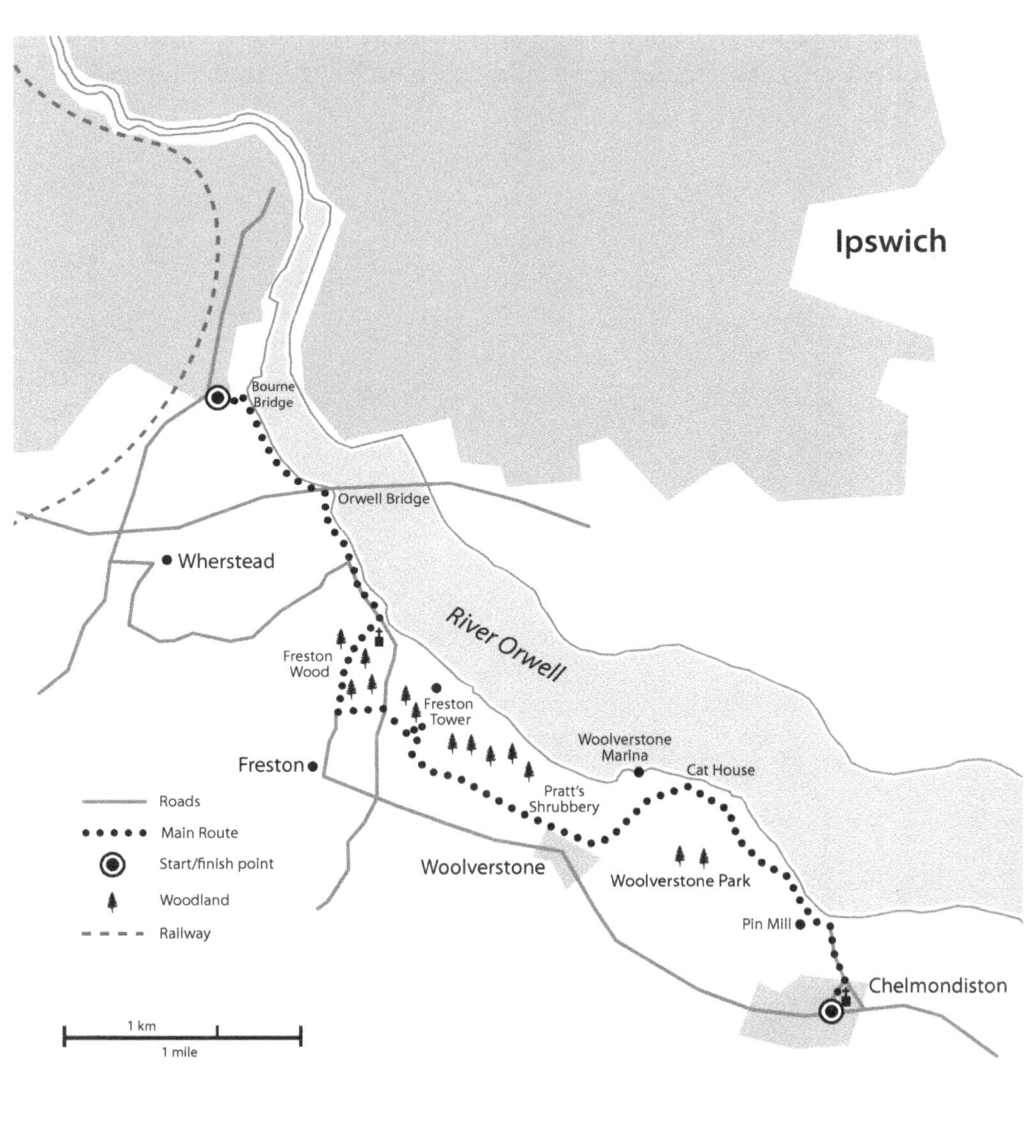

CHAPTER EIGHTEEN
IPSWICH – CHELMONDISTON

(5 Miles) 14th November

Fortified by a large bowl of steaming porridge, I set off back down the Orwell. This was the start of the last section of my coastal walk – Shotley Peninsular, perhaps the least known part of Suffolk's coast. After just two hundred yards I encountered a problem: the footpath was closed. A sign advised that this was for 'Safety Reasons' but dated from 17th May. The temporary fence across the path had been flattened and a well trodden path led to the river. You won't be surprised that I ignored the sign. The top of the river wall looked flat but the grass an unusually light shade of green. One step on the wall explained why – it was newly planted in very soft earth. My foot disappeared into the mud. Even if walking had been easier it wouldn't have been right to damage the grass. I climbed back down the bank and made my way along a muddy track running below.

After half a mile of dodging puddles and slippery mud I stopped under the Orwell Bridge, once more dwarfed by this huge structure which carries 60,000 vehicles a day. Bangs from Ipswich Docks added to the muffled traffic noise from above. The tide was high and a flock of brent geese sat on the water. The track back to the road was covered with several inches of slimy mud. To walk on it would surely mean sliding over. The river wall was still soft earth with young shoots of grass. I thought of turning back but then found I could work my way along the steep grassy bank of a drainage ditch. To slip would have meant a soaking. This wasn't to be recommended. A hissing swan by the gate to the road told me off. He was right, I should have walked on the road – this was one footpath closed sign I shouldn't have ignored.

There's no proper path on the next section, so I made my way along the beach until this turned to salt marsh. After a short stretch on the roadside verge I

Orwell Bridge from South Bank

reached a parking place where spent fireworks were lined up on the grass. They must have made a spectacular display against the backdrop of the Orwell and its bridge. From here little paths ran through the salt marsh. I stopped frequently to look back, taking photos of the contrast between man and nature – delicate colours of salt marsh with its plants and little pools, birds on the river, and looming above the water, lorries thundering over a huge concrete bridge.

Where the road headed inland I took a footpath on the right towards Freston Wood. Another path marked on the map as running parallel with the road didn't exist – it was a ploughed field. I stopped to talk to a lady walking with her dark brown labrador. She used to walk all day long but had cancer last year and was building up again, managing two hours which seemed good going to me, especially on these muddy winter footpaths. She said that at low tide you can walk to Woolverstone on the shore, but that my proposed route was fine, although there were some trees down in the wood and I should look out for falling branches. In the words of Black Adder, *'some kind of hat would be in order'*. In these days of 'health & safety' I was slightly surprised to be able to enter the wood without a man handing out hard hats and liability waiver forms. Freston Wood is an ancient wood of oak, hazel, alder, ash and sweet chestnut. The Stour and Orwell Walk was well signed through a network of paths, but with several diversions around fallen trees it would be easy to go the wrong way here. The 'falling branches' were no more than leaves and a few twigs. My woolly West Ham hat was ample protection.

Walking on a carpet of sweet chestnut husks I made my way out of the wood, emerging onto a little lane by Freston church. A notice on the door advised that the church was locked, *'Regretfully due to circumstances beyond our control'*. The original 14th century building with 15th century tower was restored from a ruined shell by local architect R.T. Orr in 1875.

Continuing along the lane I was soon back on the B1456. A pub marked on the map here, The Boot, is another to have closed in recent years. Turning right then almost immediately left, the path runs into a short cul-de-sac. Twice I walked around then turned back to the main road, seeing no way out and assuming I'd gone the wrong way. It was only on the third exploration that I found a narrow path on the right that squeezes between houses and through a low tunnel of yew trees.

Skirting Tower Plantation, the path took me alongside a field of newly germinated corn. Behind the wood is Freston Tower, a six-storey Tudor folly that looks out across the Orwell. Restored by the Landmark Trust, this is now yet another of Suffolk's unusual holiday lets. The true origin of this curious building has never come to light, but a charming explanation has been put forward by Richard Cobbold, author of *Freston Tower*, in which he says it was built by William Latimer in the 16th century, as a place of study for Ellen, the beautiful young heiress to the De Freestons. Each of the six rooms which form the tower was devoted to a different study and Ellen divided her day between them. Thus she dispensed charity from the ground floor, later going to work on her tapestries on the first floor. After this she would climb to the second floor where she played music, followed by painting on the third floor, literature on the fourth and astronomy on the fifth.

Leaving the path to the tower just before it heads into the woods, I turned sharp right along a track across fields. Ignoring a dead end path to the river, I crossed Mannings Lane and continued past Pratt's Shrubbery, notable for a distinct lack of shrubs. After crossing the entrance to Woolverstone Marina I found myself in a huge grassy playing field with a church in one corner. Approached though a line of neatly trimmed yew trees, the mostly Victorian St Michael's of Woolverstone was firmly locked.

Beyond the church is the magnificent Woolverstone Hall, built by John Johnson in 1776 for William Berners, a property developer from London who had gradually been acquiring extensive landholdings on the Shotley peninsula. The Hall's logo depicts a pair of monkeys, which according to local folklore comes from the occasion when William Berners' pet monkeys raised the alarm after Woolverstone Hall caught fire, so enabling the family to escape unharmed. Following this Berners had statues of monkeys made to adorn the estate. As home to Ipswich High School for Girls, the Hall is yet another wonderful educational setting in this part of Suffolk but sadly with senior fees almost £12,000 per year, in the main only available to those children with well off parents.

A gap in the trees behind the church led to a delightful walk through autumnal woods with glades of sunlit bracken. Looking ahead on the map I'd been intrigued by 'Cat House' marked where the path met the Orwell. It was indeed a house, one for humans not felines, but research was needed to find out more. The citation for its Grade II listing records it as Gothic style dating from 1793, adding *'said to have been used to guide smugglers'*, but with no reference to a cat. A cat is however said to have played a crucial role in the smuggling operation. The house reputedly belonged to a man sympathetic to those carrying contraband along the river, who had his favoured cat stuffed (after it had died I hasten to add) and when he could see that no customs boats were patrolling, put it in the window to signal that the coast was clear. This single house gets its name not only shown prominently on the OS map but also as a geographical feature, Cathouse Point, where the river bends to the south. Incidentally, I spotted an error on the Ordnance Survey map – '*Wolverstone Marina*' and '*Wolverstone Pier*' both missing an 'o'.

Opposite Cat House is the club house of the Royal Harwich Yacht Club. Formed in 1843, the club moved to Woolverstone after World War Two, its old club rooms having been demolished to make way for expansion of the Navy Yard at Harwich. Some very expensive looking yachts bobbed gently in the water alongside the pontoons.

My brief return to the banks of Orwell ended just after the yacht club, as with salt marsh but no sea wall, for the next mile the path runs through more woodland. To my right was Woolverstone Hall and across the choppy river the dome of Orwell Park House rose above trees. Two beautiful buildings providing

The Cat House – Woolverstone

education for some of Suffolk's more privileged children. I wonder if they serve goats' cheese for school dinners.

Pin Mill, the next settlement (or Pinmill according to the OS), has history and notoriety out of proportion to its size. Set in a sheltered anchorage, the hamlet was once a busy landing point for barges and home to many small industries. Sails were sewn, boats repaired, beer brewed and bricks made alongside the river. In 1850 more than fifty stone dredging boats worked out of Pin Mill, bringing in stone for making cement. Many men were engaged in fishing, often supplementing their income by wrecking. Boarding wrecked boats to retrieve saleable gear was a fraught with danger and in October 1862 seven men lost their lives climbing on a half submerged wreck. Four women in Pin Mill were widowed and one mother lost two of her sons.

Thames barges were used to off-load ships anchored in Butterman's Bay, which were too deep in draught to sail up the shallow winding channel to Ipswich. A horse and cart conveyed coal to the Anchor Mill steam flourmill in Chelmondiston, as well as to the villagers' hearths. By the 1950s the use of barges for transporting goods was in decline and a number became houseboats.

Some ended up as rotting hulks, while others continued sailing for recreational use. Around twenty five residents still occupy houseboats along the foreshore, an alternative lifestyle which lends a bohemian charm to the settlement.

Like much of Suffolk's coast, Pin Mill played its part in defending Britain during World War Two. Six high speed naval launches were stationed here and to facilitate landing on the Hard, the army constructed a wooden jetty. Several local barges and little ships joined in the evacuation of Dunkirk and in 1944 landing craft were assembled on the river ready to join the D Day invasion fleet.

Despite its size, unlike many of the small settlements I'd walked through, Pin Mill remains an active little place. Boats are still built and repaired here and yachts sailed from the Hard. Pin Mill Sailing Club has four hundred members and events include an annual Thames barge race.

The path into Pin Mill had taken me through Harry King & Sons boatyard. Established in 1850, the yard employs nine local people, plus Dughy the spaniel, who the company's website describes as *'office paper shredder and guard dog'*. Seven hundred dinghies have been built here, including two for Arthur Ransome, whose book *We Didn't Mean to go to Sea* was set at Pin Mill. His boat *Nancy Blackett* inspired the story of four children who find themselves adrift in a North Sea gale and end up sailing to the Dutch port of Flushing. Ransome sold *Nancy Blackett* in 1939 but always said that she was *'the best little ship'*. In 1988 she was found slowly decaying, tethered to the harbour wall in Scarborough. A car tumbling over the edge almost finished her off, but local man Michael Rines bought her back to Pin Mill for restoration. She's now owned by The Nancy Blackett Trust, which was formed to preserve and sail her, promoting the sort of sailing activities dear to Ransome.

I'd intended to eat lunch sitting by the river, but purely on grounds of research considered it my duty to explore The Butt and Oyster. A roaring fire seemed good reason to stay a while. A bacon sandwich condemned the not very appetising chicken slice I'd bought this morning to stay in my bag. Pin Mill's riverside pub remains the heart of the hamlet, but outsiders have largely replaced a clientele of men making their living from the river, sailors from ships anchored in Butterman's Bay and of course smugglers. I doubt that they would have been eating from a menu that included stilton, goats' cheese, pesto, rocket

The Butt & Oyster – Pin Mill

and sun-dried tomatoes. Most likely though they'd have been as disappointed with my bacon sandwich as I was – a huge pile of salad, not enough bacon and bread that was thick but dry. It might have looked posh but bacon sandwiches are invariably better in a 'greasy spoon'.

With no buses to Pin Mill I walked half a mile up the hill to Chelmondiston, a pleasant if unremarkable village on the road to Shotley. St Andrews church proved to be quite a surprise. Neither ancient nor Victorian, but a 1950s concrete rendered building with a stumpy tower and red tiled roof. St Andrews had followed the familiar pattern of dereliction and 19th century rebuilding, but one night in late 1944 a German V2 rocket almost completely destroyed E.B. Hakewill's 1860 church. It was not Basil Hatcher's 1951 building that I found particularly memorable, but a fine array of brightly coloured embroidered kneelers. I counted 143, many with nautical themes and brightening up an otherwise ordinary church.

With time to spare I wandered up to the Foresters Arms. It was closed and had been since 2008. The car park was overgrown and the building starting to deteriorate. Rural Suffolk seems to do better at keeping churches open than it does pubs. The bus stops outside the Red Lion. Dating from around 1750, this too was closed but only for refurbishment. Ipswich Buses' Number 202 arrived on time and dropped me back at the station. I'd enjoyed my first walk on the Shotley Peninsular but before returning was to explore Suffolk's County Town.

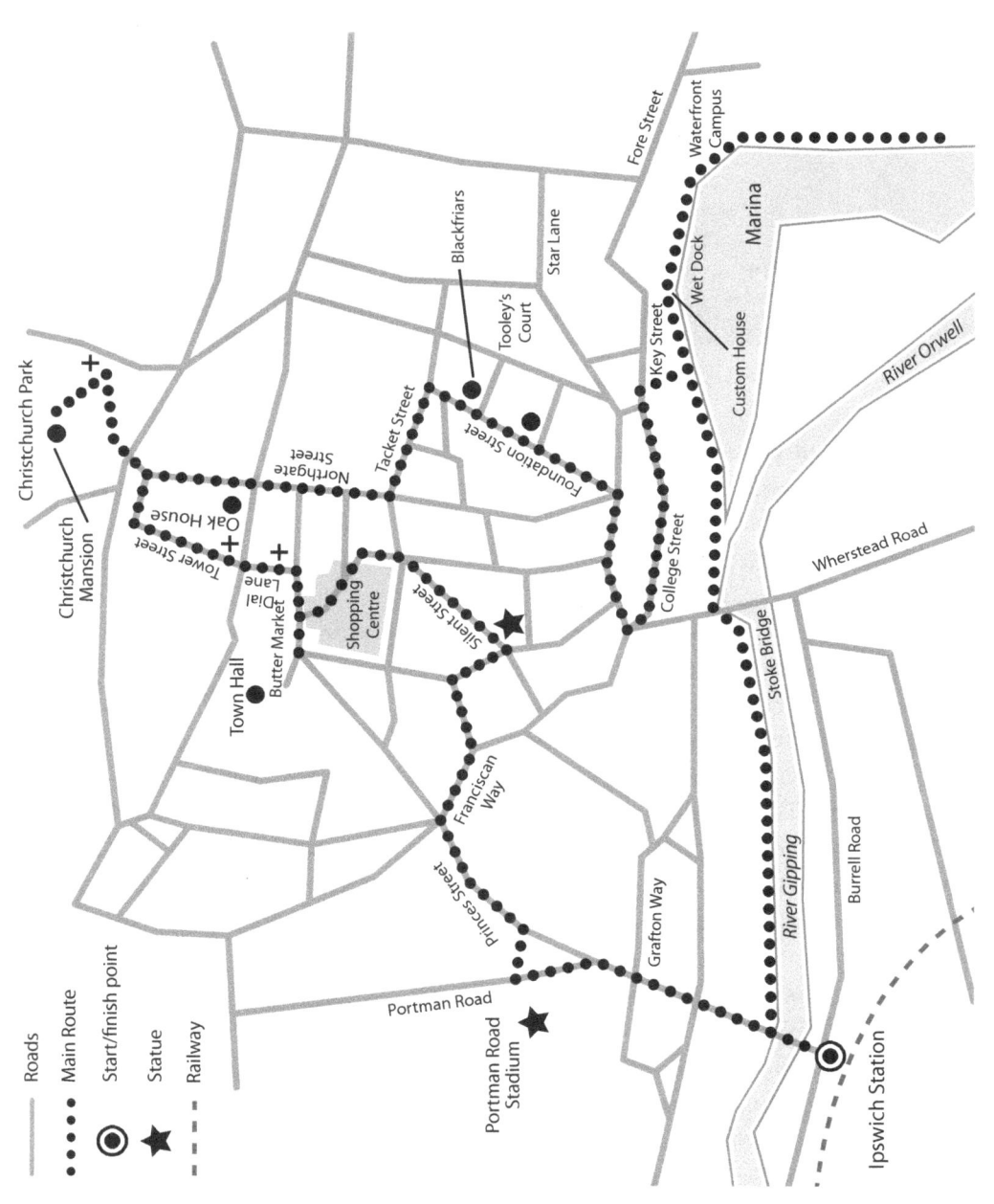

CHAPTER NINETEEN
A WALK AROUND IPSWICH

(3 Miles) 31st December

An internet search for a walking route around Ipswich suggested an article reporting that *'a walk through Ipswich town centre by members of the English Defence League has finished without incident',* the Wikipedia page for *'John Wark, a Scottish former footballer who spent most of his playing time with Ipswich Town'* and a list of hairdressers including *'John Michael, 13 The Walk, Ipswich'.* Eventually I found a leaflet and on a damp New Year's Eve, set off to explore one of Britain's oldest towns.

Crossing the bridge from the station I descended steps to the riverside and turned to the left. Had I turned right, I could have walked seventeen miles to Stowmarket along the Gipping Valley River Path. My walk today would be far shorter and entirely urban. At Stoke Bridge, an ancient crossing place a few hundred yards downstream, the river becomes tidal, changing its name to the more familiar Orwell. Its course from here was altered when New Cut was dug in the 1840s, diverting the river from Ipswich Dock and allowing fresh water from the Gipping to flow out into the Orwell.

Here I left the river as it swung to the right, continuing on to the Waterfront, a name now widely used by towns and cities for their gentrified old docks. Ipswich is no exception, with many of the fine houses and warehouses now converted to restaurants, offices and luxury apartments. One huge warehouse which is yet to be renovated was brightened by colourful paintings on hoardings, part of *The Never Ending Mural*, a community project inspired by the Ipswich Art School Fundraising Appeal and brought to life by curator John Edwards.

Ipswich Wet Dock

A dock was in operation in the 8th century on a bend in the Orwell, at what was then known as Gipeswic and was probably established even earlier. Granted a Royal Licence to export wool in 1404, the port became a major exporter of cloth woven in Suffolk's Wool Towns. Expansion in 1846, with opening of the Wet Dock, transformed Ipswich from a country market town to an industrial centre. Following the pattern of so many ports, by the late 20th century new docks downstream towards Bourne Bridge, combined with industry moving away, left the town centre dock largely derelict. There was talk of filling it in to make a lorry park but renovation has transformed what was once a noisy commercial centre into a popular place to relax beside the water.

On a cold winter's morning there were few people outside, but in the pubs and restaurants staff busily prepared for a hectic evening to come. With four bars, Isaacs, a converted 17th century merchant's house, promised a lively New Year's Eve. Focal point of the waterfront is the Old Custom House, built in classic style in 1845, with steps leading to a raised entrance beneath a four columned portico. Moored opposite was *Victor*, a Thames sailing barge which represented Suffolk and Lord Tollemache, the county's Lord Lieutenant, at the Thames Diamond Jubilee Pageant in June 2012.

Contrasting with the 19th century dock buildings is the modern six storey Waterfront Campus of University Campus Ipswich. Beyond here the dock turns to the right into a section seeing greater commercial use. Moored by the quay were *Alert*, Trinity House's Rapid Intervention Vessel, and *HMC Vigilant*, one of four patrol cutters operated by the UK Border Agency. An officer was sitting on the deck in his socks, vigorously polishing a pair of boots.

Had I have wished, from here I could have continued on a winding path through mostly parkland, joining the walk from Trimley at the Orwell Bridge. Instead I retraced my steps then headed away from the docks to College Street, where two churches stand surrounded by dereliction and wasteland. The medieval St Mary at the Quay closed following damage bomb damage in 1943. It was used by Ipswich Boys Brigade and is now in the care of Churches Conservation Trust. A partnership with Suffolk Mind is converting it into a well-being centre. The 15th century St Peter's, one of the oldest buildings in Ipswich, has fared better. Also closed in the 1970s and badly vandalised, it was re-opened in 2006 as a Heritage Centre and concert venue. Open daily in summer months, today it was firmly closed, with all gates to the churchyard padlocked.

Leaving the dock area, around which the old town of Ipswich had originally built up, in pouring rain I wandered up Foundation Street, stopping to look at Tooley's Court. Henry Tooley first provided homes for the elderly of Ipswich in 1550 and fine 19th century almshouses still serve as sheltered accommodation. In Upper Brook Street I stopped to view the remains of Blackfriars, a Dominican priory built in 1263. The ruins stand rather incongruously amidst modern flats but it is fortunate that they can be seen at all, as local opposition stopped a major road development in the 1970s. Excavation when building the flats uncovered the base of a flint rubble wall, showing the entire outline of what was once the town's largest church.

Tooley's Court

Continuing up Northgate Street my next stop was Oak House, a fine 15th or 16th century semi-timbered house that was formerly the Royal Oak Inn and now home to Jackman Solicitors. The number of historical and interesting buildings in Ipswich was proving a surprise. Even the Baptist church at the top of the road is Grade II listed – an imposing stone building constructed in 1912 with four granite columns.

Turning right I made my way into Christchurch Park, a large open space close to the centre of town and a real asset to Ipswich. Pouring rain wasn't the best weather for a stroll so I contented myself with just a quick look at Christchurch Mansion, a beautiful brick Tudor mansion which was presented to the town in 1895 by Felix Cobbold on the condition that the Corporation bought the surrounding parkland for the people of Ipswich. Open to the public, with free admission, visitors can see rooms preserved as past inhabitants would have known them, and galleries containing the finest selection of Constable paintings outside of London.

St Margaret's Church just outside the park, was firmly locked. Wandering around the churchyard I found benches chained to the ground and 'No Camping' signs amongst the graves. It's a beautiful building but was hardly welcoming. The Robert Ransome on Crown Street looked more enticing. This popular pub is named after the iron works Ransome established here in 1789, which exported agricultural machinery around the world and later built the first railway in China.

At the bottom of Tower Street I finally found a church that was open. Standing on a site occupied by churches for at least eight hundred years, St Mary-le-Tower, with its Victorian spire, is the town's civic church. A smile and hello from a kindly looking lady by the door provided a warm welcome as I came in from the wind and rain. Christmas trees decorated with lights added to the atmosphere. The parish has virtually no resident population, the congregation being drawn from a wide area, but I would concur with Simon Knott that *'it is a friendly one.'*

Along Buttermarket, a pedestrianised shopping street where, would you believe, butter was once sold, is Cornhill, an open square and the centre of the town. Stalls selling hot food were doing a busy trade, while a roundabout gave rides to small children wrapped in many layers of clothes. All a far cry from the mid 16th century when nine 'Ipswich Martyrs' were burnt at the stake here for their Protestant beliefs.

Dominating the square is the rather grand town hall, which dates from 1866 and is currently used for events and art displays. Would it be insensitive of me to mention that as a venue for civic receptions after Ipswich Town win a trophy it has seen little use for many years? Two weeks after my visit it was announced that a new development, including a tower, '*a delicate steel and glass object*', was to be built in front of the Town Hall. David Ellesmere, leader of Ipswich Borough Council, said the new design would '*transform the centre of Ipswich*'. Just a week later though it was announced that only a quarter of the £3.5 million funding was in place, so how many years until the town has its new tower is anyone's guess.

A narrow passage, 'The Walk', runs south of Buttermarket. With overhanging timber-framed buildings it seemed more the sort of street to be found in York or Chester and quite unexpected in Ipswich. In contrast, the 1992 Buttermarket shopping centre has thirty two retail units (didn't they used be called shops?) on two levels, but not an ounce of character. It did though allow a sheltered short cut to the excellent Tourist Information Centre, which provides a fitting use for St Stephen's church that closed in 1975 with the population of its parish probably in single figures.

Turning right into Falcon Street, then left down Silent Street, I reached one of the town's more recent landmarks – a statue of Cardinal Thomas Wolsey who was born in Ipswich in 1470. The bronze by David Annand was unveiled in June 2011 and stands close to the spot where he is believed to have lived.

My circular walk around Ipswich was drawing to a close but I had one more place to visit, and this time somewhere familiar. It was strange to be approaching a football ground with no sign of a crowd, but wearing a claret and blue hat and scarf I soon found myself whistling '*Bubbles*'. Portman Road is a proper football ground, close to the town centre and with four distinct stands. OK it would be better if some were terraces but West Ham fans stand up anyway! I've been here many times but today wanted to look at another statue. One that dare I say means more to most Ipswich folk than that of a 15th century cardinal.

Sir Bobby Robson

Sir Bobby Robson presided over one of the most successful periods in the history of Ipswich Town. During his thirteen years as the club's manager Ipswich were one of the best teams in England, winning both the FA and UEFA Cups. He left to manage England, a job which many believe he should have kept for longer, then despite ill health held various positions within the game, most notably as Newcastle United's manager. On learning that his cancer was terminal Robson's words were typically brave, '*I am going to die sooner rather than later. But then everyone has to go sometimes and I have enjoyed every minute*'. It is a fitting tribute to Sir Bobby that statues in his memory were erected outside both Portman Road Ipswich and St James' Park Newcastle.

Almost back at the river, my walking tour of Ipswich was at an end. And what a surprise it had been – far more to see, more history and more buildings of interest than I had expected. It had been an enjoyable stroll on a wet December afternoon. In better weather one could linger more; stop for an alfresco meal by the docks, wander round Christchurch Park or peruse market stalls. At not much more than an hour from London the town is well placed for tourists. Maybe it should try harder to attract them but perhaps it is better without, a proper English county town which the colour supplements haven't yet discovered.

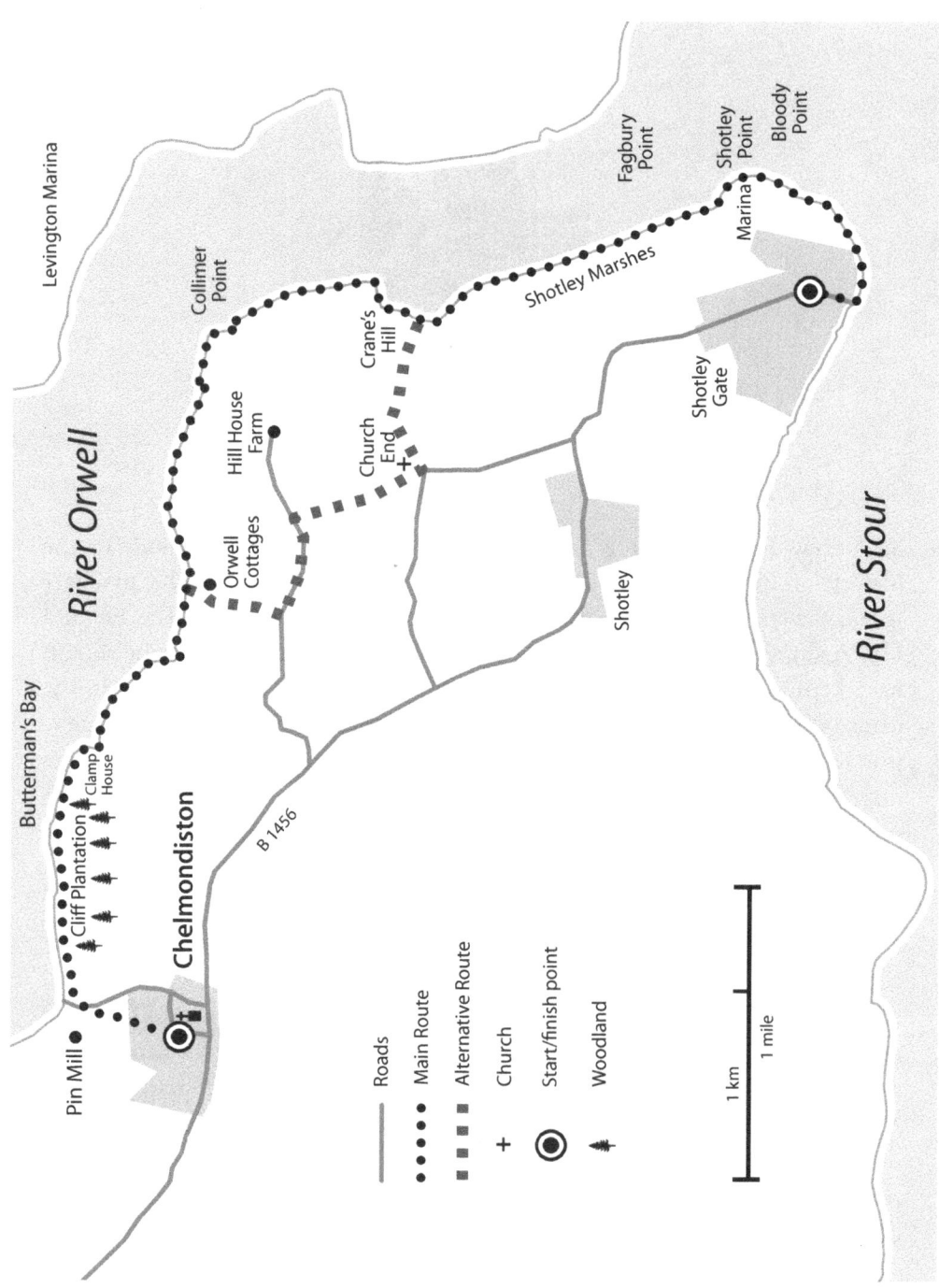

CHAPTER TWENTY
CHELMONDISTON – SHOTLEY GATE

(6 Miles) 4th February

I caught the bacon baguette Norwich express. Sadly the chef didn't. No bacon and no teacakes – I might have to turn to crayfish and basil. It took me fifteen of the twenty minutes wait to work out where the 202 bus to Chelmondiston would stop. I could have taken fifteen more – it was late – heavy traffic the driver told me. Chelmondiston is pronounced 'ChelmonDISTon' he informed me, but say 'Chelmo' and everyone will know what I mean.

Alighting by the still closed Red Lion, I found a path opposite the church down to Pin Mill, where steps up from the lane led up to a lovely path through Cliff Plantation. Donated to the National Trust by Maud Rouse in memory of her husband, this steep hillside woodland affords fine views across the Orwell. Beneath the trees was Pin Mill's community of house boats, with precarious walkways for boarding, plus its fair share of abandoned wrecks being slowly claimed by nature.

Finding a bench above a gap in the trees, I made an instant decision to stop for an early lunch. Here I could look out across the river, where the sun shone on the green dome of Orwell School's observatory. With the ground very wet after a succession of winter storms, there were likely to be few dry places to sit and probably none with such a view.

Emerging from the woods after almost a mile of wonderful walking, I was back at sea level by Clamp House, a very isolated riverside cottage. A short path through salt marsh led to a tiny beach. I stood here a while enjoying the sunshine and views – another little gem of Suffolk's coast. The Orwell Bridge was still just visible to the west, with the cranes of Felixstowe Docks to the east. Directly opposite was the grassy Nacton picnic area where I'd sat before heading inland around Orwell Park on an equally sunny day two months ago.

The path continued on a low wall around a mile of salt marsh. Birdlife abounded and patches of mud were criss-crossed with little footprints. A sign said that the land belonged to the River Orwell Sporting and Conservation Club. Once again I wondered if the latter might be more successful without the former. Ten white geese blocking the path looked determined to stand their ground, but reluctantly shuffled off as I approached.

Just beyond the wooden boathouse of Orwell Cottages a newly erected fence barred the way. 'PATH CLOSED DUE TO FLOODING' said the sign. Bother, it had all been going so well. A printed notice explained that the closure was for safety reasons, and ran from 29th January to 18th February, but that it was intended to operate until 19th August. The notice gave the email address of Martin Williams, the gentleman who had helped me with the missing path on the Deben. Again Mr Williams replied promptly to my email – what helpful people they are at Suffolk County Council. His answer was that the landowner was undertaking repairs to the damage. They would wait to see how these have worked and keep the closure in place to allow the work to stabilise.

Path Closed – Orwell Cottages

Assuming that this was a serious breach, I headed inland. The notice had said there was no alternative route but I found a very pleasant one, along the side of a field by Orwell Cottages, then up the track to Wade's Lane. Ascending the short hill to Charity Farm I passed an elderly cyclist freewheeling down, his two spaniels running enthusiastically on either side.

A sign indicated bed & breakfast half a mile ahead. This was Hill House Farm which I'd found on the internet and would have stayed at had they served evening meals. At two miles from the nearest pub by footpath and at least three by road, it doesn't really suit the walker without a car, but the philosophy of Richard and Hazel who farm 520 acres of arable land deserves repeating:

'We see ourselves as custodians of the land for our lifetime. The land is ours from which to derive our livelihood and then to pass on to the next generation in as good health (or even better) than when we took it on.'

How much better our planet would be if every individual, business and government subscribed to such worthy principles.

At Upper Lodge a footpath took me up a gentle slope towards Church End. Felixstowe Docks re-appeared, looming over the river. Like Gulliver at Lowestoft, Sizewell's white dome, and the lighthouses of Southwold and Orford Ness, the cranes standing tall against the sky are a landmark for many miles of Suffolk walking.

Ignoring a muddy path to the left, I continued to Church End, stopping for a while at the church of St Mary the Virgin. A sign asked that the door be kept shut, *'to stop any unaccompanied pets straying into church'*. In an isolated spot on the low hill overlooking the Orwell, Shotley's church is further from its village than any other in Suffolk. The few houses around the church were in fact its original village, with Shotley then just an outlying fishing hamlet. A growing wind whistled as I sat inside the strangely stumpy church (it has no tower). It must be a wild place in winter gales.

It was however the sloping churchyard looking over the river that provided the greatest surprise – hundreds of war graves. Until 1976 Shotley was home to the

Royal Navy Training College HMS Ganges and sent thousands of young men to war. Several hundred crosses mark the last resting place of brave sailors who lost their lives in unimaginable horror during the two World Wars. Some are graves of men whose bodies were brought back to Suffolk. Others are memorials to those lost in the oceans. Most are named but a few mark the last resting place of unidentified seamen. Amongst the Royal Navy graves are a few of seamen from the British Merchant Navy, some from the Dutch Navy and thirteen Germans from World War One. A fine memorial pays tribute to the many submariners who lost their lives in the Great War.

It was a sobering thought that each concrete headstone commemorates the life of a man, many still teenage lads, who would have drunk in Shotley's pubs, courted its girls and probably walked the very lanes and footpaths that I was following today. One thinks of such cemeteries in France or Belgium, and it was quite a surprise to find a Commonwealth War Graveyard here in rural Suffolk, but is perhaps fitting that this quiet churchyard overlooks the coastline which these men gave so much to defend.

War Graves, Shotley Church

A track running down the hill from the church took me past Witenagemot Wines, a nineteen acre vineyard which produces ten thousand bottles a year. It is thought that wine was first produced here in the 5th or 6th century by monks who grew grapes in the shallow valley.

Crossing a rather wet meadow to the river, I stopped twice to talk to walkers who confirmed that the path from here to Shotley Gate was intact. A new fence and notice on the river wall barred the way back to Pin Mill. The tide was high and a fierce wind whipped up waves as if the Orwell was open sea. A pair of oystercatchers stood unconcerned on the shingle. They were used to such weather but for a walker it was hard going into the strong headwind. This was nothing though; tomorrow 70mph gales were forecast.

Opposite was Fagbury Point, where on a warm autumn afternoon I'd looked across to the Shotley Peninsular, a place I then knew nothing of but was now finding quite enchanting. As the wind drowned out all sounds of the port I watched a DFDS Seaways vessel inch into dock, joining four huge ships piled high with containers. Fifty years ago Britain's docks brought in raw materials and exported finished goods. Sadly now most of the containers would have been filled with goods manufactured in the Far East at prices our declining manufacturing industry can't match.

On the grass by Shotley Point I stopped to talk to a chap with his dog, agreeing it was a bit blowy but '*a nice day for it*'. We watched a yellow rescue helicopter appear, hover low over the river for a moment, then leave as quickly as it had arrived. Behind us a host of yacht masts in Shotley Marina swayed in the wind. A water tower by the marina, another landmark from across the river, was built on the base of a Martello Tower.

The Stour and Orwell Walk crosses the lock gate to the marina, passes through a boatyard and emerges by the Shipwreck pub. Around the gentle curve of the headland was my final Suffolk river, the Stour.

The confluence of the two rivers is known as Bloody Point. The Harwich Society provides possible answers to the inevitable question, what's the bloody point? Anglo-Saxon Chronicles for AD 885 tell us that following a Viking attack on Kent, King Alfred sent a fleet to attack the invaders in East Anglia. '*As soon as they came to Stourmouth, there met them sixteen ships of the pirates, and they fought with them, took all the ships and slew the men. As they returned homeward with their booty, they met a large fleet of pirates and fought with them the same day, but the Danes had the victory*'. It is possible that Bloody Point took its name from this incident, however at that time the river entered the sea north of Felixstowe, so the area would not have been seen as the mouth of the Stour. Alternatively the name may come from the next century when Vikings returned to the estuary, twice plundering Ipswich.

A stretch of road walking behind flood barriers took me to The Bristol Arms and the village of Shotley Gate. Named after the Marquis of Bristol, who owned the land and foreshore of Shotley Gate, there has been a Bristol Arms overlooking the River Stour since the mid-1800s. The pub closed in June 2012, but bucking the trend, was reopened by landlord Shane Rolin later that year. His aims were to concentrate on food, support local farms and maintain the rustic village feel. I'd liked to have stopped, but with a bus to catch headed up the hill into the village.

Shotley Gate was deserted. I saw no one on the streets and was the village shop's sole customer as I bought my late afternoon Kit Kat. My last few walks had lacked the frequent opportunities for toasted tea cakes found on the more touristy parts of Suffolk's coast. Standing high over the village is the mast of the steam ship *HMS Cordelia,* which was erected on the parade ground of HMS Ganges in 1907. The 44 metre mast, which would once have been climbed by trainee sailors in ceremonial mast mannings, now stands forlornly over the derelict and slightly eerie abandoned site. Barbed wire and Keep Out signs abound. Just the squawks of gulls punctuated the silence, where once the chatter of two thousand young men and the shouts of their officers would have drifted across the cliffs.

A museum by the marina (open summer weekends) tells the story of HMS Ganges, detailing its history as the Royal Navy's flag-ship, a boys' training ship at Falmouth and Harwich, and the shore based training centre here at Shotley. After closing in 1976 HMS Ganges was used for police training but with years of abandonment the weather is taking its toll. In November 2013 permission was granted to build 285

HMS Ganges

homes, a hotel, a sixty bed nursing home, retail and commercial units. There were local objections, but with a commitment to use many of the existing buildings and restore the listed ceremonial mast, it seems a sensible solution to me.

I was the only passenger on the Number 98 back to Ipswich. Once again I alighted at Bourne Bridge for a night in the Premier Inn. Once again friendly staff provided a welcoming atmosphere, rather than the impersonality of so many chain hotels. I chatted to Chris on reception, mentioning Katie who'd been on duty last time, who it transpired, was his sister. Next morning she was working and as I checked out asked how my walk was going. It's nice to be remembered. I would have liked to have stayed at Shotley, but the Premier Inn had served me well on my peninsular walks.

Post Script

Alighting from the bus on a very warm June morning I noted that the Red Lion was now open and very nice it looked. It was again a lovely walk through Cliff Plantation, the wood at its best with trees in leaf but some of the winter views to the river now obscured. Some of these return walks had given me the benefit of seeing the same places in different seasons.

It was a long time since I'd needed to find a shady spot for lunch but a large tree by the salt marsh fitted the bill. A corn field red with poppies delayed me for a while as photos simply had to be taken, before reaching Orwell Cottages and the moment of truth. Would the path be open? Yes was the answer. The wooden fence had been removed and now lent against a hedge, its closure notices already partly obscured by brambles.

The mile and a half to Crane's Hill where I'd rejoined the river wall last time were a superb walk with views across the water to Levington and its marina and abundant bird life. Several partial breaches had been repaired but the damage to the wall was less severe than that I'd seen elsewhere. My recommendation would be to follow the river rather than the inland route I'd taken in February but perhaps with a diversion up the hill to see the war graves at Shotley church.

Shotley – Harwich Ferry

My plan had been to take the bus back from Shotley Gate but enjoying a cold drink sitting outside the Shipwreck I made a snap decision. In summer a ferry links Shotley with Harwich and it was due to leave in twenty minutes. I could get the train from Harwich to Manningtree and make a circular trip. What a good idea. Sea spray and a cooling breeze off the water were most welcome on the short crossing. Welcome to Essex said the boatman as we disembarked.

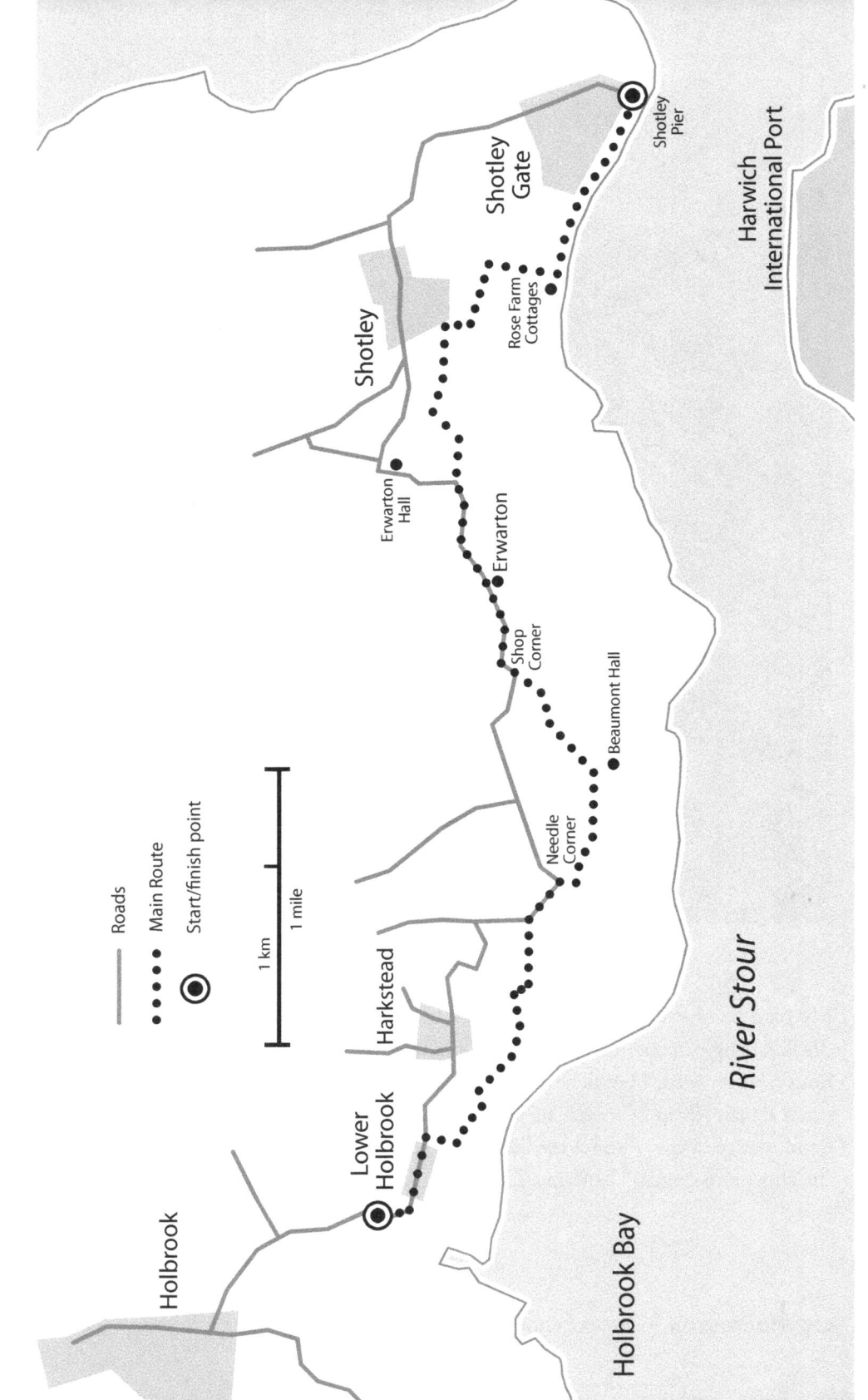

CHAPTER TWENTY ONE

SHOTLEY GATE – LOWER HOLBROOK

(6 Miles) 5th February

The weather forecast had promised fierce storms, with 70mph winds in Suffolk by lunchtime. They seemed to have arrived early. At 6am I was woken by wind howling round the hotel and hail battering the window. The TV still said that the worst of the weather would be here later, so leaving my warm bed and getting the walk done this morning seemed a sensible plan. Breakfast was enjoyed with the accompaniment of chatter of two young boys, eating here for a treat with their Mum – a pleasant change from the mobile phones of business people who generally populate the Premier Inn in midweek. As I returned to my room the car park was covered with a carpet of hailstones. It was going to be a wild day.

The bus was late – an accident on the A14 the driver said. The rain would be here at 12 o' clock he told me, with far more certainty than the weather lady had on the TV. But bus drivers are always right. I know because my wife is one. As I alighted at the Bristol Arms after a tour along what seemed to be most of the lanes of Shotley Peninsular, he bade me farewell, adding that he hoped it would stay dry. We agreed that it wouldn't. With the already strong wind due to strengthen and torrential rain on its way, I decided that today's walk would be at high speed, with few stops or diversions. My aim was to get the 12.29 bus back from Lower Holbrook.

Turning right and heading up the Stour, I set out along a footpath that gives hope to those who fear that accelerating erosion will eventually put an end to long stretches of coastal walking. After more than fifty years of exposure to the ravages of the tidal Stour, the steel piles that protected a long established footpath at the base of Shotley Cliff were breached. The path became impassable at even the most modest of high tides and with concrete piles also collapsing, access was hazardous. Shotley Parish Council responded to the concerns of local residents, but none of the bodies they turned to wanted to accept responsibility. With the cliff slumping and trees in danger of sliding onto the beach, a group of local people took matters into their own hands. The Shotley Stour Footpath Renovation Group was formed.

After much discussion with the various statutory bodies, by early 2010 a plan was in place to protect 258 metres of Shotley Cliff. Rather than sheet piles, which reflect rather than absorb energy, and tend to flood the path as splash-over water cannot drain back, the plan was to use a stepped design of gabions. Formed of wire mesh filled with local stone, these absorb wave energy and allow surface water to drain, so preventing waterlogging. This simple and relatively low cost scheme, which will protect the coastline for at least twenty five years, opened in August 2011.

Thanks to the work of those few residents of Shotley Gate it was an easy start to my walk today. The sun was still shining and although the wind seemed to be strengthening, it was directly behind, whipping up waves and blowing me up the river. The gabions would be needed later today. Across the water was the port of Harwich with its distinctive and historic railway station. I exchanged greetings with a man walking his dog, '*Bit breezy*' we agreed.

Beyond the new defences the path runs along the edge of a field. The map shows a riverside path all the way to Holbrook, but I had been told this is impassable and the Stour and Orwell Way diverts inland. With major storms forecast and the tide rising, attempting to get through along the beach seemed unwise. At Rose Cottages a footpath sign points down the river, but I took the safer option of a track heading inland.

As I studied my map by Shotley Cottage, an unusual house with six tall chimneys, a lady asked if I was lost. She often walks by the river and directed me back to the water, but as she doesn't go as far as Holbrook and wasn't sure you can get through, I opted to stick to my inland plan along the waymarked paths.

She offered me the loan of her dog for company. Doggy looked keen but I had to disappoint him as he'd need to get the bus back and didn't have the fare.

Turning left, then right, I walked across fields almost into Shotley village, before two more left turns took me into a small wood. A man coming the other way got his two black labradors to sit as I approached. We agreed it was breezy. I commented how well behaved the dogs were but was told, *'They have their moments'*.

At a small reservoir the Stour and Orwell Walk turns right towards Erwarton Hall, but I continued straight on, a more direct route, which although including a mile of road walking, would save me half an hour – essential if I was to catch the early bus and avoid the predicted downpour. I'd been past the 16th century Erwarton Hall on the bus, noting its unusual brick gatehouse. Ignoring a path back to the river, on reaching The Street (yet another – with so many roads across the county having this same name the postmen of Suffolk must have been glad when postcodes were invented), I turned left into the village of Erwarton. Despite a population of little more than a hundred the village still keeps its church, which was to be my first stop of the day.

St Mary's Church Erwarton

My notes *'looks very old'* were correct, St Mary's dates from the 15th century, although the top of the tower is a more recent repair following a lightning strike in 1837. The interior is fairly simple but with some fine stained glass. The churchyard provides a superb view across the Stour, however it is for another Suffolk legend that the St Mary's is best known. Most of our historical legends seem to involve either Mary Queen of Scots or Anne Boleyn. In Erwarton's case it is the latter.

Anne's uncle, Sir Phillip Calthorpe, who had married her aunt, owned Erwarton Hall and according to legend Anne Boleyn spent time here as a child. It is said that before her execution she was heard to say that the happiest days of her life were spent at the Hall and that she gave instructions for her heart to be buried in the church. In 1838 when the north aisle was being renovated a small, heart-shaped casket containing brown powder was discovered in the wall. The metal casket was reburied beneath the organ with a small plaque marking the spot.

Predictably historians cast doubt on this romantic tale, pointing out that heart burial had gone out of fashion in England by the end of the fourteenth century. Some say that the story could not possibly be true because Erwarton Hall was built in 1585 and Anne Boleyn beheaded in 1536, however it is the current brick hall that dates from the 16th century, and was in fact a re-build of an older hall. Anne Boleyn's paternal aunt, Jane Boleyn, did indeed marry Sir Philip Calthorpe, so Anne may well have visited the hall. But even if the dust of Anne Boleyn's heart does not lie beneath St Mary's organ, there is still intrigue and mystery. Did the workers find a casket and if so who had hidden it in the wall? Was it a Victorian hoax 'found' to support the legend? Or is there a casket at all?

Next to the church is a short line of low cottages, a gift to the poor of Erwarton from Sir Peter Parker, Calthorpe's successor at the Hall, and said to be Anne Boleyn's uncle who was responsible for burying her heart in the church. Further down the lane, the 17th century Queens Head is yet another Suffolk pub to have closed. Owner James Buckle reluctantly shut the doors in July 2009 saying, *'The Queen's Head has, in spite of the best efforts of management and staff, failed to reach a sustainable turnover. We are not the first rural local to close and sadly I don't think we will be the last.'*

Continuing on The Street, I met up with the Stour and Orwell Walk. It looked like a nice walk past Erwarton Hall and Warren Bottom, and avoids roads, so in normal weather would have been my preferred route. Mind you, the worst of the weather hadn't arrived yet. The sun still shone, just occasionally obscured by white clouds that scuttled hurriedly by, seemingly apologetic that they'd got in its way.

At Shop Corner (a corner but no shop) the path leaves the lane and descends a gentle slope towards another reservoir. After a short battle with the wind for ownership of my map, I worked out that the way forward was to follow the right bank of the water then descend towards a very muddy field and over a little wooden bridge towards Beaumont Hall. Dating from the 16th century or earlier, the hall also has its Anne Boleyn connection, a heart in the diapering which is said to represent that of the beheaded Queen.

Approaching Needle Corner, where the footpath rejoins the lane, I watched the 98 bus trundling by on its roundabout route towards Shotley Gate. It was touch and go whether I'd make it to Lower Holbrook in time to catch it returning to Ipswich. The wind was though doing its best to help – it would have been a much harder walk in the opposite direction. Clouds were gathering but the rain had only a few minutes to fulfil the bus driver's forecast.

At Boleyns Covert (Anne's favourite wood?) the footpath heads off to the left across fields. Running parallel to the Stour, the rather muddy paths afforded good views of the river and into Essex. Any walkers in need of refreshment can easily divert into Harkstead, another typically spread out Suffolk village, but unlike many, retaining its pub. The Victorian Baker's Arms reopened in 2008 and would make a convenient stop for anyone walking all the way to Manningtree. With today's weather forecast (official and bus driver) I was glad to have decided to split the Suffolk Stour into two walks.

The path continues to Holbrook Creek, but I took a right fork into the little settlement of Lower Holbrook, reaching the road by a rather overgrown pond on the green. Turning left, I slackened my pace, arriving at the car park and bus stop with a whole ten minutes to spare. A sign pointed out that there 'is no such thing as the dog poo fairy'. Still the sun shone and the rain held off. It arrived as my train home stopped at Colchester. The bus driver's prediction was late – like his bus.

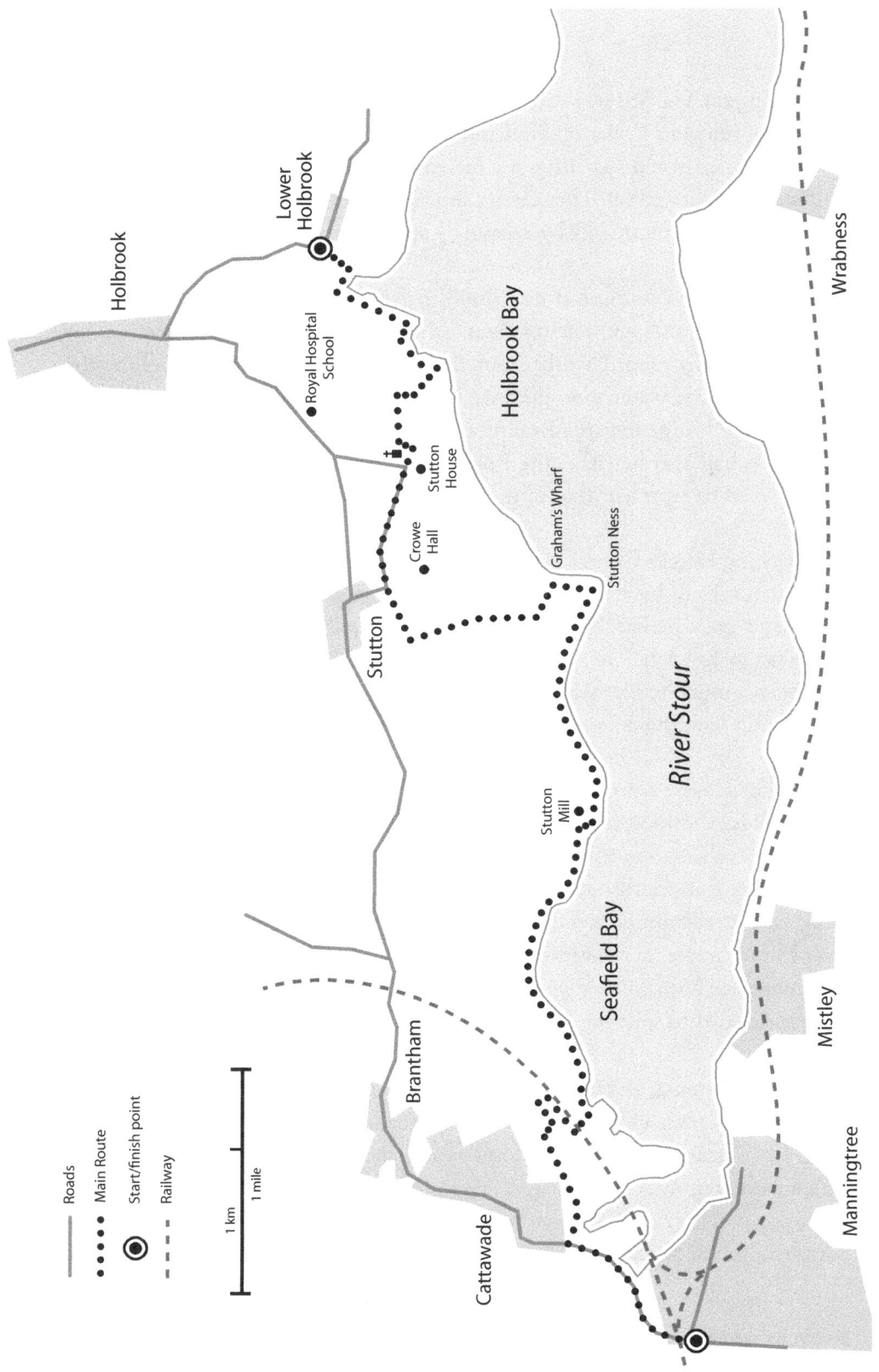

CHAPTER TWENTY TWO
LOWER HOLBROOK – CATTAWADE

(7 Miles) 3rd March

It was with a little sadness that I boarded the Norwich express, knowing that today my walk along this most varied coast was to be completed. By just one day I was to meet my aim of walking the coast of Suffolk in a year, seeing the county in all seasons.

Arriving at Ipswich in bright sunshine, I walked down to Portman Road to photograph Bobby Robson's statue in somewhat better weather than my New Year's Eve visit, before catching the 98 bus along the now familiar road under the Orwell Bridge. Lower Holbrook was considerably calmer than I'd left it three weeks ago, and after a few minutes walk down a track from the car park I was back by the Stour at Holbrook Creek.

With the sun out, the tide high and boats bobbing on the water, this was another lovely little spot on Suffolk's coast. A boathouse on the left bank belongs to The Royal Hospital School, whose grand buildings stood beyond a field to the right. A farmer and his dogs had just rounded up a flock of sheep, who were now bunched together in a pen baaaing their disapproval. As well as being an excellent area for bird watching, Holbrook Creek is one of the few places in Suffolk where the rare Lesne's earwig has been found.

The Royal Hospital School was founded in 1712 for the sons of officers and men from the Royal Navy and Royal Marines. Housed at Greenwich, in what is now the National Maritime Museum, it moved to Holbrook 1933. Until relatively recently entry was restricted to children and grandchildren of seafarers, and naval tradition is maintained with pupils wearing Royal Navy uniforms for ceremonial events. One of the country's leading independent co-educational boarding schools, and the largest in East Anglia, its neo-Georgian buildings with 60 metre high clock tower look out across the Stour, a beacon for many miles around. Its 200 acres of grounds include sports pitches and that essential for every school, a parade ground.

I must just mention a story from a few months earlier when my wife drove a coachload of school rugby teams to Holbrook for Saturday morning matches. After parking on the parade ground and enjoying food provided in the hall, she came across another coach driver staring at a 'map' on the wall. As he struggled to locate the toilets, she had to point out to him that this was not actually a map of the extensive school buildings, but a chart of the periodic table of chemical elements!

At the head of the creek are the remains of wharves that were once used to load hay and straw for the horses of London, with return cargoes of muck swept from the streets to be spread on local fields. Building materials used in the construction of the Royal Hospital School were unloaded here and locally produced bricks transported out.

It was slow going on a muddy path, with frequent stops for photos. A brief pause to greet a couple watching birds turned out to be a longer stop. Tony told me that the line of wooden posts stretching out into the river were fish traps.

The Royal Hospital School

They didn't know how old, but at least the sixty years that they had lived here. Rather longer than that is the answer; AD650 – 850 according to an archaeological study published by English Heritage. Sandy told me that her parents originated from Birmingham and moved to Holbrook in the 1930s, when her father, a plumber, came to work on fitting out the school. He met her mother here and Sandy was brought up with the freedom to roam around the school as she wished, playing on the fields and roller skating on the parade ground. It was a privilege to grow up here she said.

As we chatted, Brian, another local man joined us. He told me that if you know where to go, at low tide it's possible to walk to Cattawade on the mud, but we agreed that the paths are safer. Before heading our separate ways they pointed out a pink cottage by St Peter's church in which Griff Rhys Jones lives. I might see him cutting his hedge as I walked by.

With a mile of sea wall barred to public access, the path turns inland, running past fenced paddocks and the school playing fields, before reaching a pleasant green in front of St Peter's church. Markwell House, Griff Rhys Jones' 17th century, timber-framed farmhouse stands at the bottom of the green. With neatly trimmed hedges there was no need for the comedian turned travel presenter to be outside today.

Fish Traps, Holbrook Creek

Beautifully situated behind the green, a mile from the centre of its village of Stutton, St Peter's church was notable for a fine millennium window, and for having tea and coffee left out for thirsty visitors to make themselves a drink. The first church organ was installed here in 1902, allowing a somewhat greater range of hymns to be sung than in the previous century. From 1832 music had been supplied by a barrel organ which played only twelve tunes, although things improved in 1849 when a second was purchased, doubling the repertoire.

This was to be the last of many Suffolk churches that I'd stopped at. Other than in Ipswich, virtually all had been left open, providing a welcome, peace, shelter and a window on the communities they serve. Whatever one's religious views, few could argue that the countryside is not enhanced by these historic buildings, erected and maintained to the glory of God.

The village of Stutton once clustered around the church, but just a few houses remain, the rest, according to legend, having been purposely burnt down in an attempt to stop the spread of the plague. This part of Suffolk saw the last English cases of plague, with sixteen deaths between 1906 and 1918 in Shotley, Trimley, Freston and Erwarton. Wildlife was found to be infected and eventually it was realised that rats were spreading the disease. The Council asked farmers to exterminate them, although declined to foot the bill for the poison.

An unfenced lane heads east with fine views across the Stour. A train whistle came not from Suffolk, but the scenic Harwich branch line which runs just above the river's south bank. To the right a host of yacht masts were the only clue that a mile away was Alton Water reservoir, the largest area of inland water in Suffolk. Passing the attractive gatehouse of Crowe Hall, I got just a glimpse of the early 17th century mansion, but casual visitors were not welcome – 'Strictly Private, Trespassers will be Prosecuted'.

As the lane turns sharp right towards Stutton village, I continued straight on along Hyams Lane, a rather muddy track past a handful of cottages. A black and white cat watched me pass. A footpath continues between two fields, reaching a crossroads by a single house, where after careful studying of the map, I turned towards the river along Crepping Hall Drive. A prominent 'Private Road' sign should not deter walkers as this is a public footpath. Crepping Hall is not named on the OS map, but the red-bricked frontage of the manor house which once belonged to Colne Priory, can be seen by a small wood on the left.

A footpath continues down a gentle slope but still not a hundred percent sure I was on the right track, I asked a couple coming the other way. Yes it did lead to the river they said, but it was hard to go much further as the path was eroded and the tide too high to walk on the beach.

A grassy river bank provided a fitting place to enjoy the last lunch of my Suffolk walks. With the tide high and water just inches from my feet, this was yet another lovely spot. I reflected on the different places I'd stopped to eat over the year of walking – beaches, heaths, woods, fields, salt marsh, creeks, sea and estuaries. Such is the variety of Suffolk's wonderful coastline.

The remains of Graham's Wharf to my left illustrated how the coast has changed. Now just darkened wooden posts in the water, like many of the jetties and wharves I'd passed on my walks, barges would once have docked here, bringing materials to isolated communities and taking away local produce. Suffolk's rivers were once its highways, but although ships still sail up the Orwell to Ipswich and a few use the Stour to Mistley in Essex, most river traffic is now for pleasure rather than commerce.

River Stour near Graham's Wharf

Turning right, a short walk behind a line of trees took me to Stutton Ness, where a sand and shingle bar curves into the river. With the tide high, only a short length remained above the water, but in sunshine with good views up, down and across the Stour, this was yet another spot to add to my list of Suffolk coast gems.

From here walking became more difficult. The footpath is signed along the beach but that was completely under water. The alternative, a narrow path on the cliff top, is somewhat hairy, with erosion having left several sections on overhangs at the cliff edge. Brambles across the path suggested that few walk on it and I stopped several times to consider whether it was safe to go on. Bones of bison, lion and straight tusked elephants have been found in these soft and crumbly 200,000 year old cliffs, and I had no wish to add those of a 21st century human walker. Had the cliffs been high I would have turned back, but my conclusion that a fall would be painful rather than fatal led me to proceed with caution. Again I made my own my risk assessment but the safest advice is to avoid high tide and walk on the beach.

At Chestnut Spinney the path drops to river level. A couple picking up shells on the beach asked if I'd seen a hairy grey dog, but didn't seem too concerned that I hadn't. Patches of primroses in the woods told that spring was here. After a slow start this morning I was now making good progress, and stopped only to photograph a dead tree lying across the beach. With patches of woodland this was an enjoyable stretch of coast and reminded me of the north bank of the Deben. It is hard to say which is the most picturesque of Suffolk's river estuaries. Some say the Butley, but like the Blythe and Alde, there is limited access for walkers. These three are probably the quietest, whilst the Stour and particularly the Orwell, are still working rivers. All are beautiful rivers, but for me I think the Deben was favourite, the stretch from Ramsholt to Methersgate being one of the best of the whole walk.

At Newmill Creek the path runs along a grassy bank, passing Stutton Mill, a fine house on the water's edge. A black swan watched me walk by what is yet another lovely spot. Unable to find any published information on the mill, I contacted Stutton Local History Group, and received a most helpful reply. I have included most of the information so that it may be publicly recorded.

Dead Tree near Chesnut Spinney

Stutton New Mill is shown on Hodskinson's map of 1783 and was powered both by the tide and the Bentley and Dodnash streams. With the extra efficiency this provided the mill was able to produce sufficient to send at least part of its production to London by sea. Records show that in 1844 Stannard and Death were corn millers at the New Mill, and by 1855 the mill had been taken over by Christopher Spanton Sadler. By 1883 his place had been taken by Richard Blake, who was using a steam engine as well as water power. It appears that the New Mill was out of use by 1900, which is confirmed by the 2nd edition of the Ordnance Survey 1.2500 map which says '*Stutton New Mill (disused)*'. What remains of the mill is now the private home of Lady Green, widow of the late Sir Peter Green.

As I followed the wall around the gentle curve of Seafield Bay the sounds of human activity once more intruded into the river's peace. Bangs from Mistley Docks across the Stour and the distant roar of a Norwich-bound train, competed with the calls of birds, the sloshing of waves and rustling from a gentle wind. I had enjoyed every mile of Suffolk's coast, but like Essex, my favourite bits were probably those furthest from civilisation, where few venture to walk, and where it was just me and nature by the water.

A glance at the map showed less than two miles to go. I kept stopping to look back. This wasn't a walk I wanted to end. The Stour and Orwell Walk turns inland at Brantham Hall Sluice, but I stayed on the river bank, following a path that's shown on the map but not signed. Steps led up to a railway crossing where I waited for a train to pass. The driver who hooted and acknowledged my wave was the first person I'd seen for three miles.

The next short section was quite a contrast; a very wet path around a largely derelict industrial area. After splashing through puddles, to avoid ankle deep water I climbed the fence and walked on the side of the railway embankment until the path turns sharp left, passing a decoy pond and coming out on Factory Lane.

The 130 acre site, which spans both sides of the railway line, was purchased by BX Plastics in 1887 to relocate their plastics factory from London, as nitro cellulose explosives were employed in the process and the Capital wasn't considered a safe place to use such dangerous materials. Proximity to the Stour enabled goods to be brought in by barge. The company built an extensive array of factories, workshops and warehouses, which at one time provided work for over five thousand employees. The nearby village of Brantham was built to house the massive workforce.

In 1946 part of BX Brantham site merged with Ilford, forming a new company, Bexford, to produce the base for photographic film, as following World War Two the government had realised the importance of Britain having its own source of film for reconnaissance. Later it became an ICI plant, which twenty years ago I'd visited to assist with an adhesive problem, but closed down in 2007. Also closed is the large plastics plant, which had a series of owners, most notably Storeys who bought it for a penny in 1977.

A remnant of industry still remains on the estate and a smell of solvent in the air seemed a fitting reminder of what was once here, but most of the site is now derelict. Neat heaps of rubble show the outlines of demolished buildings. Others still stand – intriguing industrial archaeology – but for how much longer? There is talk of a new housing development. Overgrown car parks haven't seen a vehicle for years, but signs remain advising that parking is 'at owner's risk'.

It was at BX Plastics that a certain chemistry graduate took her first job in 1947 – a Miss Margaret Roberts who was to become Margaret Thatcher. How apt that this derelict concrete wasteland, which was once a site of activity, innovation and employment, should be associated with the Prime Minister who decimated so much of our country's industry.

Leaving the industrial wasteland behind and turning left along a few yards of river wall, I found one final attractive spot on Suffolk's coast. Yet another contrast – this one of motion and stillness. River water rushed through Cattawade Sluice, a foaming stream splashing over the mud. Beside the water a heron stood statuesque. Above the sluice a swan swam serenely across a pool of dark slow-flowing water. Behind the pool an 18th century red-brick bridge crosses the creek; a bridge that would have once taken packhorses across the water, then cars and now fittingly for this last quiet spot on the county's coast, just pedestrians.

Walking through a car park took me onto the main A137 road, past Cattawade Barrage and on to The White Bridge, the county boundary. 'Welcome to Suffolk' greets those crossing into the county. I stopped for a moment, looking up the Stour towards Flatford Mill, then down towards Harwich on one bank and the little known Shotley Peninsular on the other.

Those coastal walkers who take the ferry from Felixstowe miss much by not following the Orwell and Stour estuaries. Indeed my whole walk had been greatly enhanced by choosing to walk up and down the rivers, adding much to the variety of the coast. The Suffolk Coast Path from Lowestoft to Landguard Point is about sixty miles of beautiful walking along cliffs, beaches and rivers, passing through heathland, meadows, woods and dunes. My walk had been almost three times the length and complementing the glorious open coast, took me along some of England's least known but most peaceful rivers.

When I'd started my Essex Coast Walk at The White Bridge there had been no sign to welcome travellers arriving in Essex. Perhaps the Council read the book for now those leaving Suffolk receive appropriate greeting as they cross the border. Half a mile down the road I was at Manningtree station. In the absence of a toasted tea cake I chose a very sticky treacle tart in the station buffet – a treat to finish my walk.

The End!

As we'd looked across the Stour at Holbrook Creek this morning I'd commented that the southern Suffolk and northern Essex coasts are quite similar. Sandy had disagreed, Suffolk was far superior. Having now walked both counties I could perhaps try to compare. There are many similarities – both are beautiful coasts with much history, wildlife and interesting geographical features. Both have remote spots which few people visit and places that can be over-run on sunny summer weekends. The coasts of both counties are constantly changing in outline and the way they are used. Suffolk is more varied, while Essex has even greater remoteness. Suffolk definitely has more goats' cheese, rocket and basil. Rather than board the train home, I would have been just as happy to carry on walking back down the Stour to Harwich and the creeks of Essex, or to have turned round and headed back to Lowestoft.

I hope I may have inspired a few others to explore the varied coast of Suffolk. You'll like Southwold, find Dunwich is interesting and enjoy the fish and chips at Aldeburgh, but venture out onto the expanses of shingle, mysterious marshes, heaths and remote rivers, and there you will find the true glory of Suffolk's coast.

UPDATES 2026

Chapter One – There has been further erosion south of Hopton. The path is now routed around the former radar station. There is a good cliff-top path above the beach which now diverts inland slightly further north at Corton Cliffs. Lowestoft has done nothing more to mark Ness Point and Euroscope looks neglected, some of the copper plaques having been crowbarred and stolen. Gull Wing Bridge, a bascule bridge across Lake Lothing, opened in 2024, relieving congestion in Lowestoft. The number of B&B establishments in the town has reduced considerably. Edingworth Guest House is now a holiday let. I stayed at South Beach B&B. The Hatfield Hotel no longer serves a daily carvery. I enjoyed an excellent and very reasonable dinner at the Iconic Bar & Grill. Lowestoft is still cheap!

Chapter Two – Buses no longer go down to the beach at Kessingland but it is only a few minutes' walk from the Southwold bus stop on Wash Lane. The brick soakaway chamber at Benacre Beach has been lost to the sea but as the tide was high I wasn't able to see if any signs of it remain. There has been further erosion and a sign at Benacre Pumping Station advises that the beach route to Southwold is no longer passable at Easton cliffs.

Chapter Three – There is a chapter on Walberswick station and the Southwold Railway in my book *Remote Stations*. Limited clearance of the station site is being carried out by Halesworth to Southwold Narrow Gauge Railway CIO.

Chapter Four – Jasmine B&B has closed and is now a private house. My wife accompanied me on this visit and we stayed at the excellent Bay Hotel, formerly the Blyth Hotel and once the Railway Hotel. Some of the machines on the Under the Pier Show have changed. We spent two pounds on the most amusing TRUST WILDLIFE, '*All the secrets seagulls know about us human beings!*'.

Chapter Five – Whilst usually still rowed, the Walberswick Ferry is now sometimes a motorboat. The ferryman told me that they are getting old and the tides stronger.

Chapter Six – The Ebb & Flow Project sculptures in Black Heath Wood have gone. A new set of sculptures by Ryan Gander, with the title '*To Give Light (Northern Aspirations Charms), 2016*', can be seen at Snape Maltings.

Chapter Seven – There is no longer a regular bus service to Snape but Katchalift.com offers a bookable bus between Framlingham, Wickham Market & Snape. My attempt to walk from Snape to Iken was thwarted by the boardwalk being flooded. It was like walking on a wobbly raft. Beware very high tides!

Chapter Eight – Ashanwell B&B has closed.

Chapter Ten – RSPB South Suffolk Coast Warden Mike Marsh told me that the hares on Havergate Island are doing well. Numbers fluctuate and recently the population has been in the region of 12-15 individuals.

Chapter Eleven – Richmond B&B closed in 2014 but Sue & Chris still have a self-catering bungalow in Hollesely.

Chapter Twelve – There is no longer a service bus to Felixstowe Ferry. The summer open-top service ceased after Ipswich Buses sold the 43-year-old vehicle because it did not meet accessibility or emission rules.

Chapter Thirteen – In 2025 eleven miles of new access rights, forming part of a 26-mile route around the Deben from Bawdsey to Felixstowe Ferry, opened as part of the King Charles III England Coast Path. Some of the wrecks in the Deben between Melton and Woodbridge have been removed. When I walked past Melton Boatyard a decaying barge was in the process of being broken up. HMS Vale, a former Swedish Navy missile attack craft, was moored close to Melton Boatyard in 2018 and is now a café bar.

Chapter Fourteen – Woodbridge tide mill was closed for external restoration in 2025. The £60,000 cost was mainly raised from donations, topped up with grants. A full-sized replica of Sutton Hoo's King's Ship is being built in The Longshed at

Woodbridge. A new sculpture, *The Sisters*, depicting two women in a rowing boat, was installed in the Deben by Woodbridge Boatyard, celebrating Molly and Ethel Etherson, who along with their brothers managed the boatyard from 1969. The ferry from Woodbridge to Sutton has not been reopened.

Chapter Fifteen – The shore end of Felixstowe Pier has been rebuilt, with amusements, a restaurant and boardwalk, but the rest remains closed. Felixstowe now has an excellent independent bookshop, Stillwater Books. Norfolk Guest House has closed.

Chapter Sixteen – A 35-metre Ferris wheel now stands on Felixstowe seafront from February to October each year. OS maps no longer show a footpath running through Felixstowe Docks.

Chapter Seventeen – Trimley station is looking well cared for with flower beds and newly painted signs. The Victorian station building is behind hoardings and still in a bad state but Trimley Station Community Trust are working towards getting it restored for community use.

Chapter Eighteen – If walking across the Orwell Bridge the southern side is preferable and there are steps down on reaching the west bank.

Chapter Nineteen – Suffolk Mind vacated St Mary at the Quay in 2020 and it is now occupied by River Church, an Anglican church linked to Holy Trinity Brompton. The proposed glass tower in front of the Town Hall has not been built. The Ipswich Portal, a round screen linking the town with a network of identical portals around the world, was unveiled in the Town Square on 22nd October 2025.

Chapter Twenty – New houses have been built on much of HMS Ganges. A new road, Nelson Road, leads to Barrelmans Point, a '*prestigious development with a range of 2, 3, 4, & 5 bedroom homes*'. There's no sign of the proposed hotel but The Shipwreck by the marina offers B&B. The mast still stands. Several blocks of sea-facing apartments have been built overlooking the Stour upstream of Shotley Marine. The village shop has closed but the Bristol Arms is still open.

Chapter Twenty One – Only one bus a day (a school service) now runs between Shotley Gate & Lower Holbrook. A two-hourly service from Ipswich to Manningtree calls at Lower Holbrook.

Chapter Twenty Two – The path beyond the railway crossing at Cattawade, which I had found to be very wet, has been improved and now has a gravel surface. A few companies occupy parts of the industrial site and there is still a faint whiff of solvent but much of it remains derelict, with signs offering land for development. Houses have been built on some of the parking areas and other land north of the access road.

In general, I found the walks little-changed. There seems to have been less erosion in the eleven years from 2014, than occurred from the severe storms and surge tide that winter. Transport has become more difficult, with fewer rural buses and overnight accommodation more limited as many B&Bs have closed.

BIBLIOGRAPHY

The following books have provided information used in the writing of this book:

Blythburgh : A Suffolk Village
Alan Mackley & Mary Montague, Jarrold, 2003

Coastal Suffolk
Robert Simper, Creekside Publishing, 2009

Cosy in the Winter! A History of Shinglestreet
Sarah Margittai & Alec Burwood, Sigma Books, 2010

Creekside Tales
Robert Simper, Creekside Publishing, 2004

Discover the Suffolk Coast
Terry Palmer, Heritage House, 1992

East Anglian Shores
David Fairhall, Greenwich, 1988

Explore East Anglia
Mark & Elizabeth Mitchels, Countryside Books, 1989

Harbouring the Dream
Martin Treadway, Suffolk Yacht Harbour Ltd, 2011

Landguard Fort
Paul Pattison, English Heritage, 2006

Most Secret: The Hidden History of Orford Ness
Paddy Heazell, The History Press, 2010

Orford and Orford Ness
Jean & Stuart Bacon, Segment, 1992

Orford Ness
The National Trust

Suffolk Coast and Heaths Walk
Laurence Mitchell, Cicerone, 2012

Suffolk's Wildlife Coast
RSPB, Healeys Print Group, 2012

Sunrise Coast
Robert Simper, Creekside Publishing, 2002

Sutton Hoo
The National Trust, 2002

The Roaring Boys of Suffolk
Peter Cherry & Trevor Westgate, 1970

The Search for Dunwich City Under the Sea
Jean & Stuart Bacon, Segment, 1979

The Southwold Railway & Blyth Valley Walk
The Southwold Railway Trust, 2012

The Suffolk Shoreline and the Sea
Jean & Stuart Bacon, Segment, 1984

Thorpeness Guide
C. Durand & C. Everett, Mrs E. & Mr J. Everett

Two Feet, Four Paws
Spud Talbot-Ponsonby, Summersdale, 1996

Untold Tales from the Suffolk Sandlings
Valerie Fenwick & Vic Harrup, Butley Research Group, 2009

www.swanbooks.co.uk have been most helpful in tracking down some of the lesser known or out of print books.

ALSO BY PETER CATON

NO BOAT REQUIRED
EXPLORING TIDAL ISLANDS

When is an island not an island? Peter Caton takes us to all four corners of England, Scotland and Wales to find out.

Sharing our nation's fascination with islands, Peter sets out to be the first person to visit all 43 tidal islands which can be walked to from the UK mainland. Along the way he faces many challenges: precipitous cliffs, vicious dogs, disappearing footpaths, lost bus drivers, fast tides, quicksand and enormous quantities of mud, but also experiences wonderfully scenic journeys by road, rail and on foot. He contrasts the friendly welcome from most islanders and owners with the reluctance of others to permit visits, and tells how he was thrown off one secret island.

An entertaining narrative illustrated with colour photographs, *No Boat Required* contains a wealth of information as the author unearths many little known facts and stories. It tells of the solitude of the many remote islands and the difficulties of balancing the needs of people and wildlife. We learn of the islands' varied histories – stories of pirates, smugglers, murder and ghosts, of battles with Vikings, an island claimed by punks and another with its own king. He writes of the beauty of the islands and our coast, and reflects on how these may be affected by climate change.

In *No Boat Required* Peter Caton takes us to explore islands, some familiar but most which few of us know exist and even fewer have visited. He finds that our tidal islands are special places, many with fascinating and amusing stories and each one of them different. It adds up to a unique journey around Britain.

£12.99 343 Pages ISBN 9781848767010 **Published by Matador**

ALSO BY PETER CATON

ESSEX COAST WALK

When Peter Caton set out to walk the Essex coast he had no idea of the beauty, wildlife and stories that he would find on the way. He takes the reader up and down the many creeks and estuaries of the longest coastline of any English county, through nature reserves, seaside resorts, unspoilt villages, sailing centres and alongside industry past and present. On the way we read of tales of witchcraft, ghosts, smuggling, bigamy and incest. We learn of the county's varied history – stories of battles with Vikings, of invading Romans bringing elephants, a fort where the only casualty occurred in a cricket match, burning Zeppelins and of Jack the Ripper.

Whilst an entertaining narrative, not a guidebook, *Essex Coast Walk* contains a wealth of information, including many little-known facts and stories. With gentle humour to match the coastline's gentle beauty, and illustrated with photographs and maps, the book makes for easy reading.

The book highlights how climate change may alter our coast and looks at new methods of coping with rising sea levels. It tells us how tiny settlements grew into large holiday resorts and how other villages have remained as unspoilt and isolated communities. The author's thought provoking final reflections consider how the coast has changed over the centuries and what its future may be.

Written in an accessible style, *Essex Coast Walk* has been enjoyed not only by those living in the county, but by others who have been surprised to read of the beauty and history of this little known part of our coast.

£9.99 376 PAGES ISBN 9781848761162 **Published by Matador**

ALSO BY PETER CATON

THE NEXT STATION STOP
FIFTY YEARS BY TRAIN

A 10,000 mile tour of Britain, discovering what it's like to travel on our modern railways and comparing experiences with train journeys made over the last fifty years.

Inspired by finding a childhood notebook, the author revisits locations of family holidays, looking at how the journeys and places have changed, and wondering why his parents chose such unlikely destinations.

His travels take him to some of the most beautiful and remote parts of the country and on trains so eccentric that sometimes he wonders if Thomas the Tank Engine is round the corner. Sampling a selection of Inter City routes, he questions whether the pursuit of speed and efficiency has taken away some of the enjoyment of travelling by train, but on sleepers to Cornwall and Scotland finds the romance of rail travel is still alive. He ends with a journey to Italy, with a diversion up a snowy mountain, comparing European train travel with British railways.

We read of the author's experiences of missed connections, inflexible computers, waving to Marjory and upsetting a machine gun carrying policeman. He writes of his frustrations with 'health & safety' and ridiculous announcements, and how these combine to give the book its title.

Illustrated with sixty colour photographs covering the steam, diesel and electric eras of the last 50 years, The Next Station Stop will appeal to anyone who travels on Britain's trains.

£9.99 260 PAGES ISBN 978-1-78306-050-4 **Published by Matador**

ALSO BY PETER CATON

50 WALKS ON THE ESSEX COAST

A walking guide describing 50 walks along the Essex coast, the longest coastline of any English county. Peter Caton discovered the wonderful Essex coastline as he narrated his journey along its whole length, writing Essex coast walk.

He now describes walks covering the entire publicly accessible coast, helping others to follow in his footsteps. Detailed route instructions are provided, along with high-quality maps, while background information and colour photos add context and interest. Following rivers, creeks and open sea, on paths, tracks and promenades, often with circuits completed across countryside, the walking and views are varied. There is much history and wildlife to be seen as the walker discovers picturesque villages, smugglers' haunts, nature reserves and little-known gems along the coast.

Walks range from 2 to 15 miles, with most having different length options, plus the possibility of linking adjoining routes. Produced in full colour, 50 Walks on the Essex Coast is an invitation for serious ramblers, or those looking for just an afternoon stroll, to discover the hidden magic of the Essex coast.

£9.99 200 PAGES ISBN 9781785892578 **Published by Matador**

ALSO BY PETER CATON

REMOTE STATIONS
Includes chapter on Southwold Railway

Journeys to forty of Britain's loneliest railway stations.
Written for the railway enthusiast but also for anyone who enjoys travel books.
Illustrated with more than 150 colour and black & white photos, both recent and historical.

Combining a love of remote places and of travelling on our more interesting trains, Peter Caton visits forty of Britain's most lonely railway stations. His travels take him to all four corners of the country; to the top of a snowy mountain, to moors, hills and marshes, and even a mile out to sea, as he rides on some of our most scenic railway lines. Along the way he unearths stories of some bizarre accidents, tales of human endeavour and railway history. He finds a station that closed before it officially existed, wonders why some survived, laments others that should never have been lost and on finding that one of his forty stations is proposed for closure joins the battle to try to save it.

Peter enjoys walks along deserted coast and countryside and discovers five stations that closed long ago. His choice covers a wide variety of stations including a few on resurrected narrow gauge railways. Some are well known, others obscure. He often writes that the train stopped 'just for me' and the station 'serves nowhere at all'.

Remote Stations is written with a railway theme but is not a heavy or technical railway book. It will also appeal to those who enjoy an easy reading travel book describing journeys to some of the most remote parts of Britain.

£9.99 320 PAGES ISBN 9781789014082 **Published by Matador**

ALSO BY PETER CATON

DARTMOOR:
ENGLAND'S LAST WILDERNESS?

A Dartmoor narrative, exploring many aspects of the moor by means of a series of varied walks and asking the question, is Dartmoor England's last wilderness?

The author starts by telling us of the various mishaps he has experienced on Dartmoor and the lessons learned. He moves on to describing walks, each with a theme and including information on the history, legends, geography and people of the moor. Making use of his father's sixty-year-old notebooks, he refers back to some of his childhood walks in the 1960s & 70s.

Some of the many controversies and conflicts relating to Dartmoor are discussed, including access, camping and rewilding and the book includes four chapters on battles to save the moor.

The author considers what defines a wilderness, whether Dartmoor qualifies and if so, is it England's last.

Illustrated with colour and monochrome photos, the book could perhaps be described as a Dartmoor miscellany with themes of walks, wilderness, controversies, and stories of the moor.

£11.99 352 PAGES ISBN 9781805145219 **Published by Matador**

ALSO BY PETER CATON

WALKS DISCOVERING LESSER
KNOWN DARTMOOR

A guide describing routes of 1½ to 10 miles, enabling walkers to discover the beauty, history and hidden places of Dartmoor, the wildest, most remote and arguably the most beautiful area in Southern England.

The walks will take you to antiquities dating from the Bronze Age and even earlier, to hidden waterfalls and gorges, abandoned remote dwellings, fascinating industrial archaeology, majestic tors and wonderful viewpoints.

For those who don't know Dartmoor they provide routes for interesting walks of varying length and difficulty. Whilst some of the points of interest will be familiar to those who know the moor well, the walks will take you to places that very few people visit, passing little known artefacts with something new for almost everyone.

Produced in full colour with routes clearly marked on OS maps, the book includes comprehensive background information on the moor and the history, stories and legends of the many places visited on each walk.

An author of walking and travel books, Peter Caton has walked on Dartmoor for more than 50 years.

£12.99 200 PAGES ISBN 9781803132303 Published by Matador